JAMIE'S COMFORT FOOD

MICHAEL JOSEPH

an imprint of

PENGUIN BOOKS

ALSO BY JAMIE OLIVER

The Naked Chef
The Return of the Naked Chef
Happy Days with the Naked Chef
Jamie's Kitchen
Jamie's Dinners
Jamie's Italy
Cook with Jamie
Jamie at Home
Jamie's Ministry of Food
Jamie's America
Jamie Does …
Jamie's 30-Minute Meals
Jamie's Great Britain
Jamie's 15-Minute Meals
Save with Jamie

PHOTOGRAPHY

'Lord' David Loftus
davidloftus.com

DESIGN

Superfantastic
wearesuperfantastic.com

MICHAEL JOSEPH

Published by the Penguin Group

Penguin Books Ltd
80 Strand,
London WC2R 0RL, England

Penguin Group (USA) Inc.
375 Hudson Street,
New York, New York 10014, USA

Penguin Group (Canada)
90 Eglinton Avenue East, Suite 700,
Toronto, Ontario, Canada M4P 2Y3
(a division of Pearson Penguin Canada Inc.)

Penguin Ireland
25 St Stephen's Green,
Dublin 2, Ireland
(a division of Penguin Books Ltd)

Penguin Group (Australia)
707 Collins Street,
Melbourne, Victoria 3008, Australia
(a division of Pearson Australia Group Pty Ltd)

Penguin Books India Pvt Ltd
11 Community Centre,
Panchsheel Park, New Delhi – 110 017, India

Penguin Group (NZ)
67 Apollo Drive,
Rosedale, Auckland 0632, New Zealand
(a division of Pearson New Zealand Ltd)

Penguin Books (South Africa) (Pty) Ltd
Block D, Rosebank Office Park,
181 Jan Smuts Avenue, Parktown North,
Gauteng 2193, South Africa

Penguin Books Ltd, Registered Offices:
80 Strand, London WC2R 0RL, England

First published 2014
001

Printed in Germany by Mohn Media
Colour reproduction by Altaimage Ltd

A CIP catalogue record for this book is available from the British Library
ISBN: 978–0–718–15953–5

penguin.com
jamieoliver.com

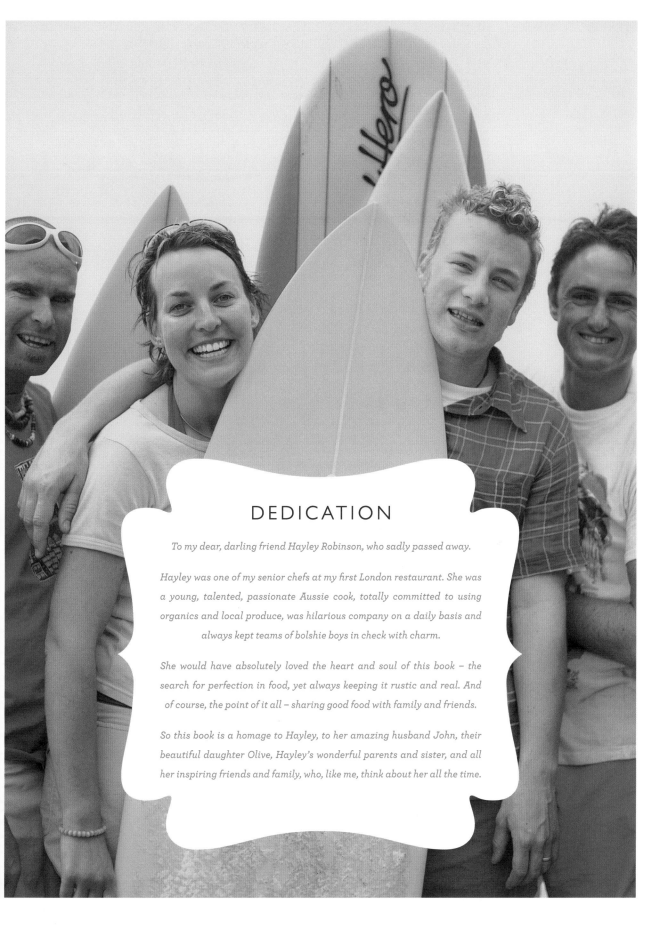

DEDICATION

To my dear, darling friend Hayley Robinson, who sadly passed away.

Hayley was one of my senior chefs at my first London restaurant. She was a young, talented, passionate Aussie cook, totally committed to using organics and local produce, was hilarious company on a daily basis and always kept teams of bolshie boys in check with charm.

She would have absolutely loved the heart and soul of this book – the search for perfection in food, yet always keeping it rustic and real. And of course, the point of it all – sharing good food with family and friends.

So this book is a homage to Hayley, to her amazing husband John, their beautiful daughter Olive, Hayley's wonderful parents and sister, and all her inspiring friends and family, who, like me, think about her all the time.

CONTENTS

COMFORT

means so many things to different people, and when you apply that to food, the volume of emotions it brings out is incredible. Without doubt, comfort food is completely subjective – it's about smells, sounds and tastes. It's about recipes that really hit the spot at a certain time, and have the capacity to pull out explicit feelings and old memories, as well as creating new ones and passing that joy on to the next generation. Comfort food has the power to make you feel safe, secure, fulfilled, excited, loved, even a bit giddy! True comfort food can wrap its arms around you and give you a great big hug, or can tickle you pink and make you laugh. It can be about the seasons, your childhood memories, your school food, the trips your grandparents took you on, your first takeaway, your first date – it's all about what a particular dish means to you. In a bowl, on a plate, handheld, wrapped in newspaper, eaten straight from the fridge or even from a tin, whether you're with a big group of loved ones, in a cosy kitchen with your family or curled up on the sofa on your own, comfort food can be elegant and nurturing, or it can be downright dirty.

ULTIMATELY FOR ME, COMFORT
FOOD IS ALL ABOUT REALLY
GOOD FOOD THAT'S JUST SO;
DONE IN A PARTICULAR WAY.

Only one hundred recipes out of the millions out there have made my comfort food cut, right now. So this book is full of the food I cook and eat when I want to celebrate, when I'm excited, when I need a little pick me up, or I feel under the weather, or frankly when I want to be a bit naughty and indulgent. All of you will have your own comfort food cookbook inside you, just as I have. In writing this book, I've talked to loads of people that I love and respect in food — good cooks, chefs and friends. The stories they've shared with me about little moments in time, as well as quirky, specific ways of creating a dish, have really helped me craft and shape the repertoire of this book. And I've embraced new dishes that are much loved from countries around the world, taking inspiration not only from close friends, but also directly from you guys via social media.

This book is the opposite of *15-* or *30-Minute Meals*. Most of the recipes aren't super-fast, nor are they for everyday cooking – this is about long summer evenings, cosy winter nights, weekends, holidays and celebrations. It's a book that I know you'll reach for when you're yearning for something special – it's about perfection, indulgence and proper good cooking, which as you know, you've always got to balance up with some lighter meals in the days that follow. As usual with my books of late, my ninja nutrition team have provided you with all the information you need to make informed choices, at the back of the book (page 388–93), making sure everything is super-clear and easy for you to navigate.

I've been writing cookbooks of solid, reliable recipes for 15 years, but I want to bring you in and take you to the next level now, to the nth degree. I've dedicated more space to the recipes and switched my usual edit filter off so I can really talk about all the slightly eccentric, geeky little details, with extra rants and pops of information. I hope you'll enjoy this, because although I'm really proud of all the recipes I'm presenting to you, hopefully there are principles and eccentricities and attention to detail and downright bonkers-ness that will help you develop your own comfort food with a little extra spring in its step. It's about perfecting a dish, getting your friends to go 'wow', and the kids to argue about which bit they get. It's not just about the food, the recipe, the ingredients or working in harmony with the seasons, it's about your swagger and attitude, about how you serve a dish, what you serve with it, at what point in a meal you serve it, where you serve it and who to. This is about that wonderful ability food has to take you on an emotional journey.

Some things are worth waiting for and getting just right. It's like all those little lessons – toast isn't great until you've let the butter melt; the best tea needs to brew for three minutes; a perfect roast potato is crispy on the outside and fluffy in the middle and nothing else will do. Comfort food is all about those tiny details – it could be the fact that something is better as a leftover, or it's better cooked at the base of the oven to create a crispy bottom, or letting gravy bubble up and bash through the crust of a pie. And a lot of us know what we want, so we need to find a way to get there – what exactly is it that makes it perfect? Now that I'm getting a bit older and starting to sound like my dad, who in turn sounds like his, I want to reflect those brilliant eccentricities of our elders, how they know what makes them happy and ensure that every one of their actions speaks volumes. That's what I've tried to bottle in this book. I've also tapped into the foods I grew up with, that made my passion for cooking get me where I am today. That said, the young talent mixing things up and bringing new ideas to the fray is also really important, and I've tried to embrace all those influences here too.

So good luck, guys – here are the keys to your brand new comfort cookbook. If I've done my job right, this book will be well used and will sit on your shelf for many years to come. I believe these are the greatest, most satisfying dishes out there today, all put in this super-tested parcel, which should really take care of you and deliver on its promise. More than that, I hope it helps you think about where you take a dish, how you cook and perfect it, so that every time you make and serve one of these scrumptious, comforting meals, there's big old smiles all around the table.

× THIS IS ALL ABOUT PERFECTING A DISH ×

CHILDHOOD FAVOURITES,
MEMORIES & TRADITIONS

NOSTALGIA

× CHICKEN TIKKA MASALA ×

SERVES 6–8
1 HOUR 20 MINUTES
PLUS MARINATING
415 CALORIES

1 level teaspoon ground cloves

1 level teaspoon ground cumin

2 heaped teaspoons each sweet
 smoked paprika, garam masala

3 lemons

6 cloves of garlic

1 thumb-sized piece of ginger

6 heaped tablespoons
 natural yoghurt

800g skinless boneless
 chicken breasts

3 fresh green or yellow chillies

SAUCE

2 onions

4 cloves of garlic

1–2 fresh red chillies

1 bunch of fresh coriander (30g)

olive oil

1 level tablespoon ground
 coriander

2 level teaspoons turmeric

6 tablespoons ground almonds

2 x 400g tins of plum tomatoes

1 chicken stock cube

2 x 400g tins of light coconut milk

Without question, chicken tikka masala is a brilliant curry that makes people very happy. Of course it's inspired by fantastic Indian cooking, but is in fact an Anglo-Indian evolution, created to suit British palates. When you make it, you'll be super-proud – you can use top-quality chicken, it's loads of fun to marinate and grill, the method rocks, and it's highly unlikely you'll find a better expression. I love to make my own paratha breads to serve with it too (page 19). Dig a hole in the garden and get grilling!

Put the cloves, cumin and 1 heaped teaspoon each of paprika and garam masala into a small pan and toast for 1 minute to bring them back to life, then tip into a large bowl. Finely grate in the zest of 1 lemon, squeeze in all its juice, crush in the garlic, peel and finely grate in the ginger, and add the yoghurt and 1 teaspoon of sea salt. Cut the chicken breasts into 5cm chunks, then massage all that flavour into the meat. Skewer up the chicken chunks, interspersing them with lemon wedges and chunks of green or yellow chilli, but don't squash them together too much. Place on a tray, cover with clingfilm and marinate in the fridge for at least 2 hours, but preferably overnight.

For the sauce, peel the onions and garlic, then finely slice with the red chillies and coriander stalks (reserving the leaves for later). Put it all into a large casserole pan on a medium-high heat with a lug of oil and cook for around 20 minutes, or until golden, stirring regularly. Add the ground coriander, turmeric and remaining 1 heaped teaspoon each of paprika and garam masala. Cook for 2 minutes, then add and toast the almonds. Pour in the tomatoes, crumble in the stock cube and add 300ml of boiling water. Simmer for 5 minutes, then stir in the coconut milk. Simmer for a final 20 minutes, stirring occasionally, then season to perfection.

When you're ready to cook the chicken, drizzle it with a little oil, then grill on a hot barbecue, in a screaming hot griddle pan or under a hot grill, turning until it's very golden and gnarly on all sides. Slice the chicken off the skewers straight into the sauce, reserving the lemons. Simmer for 2 minutes while you use tongs to squeeze some jammy lemons over the curry, to taste. Swirl through some more yoghurt, sprinkle with the coriander leaves, and serve with parathas (page 19) or fluffy basmati rice.

Here's a nice little game-changer – make your own paratha to enjoy with your chicken tikka. For 8 people, put 300g each of wholemeal bread flour and plain flour into a bowl with a goood pinch of sea salt. Gradually add 2 tablespoons of olive oil and 400ml of semi-skimmed milk, mixing until combined, then knead for a few minutes on a flour-dusted surface. Leave to rest for 20 minutes, then divide the dough into 8 and thinly roll out each piece to A4 size. One-by-one, drizzle and rub lightly with oil, roll up into a loose log, roll the log up like a Catherine wheel, then roll out with a rolling pin again to a flat round just under ½cm thick. Cook in a hot oiled frying pan on a medium heat for 3 minutes on each side, or until nicely charred, then sprinkle lightly with salt. Transfer to a board and smash together to expose the layers.

SHEPHERD'S PIE

I believe this is the ultimate shepherd's pie – a recipe designed to use up leftover roasted meat. Historically, you'll find it had potato on the bottom, sides and top, so I was inspired to run with this, giving you a pie with crispy potato all the way round, gorgeous tender meat and veg in the middle, and the best gravy to pour over your portion. This is definitely next-level cooking. To be honest, it's so damn good that I'll usually roast a small lamb shoulder specially in order to make a big shepherd's pie for eight to ten people, which also gives you enough filling to freeze for another day – always a bonus.

✕ SHEPHERD'S PIE ✕

SERVES 8–10

6 HOURS 30 MINUTES
PLUS COOLING
508 CALORIES

ROAST LAMB

1 small shoulder of lamb,
    bone in (2kg)

olive oil

FILLING

4 red onions

4 carrots

4 sticks of celery

1 medium swede

a few sprigs of fresh rosemary

1 heaped tablespoon plain flour

TOPPING, SIDES & BOTTOM

2.5kg Maris Piper potatoes

2 good knobs of unsalted butter

100g Cheddar cheese

2 sprigs of fresh rosemary

60g fresh breadcrumbs

Preheat the oven to 170°C/325°F/gas 3. In a snug-fitting high-sided roasting tray, rub the lamb all over with a little oil and a good pinch of sea salt and pepper. Add a splash of water to the tray, then roast for 4 hours, or until the meat is tender and will fall away from the bone. Remove from the oven and leave to cool in the tray, then lift the lamb out onto a board, take all the meat and crispy skin off the bone and roughly chop it, reserving the bones. Skim away any fat from the tray and pop it into a clean jam jar. Add a splash of boiling water to the tray and stir around to pick up all the lovely sticky bits from the bottom. Keep it all to one side.

For the filling, peel and roughly dice the onions, carrots, celery and swede, then put them into your biggest pan on a medium-high heat with 2 tablespoons of reserved lamb fat. Strip in the rosemary leaves, then fry the veg for 20 minutes, or until lightly caramelized, stirring regularly. Stir in the flour, lamb, bones and tray juices, then pour in 1.5 litres of water. Bring to the boil, then put the lid on and reduce to a gentle simmer for 40 minutes, or until you've got a loose, stew-like consistency, stirring occasionally. To guarantee intense gravy and a tender but dense filling, remove and discard the bones, then place a large coarse sieve over a pan and, in batches, spoon the lamb stew into the sieve. Let the gravy drip through, and after a couple of minutes, when you get a dense pile of meat and veg in the sieve, transfer that to a bowl, leaving the gravy in the pan. Separately freeze half the cool meat and gravy for another day.

For the topping, sides and bottom, peel and roughly chop the potatoes and cook in boiling salted water for 12 to 15 minutes, or until tender. Drain and leave to steam dry, then add the butter, grate in half the cheese, season to perfection with salt and pepper, mash well and cool completely. Preheat the oven to 200°C/400°F/gas 6. Use a little reserved lamb fat to grease the inside of a large pie dish (25cm x 30cm), then pick and tear over the rosemary leaves and sprinkle with half the breadcrumbs – they'll stick to the fat and add an incredible crunch. A handful at a time, press the cooled mash into the dish, covering the bottom and sides with a 1cm-thick layer (like you see on pages 22–3). Spoon in the filling and a couple of spoonfuls of gravy, smooth out, then top with the remaining mash, pat it flat, scuff it up with a fork and pinch it at the edges. Grate over the rest of the cheese, scatter with the remaining breadcrumbs and drizzle lightly with oil. Importantly, bake on the bottom of the oven for 1 hour 10 minutes, or until crisp and golden. Warm your gravy through (reducing if desired), then serve the pie with loads of seasonal greens or peas and lots of condiments.

BEANS

ON

TOAST

· · · · · · · · · · ·

✕ BEANS ON TOAST ✕

SERVES 4
1 HOUR 45 MINUTES
450 CALORIES

4 cloves of garlic

1 onion

1 level teaspoon smoked paprika

2 tablespoons balsamic vinegar

2 x 400g tins of cannellini beans

1 x 400g tin of plum tomatoes

Worcestershire sauce

Tabasco sauce

4 thick slices of quality bread

Cheddar cheese

ROSEMARY & CHILLI OIL

2 fresh red chillies

2 sprigs of fresh rosemary

olive oil

So many British people absolutely adore baked beans, but internationally they get a bad rep. I think they're seen not to be great-quality beans or sauce, so no one understands why we get so excited by them. But that humble tinned baked bean does have a special place in our British heart, so I've come up with the best home-baked beans that I'm sure will please everyone, yet retains that sweetness and simplicity us Brits are used to.

Start by making the rosemary and chilli oil. Deseed and finely chop the chillies, put them into a pan and tear in the rosemary sprigs. Cover with oil, place on a very low heat for 20 minutes, to let those flavours really infuse, then remove from the heat.

Preheat the oven to 160°C/325°F/gas 3. Peel and finely slice the garlic and put it into a shallow ovenproof pan (26cm in diameter) on a low heat with a good lug of your rosemary and chilli oil, while you peel, finely chop and add the onion, along with the paprika. Cook for 10 to 15 minutes, or until soft and sticky, stirring regularly. Add the balsamic and let it reduce and soak into the veg. Drain most but not all of the liquid away from the beans and add them to the pan. Pour in the tin of tomatoes through your hand, crushing the tomatoes as you go, then add a few good splashes of Worcestershire sauce and a few drips of Tabasco. Cook for a further 5 minutes, then season to perfection. Scrunch up a sheet of greaseproof paper, wet it under the tap, and place it lightly on the surface of the beans. Transfer to the oven to bake for 50 minutes to 1 hour, or until thick, dark and smelling totally irresistible.

When you're ready to serve, toast the bread, then divide up the beans between the slices. Finely grate over a little Cheddar, to your liking, then finish with a drizzle of the rosemary and chilli oil and tuck right in (keep leftover oil in a jar for future meals).

SUPER
SCHNITZEL

× SUPER SCHNITZEL ×

SERVES 4

1 HOUR 10 MINUTES
690 CALORIES

50g plain flour

2 large eggs

150g fresh breadcrumbs

4 x 110g veal or
  pork escalopes

1 shallot or small onion

1 large gherkin

4 sprigs of fresh flat-leaf parsley

1 tablespoon baby capers

4 quality anchovy fillets

sunflower oil

4 small knobs of unsalted butter

blackcurrant or bramble jam

POTATO SALAD

800g new potatoes

3 tablespoons soured cream

1 teaspoon English mustard

½ a bunch of fresh chives (15g)

APPLE SALAD

2 lemons

extra virgin olive oil

2 eating apples

2 handfuls of watercress

The concept of schnitzel, or floured crumbed fried meats, dates back a long way, and making things prettier, tastier and more tender like this is a real no-brainer. You can use any meat, and served with pickles, potato salad and bramble jam, it's a joy. At home, perfection is achieved by cooking the schnitzel one at a time, so that each plate is loved.

For the potato salad, cook the potatoes in a pan of boiling salted water for 12 to 15 minutes, or until tender, then drain, leave to steam dry and cool slightly. Roughly chop and place in a bowl with the soured cream and mustard, then finely chop and add the chives (reserving the tender tips). Squeeze in the juice of ½ a lemon, toss to coat, then have a taste and season to perfection.

Put the flour on a large plate, whisk the eggs in a large shallow bowl and scatter the breadcrumbs onto a large tray. One at a time, bash out and tenderize the meat slices with a meat hammer, or between sheets of clingfilm using a heavy pan, until you have ½cm-thick escalopes. Cover each one in flour, shake off the excess, dip in the egg, let any excess drip off, then cover with breadcrumbs, pressing to coat. Place in the fridge.

To make a quick sprinkle, peel the shallot or onion, then finely chop with the gherkin, parsley (stalks and all), capers and anchovies, mixing well as you go.

For the apple salad, squeeze the juice of half a lemon into a bowl with a little drizzle of extra virgin olive oil. Finely slice the apples into rounds, ideally on a mandolin (don't worry about the pips, and use the guard!), then toss gently in the dressing. Pile the watercress and reserved chive tips on top, tossing together just before serving.

One at a time, cook each schnitzel in a large non-stick pan on a medium-high heat with enough sunflower oil to coat the bottom of the pan. When the schnitzel is golden on one side (about 2 minutes in), turn it over and add a knob of butter. Gently jiggle the pan, angling it slightly, and spoon the oil and butter back over the schnitzel to create the most wonderful flavour and golden outside. Once golden and cooked through, delicately pat dry on kitchen paper, then give to your first lucky guest, serving with the potato and apple salads, a good dollop of jam, the sprinkle and a wedge of lemon. Wipe out your pan, use fresh butter and oil for the next schnitzel, and repeat.

× CURRIED FISH PIE ×

SERVES 6

1 HOUR 45 MINUTES
PLUS COOLING
430 CALORIES

4 cloves of garlic

1–2 fresh red chillies

groundnut oil

2 small handfuls of curry leaves

1½ teaspoons black mustard seeds

1.2kg Maris Piper potatoes

2 large eggs

1 small knob of unsalted butter

semi-skimmed milk

2 onions

1 thumb-sized piece of ginger

1 teaspoon fenugreek seeds

1 teaspoon turmeric

1 x 400g tin of light coconut milk

200g baby spinach

½ a lemon

4 ripe vine tomatoes

3 x 60g lemon sole fillets, skin off
   and pin-boned

150g haddock or ray fillets, skin off
   and pin-boned

150g salmon fillets, skin off
   and pin-boned

6 large raw peeled king prawns,
   deveined

I've done a few fish pies in my time, and very nice they are too, but there's no way I could do this book without including one, so I was faced with the question of legitimately where I could go that's different from where I've been before. Well, the answer is India. This comforting curried fish pie has amazing perfumed layers of flavour that will slap you round the face yet still give you delicate fish and a crispy potato top. Throw this into the mix at a dinner party and you'll be winning on both the surprise and the flavour fronts.

Peel the garlic and finely slice with the chilli (seeds and all), then put into a frying pan on a medium-low heat with a good couple of lugs of oil. Add the curry leaves and mustard seeds and fry gently for 5 minutes, or until the garlic is lightly golden, then remove from the heat and put aside (this is called a temper).

Peel and roughly chop the potatoes and cook in boiling salted water for 12 to 15 minutes, or until tender. Boil the eggs in the same pan for the first 7 minutes too, then remove them to cold water. Once cooked, drain the potatoes and mash really well with the butter, a few splashes of milk and a pinch of sea salt and pepper.

Meanwhile, peel and finely chop the onions and ginger and scrape into a heavy-bottomed pan with half the temper, the fenugreek and turmeric. Cook on a medium heat for 5 minutes, stirring regularly. Pour in the coconut milk, tear in the spinach and finely grate in the lemon zest. Bring to the boil, removing from the heat once the spinach has wilted and the sauce has thickened. Transfer to a nice high-sided baking dish (28cm square). Roughly chop and scatter over the tomatoes, then leave to cool.

Preheat the oven to 180°C/350°F/gas 4. Peel and quarter the eggs, then dot over and poke them into the sauce. Cut all the fish into bite-sized chunks, and intersperse around the dish with the prawns. Top with your mash – go rustic and scuff it up with a fork, or, as this dish is a bit more elegant, go 80s retro-style and pipe it on with a star-shaped nozzle (it creates a larger surface area and looks and eats very well). Bake for 40 minutes, or until golden and bubbling at the edges. Reheat the remaining temper with a splash of oil just before serving, and spoon over the top to finish.

× RETRO LAYERED SALAD ×

SERVES 6–8

1 HOUR
PLUS CHILLING
388 CALORIES

½ a cucumber

1 heaped teaspoon dried dill

2 tablespoons white wine vinegar

250g dried mini pasta shells

2 tablespoons sun-dried
    tomato paste

1 tablespoon balsamic vinegar

1 x 340g tin of sweetcorn

2 spring onions

extra virgin olive oil

cayenne pepper

½ an iceberg lettuce

2 punnets of cress

400g peeled cooked prawns

2 large carrots

½ a bunch of fresh basil (15g)

100g Red Leicester cheese

MARIE ROSE SAUCE

2 tablespoons tomato ketchup

4 heaped tablespoons mayonnaise

1 splash of Worcestershire sauce

1 splash of brandy

a few drips of Tabasco sauce

juice of 1 lemon

This is inspired by those moulded salads from Marks & Spencer. As a child, it was always a bit of a treat to get one with a sandwich and a drink – me and Mum used to go back to sit in the car in a concrete multi-storey car park in our local town, spread out a little in-car picnic and tuck in. As unglamorous as that might sound, it was really precious Mum-time and this little beauty brings back all those happy memories for me – I hope you love it as much as I do. It's quite epic, looks incredible and is loads of fun to make.

Cut the cucumber into 1cm dice, toss in a bowl with a pinch of sea salt and pepper, the dill and white wine vinegar, then leave to pickle. Cook the pasta according to packet instructions, then drain and toss with the sun-dried tomato paste and balsamic vinegar. Drain the sweetcorn and place in a separate bowl, finely slice and add the spring onions, drizzle with a little oil, add a pinch each of black and cayenne pepper, then mix together. To make the Marie Rose sauce, simply combine all the sauce ingredients, then have a taste and season to perfection.

Line a 24cm-wide mixing bowl with a double layer of clingfilm, letting it hang well over the edges. Spoon the sweetcorn into the base and pat down into an even layer. Finely slice the lettuce and scatter half into the bowl. Snip over 1 punnet of cress, evenly scatter over the prawns, then spoon over the Marie Rose sauce and spread out in an even layer. Peel and coarsely grate over the carrots, then layer the dressed pasta on top. Pick over most of the basil leaves, then evenly grate over the Red Leicester and scatter over the remaining lettuce. Press everything down with your hands, then spoon over the cucumber and any dressing. Fold in the clingfilm to seal the salad, then get yourself a plate that just fits inside the bowl, place on top, and add something heavy like a pestle and mortar to weigh it down. Refrigerate for at least 2 hours.

When you're ready to serve, turn out the layered salad – think sandcastle – and carefully peel away the clingfilm. Snip over the remaining punnet of cress, scatter with the remaining basil leaves and drizzle with a little oil. Great served as it is, or as part of a bigger spread with a roast chicken, bread and lots of other salads.

✕ GIANT SAUSAGE ROLL ✕

SERVES 8

2 HOURS
PLUS CHILLING
530 CALORIES

75g dried apple rings

4 rashers of smoked streaky bacon

2 onions

½ a bunch of fresh sage (15g)

olive oil

500g minced pork shoulder (ask
your butcher to do this for you)

50g fresh breadcrumbs

white pepper

25g mature Cheddar cheese

1 whole nutmeg, for grating

1 large egg

1 tablespoon sesame seeds

PASTRY

300g plain flour, plus extra
for dusting

100g unsalted butter (cold)

50g lard (cold)

The great British sausage roll is a beautiful thing to behold. It's perfect hot or cold, on its own, or as part of a picnic, lunchbox or ploughman's with a pint. In fact, sod it, you can even have it as a canapé with a glass of Champagne. I've blessed this sausage roll with length and breadth, to be enjoyed family service style on a big board so everyone can cut off exactly how much they want. If served hot, it's wonderful with mustard, ketchup or brown sauce, and if warm or cold, it's better with pickles, savoury jams or piccalilli.

To make this rough puff pastry, put the flour into a bowl with a good pinch of sea salt. Chop the cold butter and lard into ½cm cubes and add to the bowl, then use a table knife to roughly chop them into the flour until you've got smaller, evenly coated pieces. Add 150ml of ice-cold water and continue chopping and mixing with the knife – keep your hands away – retaining some chunky bits of fat and keeping everything super-cold. If there are any dry bits, just add another splash of water. Quickly pat and bring together with your hands, then wrap in clingfilm and refrigerate for 1 hour.

Meanwhile, blitz the dried apple rings and bacon in a food processor until finely chopped. Peel, roughly chop and add in the onions, pick in the sage leaves, then pulse a good few times until combined. Put a lug of oil into a frying pan on a medium heat, tip in the onion mixture and cook on a low heat for 15 minutes, or until softened, stirring occasionally. Remove from the heat and leave to cool.

Once cool, put the onion mixture into a bowl with the pork, breadcrumbs, a pinch of salt and a doubly good pinch of white pepper. Coarsely grate in the cheese, finely grate in half the nutmeg, then scrunch and mix together with your clean hands. To check the seasoning is right, simply cook a tiny amount in a pan and taste it – there's nothing worse than an under-seasoned sausage roll, so get it right now.

Preheat the oven to 190°C/375°F/gas 5. Roll out your pastry on a flour-dusted surface to a rectangle about 25cm x 40cm, then transfer it to a flour-dusted tray of roughly the same size. Place the cooled meat just off centre on the pastry and shape it into a nice, thick, even sausage. Beat the egg and use it to lightly brush all the exposed pastry, then fold the pastry over the meat. Trim the edges, then use a fork to seal the pastry together. Lightly brush all over with more eggwash and scatter over the sesame seeds from a height. Bake for 40 minutes, or until dark golden and cooked through.

JERK HAM

× EGG & CHIPS ×

× JERK HAM, EGG & CHIPS ×

SERVES 4

WITH LOADSA LEFTOVER HAM

4 HOURS 20 MINUTES
PLUS MARINATING

817 CALORIES

3.5kg leg of ham, bone in

1 × the perfect chips (page 66)

4 large eggs

1 ripe pineapple

olive oil

JERK

6 cloves of garlic

2 red onions

5 fresh Scotch bonnet chillies

1 tablespoon golden caster sugar

12 sprigs of fresh thyme

6 fresh bay leaves

2 level tablespoons each
    ground allspice, ground nutmeg,
    ground cloves

125ml golden rum

125ml malt vinegar

GLAZE

3 tablespoons marmalade

golden rum

Ham, egg and chips is an absolute classic in the UK, but as lovely as it is I think the rest of the world has moved on. So, this jerk ham is off-the-chart delicious, and with homemade chunky chips turns this great old staple into a luxurious treat that will blow people away. Make sure you order your meat from the butcher in advance to avoid disappointment – it's a big old hunk, but if you're going to the trouble of making something this beautiful, it's worth going big and embracing those lovely leftovers in the days that follow.

Place the ham in an appropriately sized pan, cover with water and bring to the boil, then simmer for 2 hours. Skim the surface occasionally and top up with water if needed. Carefully remove the ham to a board (keep the broth to make amazing soups and risottos) and use a knife to remove the skin. You want the layer of fat to be about 1cm thick, so shave off any excess, then score the remaining fat in a criss-cross fashion.

To make the jerk, peel the garlic and onions, and carefully deseed the chillies. Put them into a blender with the rest of the jerk ingredients and blitz until smooth. Wearing rubber gloves, rub the jerk all over the ham so it sticks. Place in a snug-fitting roasting tray, cool, then cover and refrigerate overnight so those flavours really penetrate.

The next day, preheat the oven to 180°C/350°F/gas 4. Scrape the jerk off the ham into the tray, drizzle the ham with oil, then add a decent swig of water to the tray – don't let it dry out and you'll end up with a beautiful jerky sauce. Cut all the skin off the pineapple, remove the core and slice into rough 2cm chunks. Dot the pineapple in and around the ham, turning in the jerk to coat. Roast the ham for 1½ hours, basting regularly. To glaze, loosen the marmalade with a decent swig of rum, then spoon all over the meat and roast for another 30 minutes, or until beautifully golden and crisp, again basting regularly.

Meanwhile, make your perfect chips (page 66). When the ham is just right and the chips are almost ready, fry the eggs to your liking. Carve up the ham, then serve it all together with lemon-dressed green salad leaves on the side.

✕ MUSHROOM SOUP & PASTA BAKE ✕

SERVES 6
50 MINUTES
242 CALORIES (SOUP)
388 CALORIES (PASTA BAKE)

20g dried porcini mushrooms

1 onion

1 stick of celery

1kg button mushrooms

olive oil

50g unsalted butter

1 good pinch of dried chilli flakes

75g plain flour

2 chicken or vegetable stock cubes

80ml single cream

50g Cheddar cheese

PASTA BAKE

480g dried penne

1 handful of button mushrooms

2 cloves of garlic

10 sprigs of fresh thyme

Here's my tribute to cream of mushroom soup. Nostalgia is a big part of comfort food, and almost everyone I've spoken to has that shared memory of tucking into a steaming bowl of this soup as a child, particularly when they were poorly. I've taken it up a notch, while still giving you that old-school familiar flavour. It's a total beauty in its own right, but I've also shown you how to turn the soup into a pasta bake, which was fashionable in the 80s.

In a small bowl, just cover the porcini with boiling water and leave to soak for 5 minutes. Peel the onion, trim the celery and roughly chop both, then clean the button mushrooms and put it all into a large saucepan on a medium-high heat with a good lug of oil, the butter, chilli flakes and flour. Scoop in the porcini, reserving the soaking water for later. Cook it all for around 25 minutes, or until soft, dark and intense, stirring regularly.

Make up 1.5 litres of stock. Gradually add the hot stock to the pan, stirring continuously, along with 90% of the reserved porcini liquid. Bring back to the boil, then reduce to a simmer for 15 minutes. Stir in the cream and grate in the Cheddar, then blend until smooth. Season to perfection and there you have it – mushroom soup for six!

PS: To turn the soup into a pasta bake for six, preheat the oven to 170°C/325°F/gas 3. Cook the pasta in a pan of boiling salted water according to packet instructions, until just al dente, then drain and return to the pan. Pour over half the soup (eat the rest or save for another day), gently mix together, then tip into a baking dish (20cm x 30cm) and top with an extra grating of Cheddar. To make it extra special, use a mandolin (use the guard!) to shave the mushrooms and garlic into a bowl, strip in the thyme leaves, then toss it all in a drizzle of oil and scatter over the pasta. Bake for around 30 minutes, or until golden and starting to crisp up at the edges. Yum.

✕ CHICKEN KIEV ✕

SERVES 4

1 HOUR 10 MINUTES
PLUS CHILLING
878 CALORIES

4 rashers of smoked streaky bacon

olive oil

4 x 150g skinless chicken breasts
   (I got mine from the butcher with
   the bone in, but either way is fine)

3 tablespoons plain flour

2 large eggs

150g fresh breadcrumbs

sunflower oil

2 large handfuls of baby spinach
   or rocket

2 lemons

BUTTER

4 cloves of garlic

½ a bunch of fresh flat-leaf
   parsley (15g)

4 knobs of unsalted butter
   (at room temperature)

1 pinch of cayenne pepper

BROCCOLI MASH

800g Maris Piper potatoes

1 head of broccoli

1 knob of unsalted butter

Making a really great expression of a chicken Kiev will put smiles on people's faces. Good-quality chicken stuffed with gorgeous garlicky butter and crispy crumbled bacon, then coated with golden breadcrumbs – you know it's going to be good. This is pure indulgent pleasure, so simply make sure you balance up your meals in the days that follow.

Fry the bacon in a pan on a medium heat with a tiny drizzle of olive oil, until golden and crisp, then remove. For the butter, peel the garlic, then finely chop with the parsley leaves and mix into the softened butter with the cayenne. Firm up in the fridge.

Working one-by-one on a board, stuff the chicken breasts. To do this, start by pulling back the loose fillet on the back of the breast – put your knife in the opposite direction and slice to create a long pocket (check out the step-by-step pictures on page 55 or watch a video on jamieoliver.com/how-to). Open the pocket up with your fingers, cut the chilled butter into four and push one piece into the pocket, then crumble in a rasher of crispy bacon. Fold and seal back the chicken, completely covering the butter and giving you a nice neat parcel. Repeat with the 3 remaining breasts.

Preheat the oven to 180°C/350°F/gas 4. Place the flour in one shallow bowl, whisk the eggs in another, and put the breadcrumbs and a pinch of seasoning into a third. Evenly coat each chicken breast in flour, then beaten egg, letting any excess drip off, and finally, turn them in the breadcrumbs, patting them on until evenly coated. Shallow-fry in 2cm of sunflower oil on a medium to high heat for a couple of minutes on each side, or until lightly golden, then transfer to a tray and bake in the oven for 10 minutes, or until cooked through. You can bake them completely in the oven and skip the frying altogether, you just need to drizzle them with olive oil and bake for about 20 minutes – they won't be as golden, but they'll be just as delicious.

Meanwhile, peel and roughly chop the potatoes and cook in a large pan of boiling salted water for 12 to 15 minutes, or until tender. Chop up the broccoli and add it to the potatoes for the last 8 minutes. Drain and leave to steam dry, then return to the pan and mash with a knob of butter and a pinch of salt and pepper. Divide the mash between your plates and place a Kiev on top of each portion. Lightly dress the spinach leaves or rocket in a little oil and lemon juice, then sprinkle over the top as a salady garnish. Serve with a wedge of lemon on the side.

× BIG BRITISH MEATBALLS ×

SERVES 8
2 HOURS
363 CALORIES

MEATBALLS

2 large onions

2 sprigs of fresh rosemary

olive oil

2 tablespoons Worcestershire
   sauce

500g minced pork

500g minced chuck steak

1 handful of breadcrumbs

80g Westcombe Cheddar cheese

GRAVY

200g finely minced chuck steak

1 large onion

2 sprigs of fresh rosemary

1 beef stock cube

200ml pale ale

2 heaped tablespoons plain flour

1 tablespoon blackcurrant jam

2 teaspoons English mustard

2 tablespoons malt vinegar

Many of us are meatball fans, but I wanted to create a super-British, extra-comforting version, so here we're talking about the ULTIMATE meatballs: big in size, made with sweet onions, stuffed with great artisan Cheddar that melts as they cook then oozes out of the middle, plus a ridiculous, filthy-good onion and ale gravy that'll keep you going back for more. There's not much more to say really – once you start, you just have to finish.

For the meatballs, peel the onions, pick the rosemary leaves, then finely chop them together (or blitz in a food processor) and put into a large pan on a medium heat with a lug of oil, the Worcestershire sauce and a good splash or two of water. Cook for around 20 minutes, or until the liquid has disappeared and the onions are sweet and lightly caramelized, stirring occasionally. Season to taste, leave aside to cool, then put into a bowl with the minced meat and breadcrumbs. Using clean hands, mix it all together beautifully, scrunching for a minute to create a delicious texture. Divide into 16 equal-sized balls, then wash your hands and cut the cheese into 16 cubes. Poke and push a piece of cheese into the centre of each ball, then gently roll into perfect balls. Take pride in your balls, repeat until they're all done, and place in the fridge.

For the gravy, put the minced meat into a large pan with a little oil and cook until golden, stirring regularly. Meanwhile, peel the onion and finely chop with the rosemary leaves, then add to the mince and cook for another 5 minutes, or until lightly golden. Crumble in the stock cube, then pour in the ale. Cook away until nice and dark, then stir in the flour, jam, mustard, vinegar and 750ml of water. Simmer for around 30 minutes, or until rich and thick, then season to perfection. Preheat the oven to full whack (240°C/475°F/gas 9) and preheat a high-sided roasting tray.

When you're ready to go, drizzle the preheated tray with oil and add the balls, leaving nice gaps between them. Blast at the top of the oven for around 15 minutes, or until golden. Remove the tray, pour the gravy over the balls and pop them back into the oven for about 5 more minutes, to get everything cooking into each other – sometimes I even baste the balls with a little gravy to give them a lovely shine. Serve on mashed potato or smashed root veg, with some lovely seasonal greens on the side.

POSH POT NOODLE

What I wanted to do in this recipe was go back to the retro 80s Pot Noodle and freshen it up. As a kid I loved the idea that with a swig of boiling water anyone could cook . . . OK, so that's not quite true, but boy did the romance of it suck me in. I've gone for the flavour that sums it up for me here, with a wonderful prawn curry version, but feel free to mix it up with cubes of tofu or strips of steak if you prefer. I hope you enjoy this slurpy, tasty Posh Pot Noodle experience.

PRAWN CURRY POT NOODLE

SERVES 1
10 MINUTES
316 CALORIES

BASE

½ a vegetable stock cube

1 teaspoon tomato ketchup

1 heaped teaspoon curry powder

1 teaspoon creamed coconut

2cm piece of ginger (very finely grated or sliced)

1 teaspoon cornflour (mixed with a splash
of cold water)

NOODLE, VEG & PROTEIN

1 x 150g vac-packed
cooked noodles

¼ of a red pepper (finely sliced)

2 tablespoons frozen peas

1 handful of baby spinach

4 cooked peeled king prawns (halved)

TOPPINGS

1 handful of fresh coriander leaves

1 wedge of lemon

Sticking to the order that I've given you above, put the base ingredients into a 1-litre jug, pot or bowl, then layer up the noodle, delicate veg and protein elements. Carefully top up with around 400ml of boiling kettle water. Mix together really well, then cover with clingfilm and leave for a couple of minutes. During this time, the flavours will mingle, the noodles will swell and suck up all that flavour and you'll have a lovely hot Posh Pot Noodle at the perfect temperature for eating. But if you prefer it screaming hot, just blast it in the microwave for 2 minutes as well. Season to taste, add the toppings to finish off and tuck in.

Pot Noodle is a registered trademark owned by Knorr-Nahrmittel AG in the UK and other countries and is used here with permission.

× MINI FISH & CHIPS ×

SERVES 8

2 HOURS
828 CALORIES

4 x 170g fillets of firm white fish,
    skin on or off (whichever
    you prefer) and pin-boned

120g self-raising flour,
    plus extra for dusting

½ teaspoon baking powder

200ml cold golden ale or IPA

sunflower or sunseed oil

TO SERVE

1 x the perfect chips (page 66)

condiments (page 68)

malt vinegar

Maldon sea salt

×

*Cod and haddock are always
going to be amazing in batter,
but please try to mix things
up a bit – pollock, megrim,
bass, bream, and lots of other
fish are equally wonderful.
Talk to your fishmonger and
find out what's sustainable –
ultimately if it's flaky white
fish, about 2cm thick, you're
laughing. You can even use
smoked fish to great effect.*

*How could I not put fish and chips in this book? It's a British classic. I've often dreamt of
my own fish and chip shop. I love all the condiments that go with beautifully battered fish
and well-cooked chips. I'm so excited by proper homemade tartare sauce, curry sauce
and mushy peas (page 68), quality vinegar, sea salt and an array of pickles – all of this
takes fish and chips to a new level. At home, I don't like to stink the house out, so I set
myself up outside with a portable gas stove, get everything around me and let everyone
take their portion and help themselves to condiments. Because you won't have a huge fryer
at home, we're going with smaller pieces of fish, which are easier to cook to perfection.*

Slice your chosen fish up into chunky pieces the size of a playing card, checking that
there are no little bones. Season with sea salt, cover with clingfilm and allow to sit in
the fridge for 1 hour to draw out the excess moisture. Just before you're ready to
cook, make your batter. Put the flour and baking powder into a mixing bowl, pour in
the ale and whisk gently until smooth, thick and coating the back of a spoon nicely.

Just under half fill a large sturdy pan with oil (unless you own a deep-fat fryer, of
course) – the oil should be 8cm deep, but never fill your pan more than half full – and
place on a medium to high heat. Use a thermometer to get it to 180°C, or add a raw
chip as it's heating up and when it's golden and floating you'll be about right.

Pat all the fish dry with kitchen paper. Put 2 or 3 handfuls of flour in a shallow bowl.
Cooking one person's portion at a time is really advisable in a home situation, and
also means you can cook off a portion of blanched chips at the same time (page 66).
You want 2 pieces of fish per portion, so with 1 piece in each hand, dust the fish
well with flour then dredge through the batter, wiping on the edge of the bowl
to remove any excess. Carefully dip them in the oil so half the fish is submerged,
then after a few seconds, when it starts to float, gently plop the fish away from you.
Fry for 3 or 4 minutes, or until golden and crisp, depending on the thickness of your
fish. Remove with a slotted spoon to kitchen paper, season and let your guests tuck
straight in while you get on with cooking the next portion.

✕ THE PERFECT CHIPS ✕

SERVES 4   40 MINUTES   330 CALORIES

Without question, the humble fried potato, the chip, is a gastronomic phenomenon in itself. The ability potatoes have to get mega crispy on the outside and super-fluffy in the middle when cooked is so good. Skinny and shoestring fries are delicious, but a proper fat handcut chip is something else. It's just a shame that they're not very good for you, but, like a good old cake, life wouldn't be quite the same without them. At home, we don't cook chips very often, so when we do have them, we definitely want the real deal. So let me tell you how I make the perfect chip – if you're going to do it, do it right.

Three obvious things are important on your journey to perfection – your choice of potato, your choice of oil and your choice of salt. For me, the Maris Piper potato wins every time, and you want to use nice large ones. On oil, sunflower and sunseed are very efficient, and many people swear by using groundnut oil. But, if you're after flavour, cooking chips in beef tallow (rendered beef fat you can get from your butcher) gives you better flavour and colour – the choice is yours. Finally, on salt, being an Essex boy, in my house it has to be Maldon sea salt.

So down to business: chop 800g of Maris Piper potatoes into finger-sized chips, leaving the skin on – don't be too exact. Chip shops have massive industrial fryers, which you can't recreate at home, so you need to use a large sturdy pan on a medium to high heat (unless you own a deep-fat fryer, of course). Your oil should be 8cm deep, but never fill your pan more than half full. If you don't have a thermometer, use a raw chip, and as it starts to float and fry the temperature should be about 140°C, which is perfect for blanching. Use a large metal sieve to gently lower the chips into the pan for around 8 minutes, or until soft but not coloured, then remove to a tray to cool.

Turn the heat up under the oil and return one blanched chip to the oil as a guide again. Once it's floating and golden the temperature should be about 180°C, which is perfect for frying and will give you chips with those all-important crispy outsides and fluffy middles. At this stage you may want to cook your chips in 2-portion batches, so you don't decrease the temperature of the oil too much or overcrowd the pan. Fry the chips until beautifully golden, then remove to a bowl lined with kitchen paper, shake around a bit, season with sea salt and serve right away.

× CONDIMENTS ×

SERVES 4

1 HOUR 30 MINUTES
605 CALORIES

CURRY SAUCE

2 onions

5 cloves of garlic

2 carrots

olive oil

3 heaped teaspoons medium
   curry powder

3 tablespoons cornflour

2 tablespoons mango chutney

2 tablespoons white wine vinegar

low-salt soy sauce

TARTARE SAUCE

1 heaped tablespoon capers

5 baby cornichons

2 anchovy fillets

6 sprigs of fresh flat-leaf parsley

1 lemon

½ x basic mayo (page 258)

MUSHY PEAS

500g fresh or frozen garden peas

1 large knob of unsalted butter

½ a bunch of fresh mint (15g)

CURRY SAUCE

Peel and roughly chop the onions, garlic and carrots. Put a lug of oil into a large pan on a medium heat, add the chopped veg and cook for 20 minutes, stirring regularly. Stir in the curry powder, cornflour and mango chutney, then gradually stir in the vinegar and 350ml of boiling water. Simmer for 5 minutes to thicken, then blitz in a blender to the consistency that you like and season to perfection with soy sauce.

TARTARE SAUCE

Pile the capers, cornichons, anchovies and parsley leaves on a board. Finely grate over the lemon zest, then chop and mix it all together until fine. Stir into your basic mayo (page 258) with a squeeze of lemon juice, then taste and season to perfection.

MUSHY PEAS

Simply cook the peas in a pan of boiling salted water until tender. Drain and mash with the knob of butter to the consistency that you like. Pick and finely chop the mint leaves, stir them through the peas and season to perfection.

LET'S CHAT PICKLES

First up, you can make your own pickled veg by mixing 1 cup of water and 2 cups of your chosen vinegar with 1 heaped teaspoon each of sea salt and caster sugar, stirring until dissolved, then pouring it over cut-up pieces of veg (baby carrots, radishes, small turnips, sliced beets, blanched green beans – experiment) in a sterilized airtight jar. Feel free to scent them with different spices or fresh herbs, and if you define each one with a particular herb or spice, it makes them even more useful and delicious. These will be ready to go in a matter of hours, will easily last a couple of months and will improve with time. But a fun, if not slightly lazy, thing to do is just buy supermarket pickles – onions, dill pickles/cornichons, carrots, beans, chillies, even eggs – then jazz them up by draining the contents into a bowl and spicing up with fresh sliced chillies, some chopped fresh herbs, and mustard seeds or crushed peppercorns, to use right away. I often do this with large dill pickles, using my crinkle-cut knife (you should get one!) to slice them in an interesting way, then hitting them with lots of fresh dill and sliced chilli. So, whether making your own or pimping, have fun.

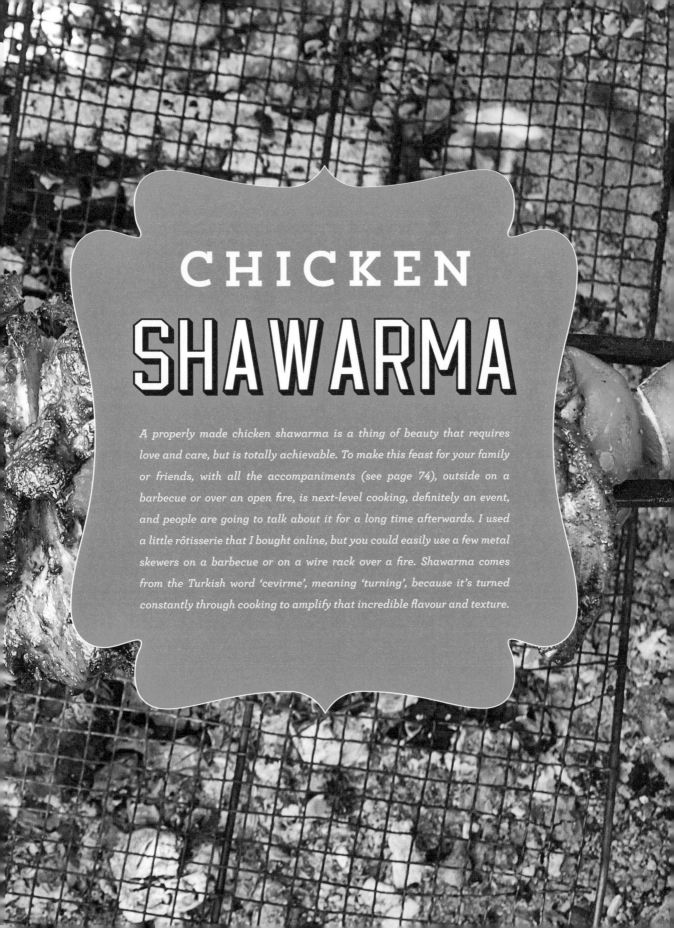

CHICKEN
SHAWARMA

A properly made chicken shawarma is a thing of beauty that requires love and care, but is totally achievable. To make this feast for your family or friends, with all the accompaniments (see page 74), outside on a barbecue or over an open fire, is next-level cooking, definitely an event, and people are going to talk about it for a long time afterwards. I used a little rôtisserie that I bought online, but you could easily use a few metal skewers on a barbecue or on a wire rack over a fire. Shawarma comes from the Turkish word 'cevirme', meaning 'turning', because it's turned constantly through cooking to amplify that incredible flavour and texture.

× CHICKEN SHAWARMA ×

SERVES 12
4–5 HOURS
PLUS MARINATING
498 CALORIES

10 cardamom pods

1 heaped teaspoon each
fennel seeds, cumin seeds,
coriander seeds

1 level teaspoon each ground
cinnamon, ground allspice,
ground cloves, sweet smoked
paprika

8 cloves of garlic

4 fresh bay leaves

4 tablespoons natural yoghurt

1 heaped tablespoon
smooth peanut butter

olive oil

16 boneless chicken thighs
(skin on)

3 large red peppers

3 onions

1–2 lemons

1–2 large tomatoes

FLATBREADS

2 heaped tablespoons
sesame seeds

900g strong white bread flour,
plus extra for dusting

100g wholemeal flour

1 teaspoon baking powder

Crush and pod the cardamoms, then toast all the spices in a dry frying pan for 2 minutes. Tip into a blender with a good pinch of sea salt and pepper and blitz until fine. Peel and add the garlic, then remove the stalks from the bay and tear the leaves into the blender. Add the yoghurt, peanut butter and a good drizzle of oil and blitz to a smooth paste, loosening with a splash of water, if needed. Put the chicken into a large bowl and massage with the paste, then cover and place in the fridge overnight.

The next day, tear the peppers into quarters, ripping out the seeds, and peel and quarter the onions. Using a spit or a couple of large skewers, start with half a lemon followed by half a tomato, then thread on all the chicken thighs, interspersing them with pieces of red pepper and onion. Finish with another tomato and lemon half, and drizzle with oil. At this point, my message to you is to remember that this should be a sociable experience. Set up your firepit or barbecue so you have a hot and a cool side, and let the hot side cool down while you prepare the flatbreads and make all the accompaniments (page 74). For the flatbreads, put the sesame seeds, flours, baking powder, a good pinch of salt and a lug of oil into a food processor. Pour in 550ml of cold water and blitz into a rough dough, then knead with your hands on a lightly floured surface for 2 to 3 minutes, or until smooth. Place in a large oiled bowl, cover with a damp tea towel and put to one side.

Now, whether you're using a rôtisserie or skewers, the emphasis is on you to control the heat. You want to spend about 1 hour getting your chicken from raw to dark, crispy, gnarly and sizzling, turning it every few minutes – you'll find your mojo. You've already created amazing flavours from the marinade so now it's about cooking and letting the fat drip onto the hot coals, explode into smoke and kiss your meat with even more flavour. When you feel that it's looking really good, carve off the outside layer of crispy skin and meat into a tray, just like at a kebab shop, then continue to cook and crisp up the next layer, simply continuing until it's all gone. Meanwhile, knock out your flatbreads pretty much to order. To cook them, divide the dough into 12 equal-sized balls and roll each one out as thinly as you can. Cook on a cake rack over a firepit, turning when golden, or on the barbecue over hot coals. Have all those lovley accompaniments around you ready for shawarma building. It's your shop so do a good job and, most importantly, have fun!

× SHAWARMA ACCOMPANIMENTS ×

AMBA SAUCE

2 ripe mangos

2 limes

2 cloves of garlic

olive oil

½ teaspoon each mustard seeds,
   fenugreek seeds, cayenne pepper,
   sweet smoked paprika, turmeric

SILKEN HOUMOUS

1 x 660g jar of quality chickpeas

1 lemon

1 clove of garlic

1 good pinch of ground cumin

2 tablespoons tahini

extra virgin olive oil

TABBOULEH

200g bulgar wheat

6 spring onions

1 big bunch of fresh
   mint leaves (60g)

1 big bunch of fresh
   flat-leaf parsley (60g)

3 small preserved lemons

3 large ripe vine tomatoes

red wine vinegar

PICKLED VEG

200g radishes or beets

2 tablespoons golden caster sugar

The amba sauce, houmous, tabbouleh and pickled veg, along with your ancient-style sesame flatbreads, are the exciting essentials that make your shawarma (page 72) so special. All but the cooking of the flatbreads can be done well in advance, so when you're ready, one at a time simply cook up the flatbreads, slice off some of that wonderful chicken, and let your guests tuck in to the mother of all kebabs. One thing to note: this isn't a traditional amba sauce – I've taken the liberty of freshening the recipe up to my taste, which I think works really well and cuts through the richness and char of the meat.

For the amba sauce, peel and destone the mangos, put the flesh into a blender with the lime zest and juice, then blitz until smooth. Peel and finely slice the garlic cloves and put into a frying pan on a medium heat with a little olive oil and all the spices. Toast until lightly golden, then stir in the mango. Season to taste, then leave to cool.

For the houmous, pour the chickpeas and their juice into a blender and squeeze in the lemon juice. Peel and add the garlic, along with the cumin, a good pinch of sea salt, the tahini and a good lug of extra virgin olive oil. Blitz until shiny and creamy, then have a little taste and tweak the seasoning to your liking.

For the tabbouleh, cook the bulgar wheat according to packet instructions, then leave to cool. Trim the spring onions, pick the mint leaves, then finely chop both with all the parsley and the preserved lemons and scrape into a bowl. Quarter the tomatoes, discarding the seeds, then finely chop and add to the bowl along with the cooled bulgar wheat. Mix together well, then drizzle over 3 tablespoons of red wine vinegar and 6 tablespoons of extra virgin olive oil and toss to coat. Season to perfection.

For the pickled veg, simply finely slice or shred all the radishes or beets (peeled), put into a shallow bowl and just cover with red wine vinegar. Add the sugar and a pinch of salt, then scrunch and mix to make a quick pickle.

With your chicken shawarma and flatbreads, all of the above accompaniments create an absolute feast. It's always nice served with some thinly sliced red onion, a few fresh coriander leaves, some pickled chillies, lemon wedges, a bottle of hot chilli sauce, and, of course, a few ice-cold beers on the side too.

DOUBLE WHAMMY

TOAD IN THE HOLE

× DOUBLE WHAMMY TOAD IN THE HOLE ×

SERVES 8

1 HOUR
764 CALORIES

3 red onions

sunflower oil

9 large sausages

14 large eggs

700g plain flour, plus 2 tablespoons

500ml semi-skimmed milk

450ml Hoegaarden beer or similar

a few sprigs of fresh rosemary

2 tablespoons HP sauce

1 chicken stock cube

Toad in the hole is a crazy name. The tradition of putting sausages or leftover chunks of stewed meat into Yorkshire pudding batter goes back hundreds of years, and presumably the meat poking out of the batter looked like a toad in a hole? Anyway, who cares, it's a great recipe and will become a central part of your comfort food repertoire. Your ability to hunt out the most spectacular fresh sausages your neighbourhood can offer is really important – pork, game and venison all work. You also need a killer Yorkshire pudding recipe, which I've given you here. I'm cooking one batch with the sausages so it's nice and gooey and stodgy, then doing a larger dedicated tray of unadulterated Yorkshire pudding that'll get really tall and crispy. With killer gravy too, this will never cease to wow.

Preheat the oven to 220°C/425°F/gas 7. To start your gravy, peel and finely slice the onions. Place them in a large pan on a medium heat with a lug of oil. Squeeze the meat out of one sausage into the pan and fry it all for 20 minutes, or until lightly golden, stirring occasionally and breaking the meat up with a wooden spoon as you go. Place the remaining 8 sausages in a large tray (30cm x 40cm), toss with a good drizzle of oil, then line them up and bake for 10 to 15 minutes, or until lightly golden. Pour ½cm of oil into an equally large tray and place under the sausages for 10 minutes to get nice and hot.

Meanwhile, whisk the eggs in a large bowl with 700g of flour and a good pinch of sea salt. Gradually whisk in the milk, then the beer, until you have a nice, smooth batter and, to make your life easier, divide it equally between two jugs.

Pick the rosemary leaves and, acting quickly and safely, slowly pull the tray of oil out of the oven, sprinkle in the leaves and pour in one jug's worth of batter. Pour the other jug's worth around the sausages. Gently close the door and try not to look for 30 minutes, or until the Yorkshires are beautifully golden and puffed up. Meanwhile, stir the HP and remaining 2 tablespoons of flour into the onions, crumble in the stock cube and gradually stir in 750ml of boiling water. Simmer to the consistency you like, then season to perfection. Serve everything in the middle of the table with a jug of that delicious gravy and a big heap of mixed steamed seasonal greens. Heaven.

× MUM'S SMOKED HADDOCK ×

SERVES 2
30 MINUTES
317 CALORIES

1 large onion

2 rashers of smoked streaky bacon
   or pancetta

olive oil

2 sprigs of fresh marjoram

200g baby spinach

1 lemon

2 x 100g fillets of undyed
   smoked haddock, skin on,
   scaled and pin-boned

2 fresh bay leaves

1 level teaspoon black peppercorns

2 large eggs

cayenne pepper

This lovely little recipe has found its way into the nostalgia chapter because the flavours evoke good memories of my mum cooking a version of this for me when I lived at home. It's one of those perfect quick, easy suppers that's always delicious. Admittedly the odd bone used to upset me if I had the top part of the fish, so always give your loved ones the tail portion, where there's no bones. Or, simply serve it with brown bread and butter – my nan and mum used to say it would remove any 'blasted' bones on the way down!

Peel and finely chop the onion. In a large frying pan on a medium-high heat, fry the bacon or pancetta in a drizzle of oil until golden and crisp, then remove to a plate and add the onion to the bacon fat in the pan. Pick in the marjoram leaves, add a good pinch of pepper, then cook for 5 minutes, stirring occasionally. Add the spinach to the pan and let it cook down for 5 minutes, or until dark, dense and delicious, and the excess water has cooked away. Squeeze in the juice of ½ a lemon and leave on the lowest heat.

Meanwhile, put the haddock, skin-side up, into a large wide pan of simmering water with the bay leaves and peppercorns. Squeeze in the remaining lemon juice, then add the squeezed half to the water. Simmer gently for around 7 minutes, then simply crack in the eggs in a fluid movement and poach for 2 to 4 minutes, depending how soft or firm you like them. To check they're done, lift one out with a slotted spoon and gently push it with your finger – use your instincts and if it needs firming up, return it to the water.

Use a fish slice to transfer the haddock to your plates. Divide the spinach between them, denting little holes in the middle to house the poached eggs. Lay over the crispy bacon or pancetta, sprinkle with a pinch of cayenne and enjoy. Simple, but totally classic.

PROPER
PORRIDGE

One of my earliest recollections of comfort food is also one of my earliest memories, full stop. I was about five years old and I'd been dropped off with my sister, Anna, to stay at my nan and grandad's. They lived in a cute little bungalow, stuck to a budget and cooked every single day. Because me and Anna lived in a pub, there wasn't really a routine, but over at Nan and Grandad's however, there was a real pattern to the day, starting at 7 a.m. sharp with Nan's ritual of proper porridge-making.

There'd always be steaming cups of tea waiting for us on the table, and we'd climb into our chairs, feet swinging above the floor. I can still picture the strange turquoise paper that lined the walls, the array of classic family photos on the mantelpiece, and the retro drinks cabinet where sometimes, if I was really lucky, Grandad would pull me to the side and pour me just a tiny taster of ginger wine. The radio – or the wireless as they called it – would always be on Radio 4 and we'd laugh as Grandad berated all the politicians during the news. Although he was a complete gentleman, he found it impossible not to let a few F-words slip out, which even at that early age I knew was funny because Nan used to tell him off.

Anyway, back to the porridge-making. Nan's porridge was like nothing I'd ever tasted before – having researched it, hers was a classic Scottish method, and it was delicious. It was about this same time that Ready Brek launched with a brilliant campaign where a kid went to school absolutely glowing after tucking into a bowl. Certainly my nan's porridge gave me a glow – it was on another level.

THE PORRIDGE RITUAL

*Proper porridge should take around 18 minutes from start to finish. For four people, add **1 big builder's mug of coarse rolled large porridge oats**, such as Flahavan's, to a high-sided pan with 3 mugs of boiling water and a pinch of sea salt. However you want to flavour or finish your porridge, it's important to start it with water, as milk often scalds or boils over and doesn't smell or taste great when it does. Place the pan on a medium heat until it just starts to boil, then reduce to a simmer for 15 minutes, or until thick and creamy, stirring regularly, and adding a good splash of **whole milk or cream** towards the end to enrich the porridge and make it super-luxurious.*

Nan would never be rushed when she made porridge, and all those torturous minutes later it would be poured a couple of centimetres thick into wide soup bowls and given to Grandad, Anna and me. We'd go to tuck straight in, but Grandad always stopped us, so I'm going to stop you now. It's important to wait another 3 minutes for the residual chill of the bowl to slightly cool down the porridge from the outside in, so it remains soft, silky and oozy in the middle, but goes almost firm and jellified round the edges. Grandad would always sprinkle his porridge with granulated brown sugar, and insist that you waited a minute and a half for it to pull out the moisture from the porridge and turn into a bizarrely impressive caramelly glaze. I loved this, but couldn't help opting for a good spoonful of golden syrup instead. What I found extraordinary was the way that over a couple of minutes, with a little jiggling of the bowl, the syrup always managed to creep down around and underneath the porridge, elevating it as if it were some sort of floating island. It baffles me to this day how that works, but I love it.

We'd then marvel as Grandad got out an eating knife and cut the porridge into a chequerboard. He'd then pick up a jug of cold whole milk and ease it to one side of the bowl, gently pouring so it filled up every crack of the chequerboard like some crazy paddy field drainage system. Then, and only then were we given the signal to attack. And I have to say, that porridge was as good a breakfast as I've ever had.

SOME OTHER IDEAS FOR SERVING PORRIDGE

The possibilities are endless . . . quarter a few figs or any stone fruit, roast or fry with honey, then spoon over your porridge. Smash up and fold through some quality chocolate for a rare treat that's to die for. Sprinkle seasonal berries with a little sugar and lemon juice, break a few up with a fork and stir through the porridge, or do exactly the same but simmer the berries in a pan first to create a delicate compote to stir through. You could achieve a similar effect by heating some sour apricot jam. I also like to lightly toast some sunflower, sesame and poppy seeds, crush them in a pestle and mortar with a pinch of ground cinnamon, mix them with some chopped dried fruit, then fold through. Or even take the latter combo, cook it fairly thick, pour it into an oiled tray about 2½cm thick, leave to set, cut into bars, and the next day, fry them in a little butter until golden and crispy on all sides, then serve with yoghurt and honey. Delicious.

· · · · · · · · · ·

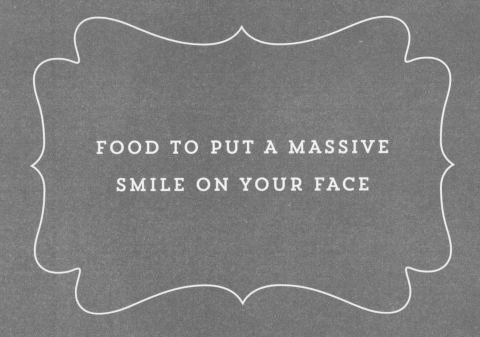

FOOD TO PUT A MASSIVE
SMILE ON YOUR FACE

GOOD
MOOD
FOOD

GORGEOUS GADO GADO

× GORGEOUS GADO-GADO ×

SERVES 4

40 MINUTES

505 CALORIES

SALAD

400g new potatoes

4 large eggs

400g firm silken tofu

sesame oil

½ a Chinese cabbage

2 ripe tomatoes

1 handful of radishes

½ a cucumber

2 handfuls of beansprouts
  (ready to eat)

½ a bunch of fresh coriander (15g)

optional: prawn crackers

optional: 1 fresh bird's-eye chilli

SAUCE

1 clove of garlic

50g palm sugar

120g crunchy peanut butter

1–2 fresh red chillies

juice of 2 limes

2 teaspoons fish sauce

1 tablespoon low-salt soy sauce

1 tablespoon tamarind paste

This is a mega salad that has its roots in Sundanese cooking and has now become the typical street food of Jakarta in Indonesia. Gado-gado means medley or potpourri, which refers to all the different seasonal veggies and ingredients that are used, making it slightly different wherever you go and whatever the time of year. Tossed with the most incredible peanut dressing, which to be honest is more of a substantial sauce, and served with something crunchy on the side, such as prawn crackers, it's a winning combination.

Start by prepping all your salad ingredients. Scrub the potatoes and cook in boiling salted water for around 15 minutes, or until tender, then halve or slice up. Soft-boil the eggs for 6 minutes, or longer if you prefer them more cooked. Cut the tofu into 2½cm chunks and fry in a splash of sesame oil for around 15 minutes, or until golden, then sprinkle lightly with sea salt. Finely shred the cabbage if you want it raw or, if you'd rather cook it (which is traditional), cut it into 2cm slices, place in a colander and slowly pour a kettle of boiling water over the top. For me, this is the perfect amount of heat to soften the cabbage but means you keep much of the delicious nutrients in there – feel free to apply this to any other seasonal greens you can find too. Cut the tomatoes into wedges, quarter the radishes and slice the cucumber (I use my crinkle-cut knife – you should get one!). Season everything from a height with a little salt.

Next, put all the sauce ingredients into a blender, peeling the garlic and grating in the palm sugar (if needed), then blitz until smooth. Have a taste and adjust the seasoning, making sure the acidity of the lime sings through, so tweak with more, if needed.

Traditionally, you'd take a little bit of everything, put it into a bowl and pour the sauce over the top, which is a fine way to serve it. I like to do the reverse, because I feel that once you pour the sauce over you can't see the care and attention that has gone into the preparation of the ingredients. So I spoon the sauce between four bowls, spread it up around the sides, then divide the ingredients around the bowls, taking a bit of pride in making them look nice. Pick over a few coriander leaves, add the prawn crackers and some finely sliced fresh chilli (if using), then show everyone what a celebration of food this is by getting them to toss together their very own portion.

× INSANITY BURGER ×

SERVES 4
35 MINUTES
PLUS CHILLING
694 CALORIES

800g minced chuck steak

olive oil

1 large red onion

1 splash of white wine vinegar

2 large gherkins

4 sesame-topped brioche
  burger buns

4–8 rashers of smoked
  streaky bacon

4 teaspoons American mustard

Tabasco Chipotle sauce

4 thin slices of Red Leicester
  cheese

4 teaspoons tomato ketchup

BURGER SAUCE

¼ of an iceberg lettuce

2 heaped tablespoons mayo

1 heaped tablespoon tomato
  ketchup

1 teaspoon Tabasco Chipotle sauce

1 teaspoon Worcestershire sauce

optional: 1 teaspoon brandy
  or bourbon

Competition for the best burger in London has gone mad. Some burgers are gourmet and piled high with toppings, whereas others are thinner, simpler, wrapped in paper, steamy and sloppy. All I can say is my insanity burger is going to be right up there – the method is almost ritualistic in what it requires you to do to get close to burger perfection. I've also used the brilliant technique of brushing the burgers with mustard and a dash of Tabasco Chipotle sauce as they cook to build up an incredible gnarly layer of seasoning.

For the best burger, go to your butcher's and ask them to mince 800g of chuck steak for you. This cut has a really good balance of fat and flavoursome meat. Divide it into 4 and, with wet hands, roll each piece into a ball, then press into flat patties roughly 12cm wide and about 2cm wider than your buns. Place on an oiled plate and chill in the fridge. Next, finely slice the red onion, then dress in a bowl with the vinegar and a pinch of sea salt. Slice the gherkins and halve the buns. Finely chop the lettuce and mix with the rest of the burger sauce ingredients in a bowl, then season to taste.

I like to only cook 2 burgers at a time to achieve perfection, so get two pans on the go – a large non-stick pan on a high heat for your burgers and another on a medium heat for the bacon. Pat your burgers with oil and season them with salt and pepper. Put 2 burgers into the first pan, pressing down on them with a fish slice, then put half the bacon into the other pan. After 1 minute, flip the burgers and brush each cooked side with ½ a teaspoon of mustard and a dash of Tabasco. After another minute, flip onto the mustard side and brush again with another ½ teaspoon of mustard and a second dash of Tabasco on the other side. Cook for one more minute, by which point you can place some crispy bacon on top of each burger with a slice of cheese. Add a tiny splash of water to the pan and place a heatproof bowl over the burgers to melt the cheese – 30 seconds should do it. At the same time, toast 2 split buns in the bacon fat in the other pan until lightly golden. Repeat with the remaining two burgers.

To build each burger, add a quarter of the burger sauce to the bun base, then top with a cheesy bacon burger, a quarter of the onions and gherkins. Rub the bun top with a teaspoon of ketchup, then gently press together. As the burger rests, juices will soak into the bun, so serve right away, which is great, or for an extra filthy experience, wrap each one in greaseproof paper, then give it a minute to go gorgeous and sloppy.

× BRAZILIAN FEIJOADA ×

SERVES 8–10

<u>4 HOURS</u>
PLUS SOAKING
<u>738 CALORIES</u>

750g black beans

1 pig's ear, tail and trotter
   (ask your butcher to cut them
   into 2cm chunks)

2 onions

5 cloves of garlic

olive oil

250g pork belly (skin on – ask
   your butcher to cut it into
   2cm chunks)

3 fresh bay leaves

1 teaspoon smoked paprika

75g chunk of smoked streaky bacon

100g fresh smoked chorizo

150g smoked pork ribs

500g spring greens

toasted cassava flour

SALSA

1 large red onion

5 large ripe tomatoes

1 red or yellow pepper

1 bunch of fresh flat-leaf
   parsley (30g)

1 lemon

3 tablespoons extra virgin olive oil

1 tablespoon white wine vinegar

Considered to be the national dish of Brazil, this is an outrageously good combination of pork and beans, slow-cooked to perfection, which traditionally includes the extra odds and ends from the pig so that absolutely nothing goes to waste. You'll easily find all these ingredients at your butcher's – smoked ribs are sold in Portuguese and Brazilian butchers up and down the country, but if you can't get them, simply use regular ribs instead. I'm excited to share my Brazilian brother Almir Santos' recipe here – he's a wonderful man, a fantastic cook, and I've had the pleasure of working with him since I was twenty years old. Get a crowd together – double or treble this recipe if you like – and have a party.

The day before, place the black beans in a large pan, cover with plenty of water and put the lid on. Do the same with the chunks of pig's ear, tail and trotter, then leave both to soak overnight. The next day, place the black beans pan on the hob, topping up with water to cover the beans if needed, then bring to a gentle boil and simmer for 30 minutes (it's important to keep them in the same water to achieve the most vibrant colour). Meanwhile, peel and finely chop the onions and garlic. Heat a splash of olive oil in a very large casserole pan on a medium-high heat, drain and add the chunks of pig's ear, tail and trotter and pork belly and fry for 15 minutes, or until golden and gnarly. At this point, go in with three-quarters of the chopped onions, and all the garlic, bay leaves and paprika. Slice up the bacon and chorizo 2cm thick, cut the ribs up, then add it all to the pan and cook for 15 minutes, stirring regularly.

When the time's up, pour the beans into the meat pan with enough of their cooking water to cover everything nicely. Cook on a low heat for 3 hours, or until the meat is tender, stirring occasionally, and topping up with a little more water, if needed.

To make the salsa, peel the onion, deseed the tomatoes and pepper, then very finely chop them with the top leafy half of the parsley, mixing as you go. In a bowl, dress with the lemon juice, extra virgin olive oil and vinegar, then taste and season to perfection.

Just before you're ready to serve, tear off the leaves of the spring greens, roll up and slice them 1cm thick, then cook with the remaining chopped onions and a splash of olive oil in a large pan on a high heat for 5 minutes. Season the feijoada to taste, then serve with fluffy rice, your spring greens, salsa and plenty of cold beers. To be truly authentic, you want a little bowl of toasted cassava flour on the side to dip each mouthful in, and some hot pickled chillies. Santos also recommends a few fresh wedges of orange to cut through the intensity of the sauce – delicious.

× KATSU CURRY ×

SERVES 4

1 HOUR 30 MINUTES
PLUS MARINATING
981 CALORIES

4 x 150g skinless boneless
    chicken breasts

250ml buttermilk

2 heaped teaspoons medium
    curry powder

2 cloves of garlic

120g panko breadcrumbs

1 mug of basmati rice (320g)

25g creamed coconut

2 litres vegetable oil

SAUCE

1 onion

2 cloves of garlic

1 thumb-sized piece of ginger

1 medium carrot

1 bunch of fresh coriander (30g)

olive oil

1 teaspoon each garam masala,
    medium curry powder, turmeric

2 heaped tablespoons plain flour

1 heaped teaspoon mango chutney

PICKLE

1 red onion

1 lemon

1 fresh red chilli

Katsu curry is super-delicious and is one of Japan's most popular dishes. Its heart is Indian spices, which were brought through the spice trade to Britain, where we manufactured our first curry powder; then, back again through trade, they went to Japan, along with the French technique of thickening sauces with a roux (fat and flour) – and the katsu curry was born. Katsu was traditionally made with pork, but I have to say, chicken is my favourite.

Press down firmly with the palm of your hand to slightly flatten each chicken breast. Place them in a bowl and pour over the buttermilk. Add the curry powder and a pinch of sea salt, crush in the garlic, then toss to coat. Cover and marinate in the fridge for at least 2 hours, but preferably overnight. When the time's up, sprinkle the breadcrumbs on a tray. Remove the chicken from the buttermilk, shake off the excess, then turn in the breadcrumbs, pressing down to make them stick and flatten them a little more. Keep in the fridge until you're ready to cook.

For the sauce, peel the onion, garlic, ginger and carrot, then finely chop with the coriander stalks (reserving the leaves). Fry in a large pan over a medium-low heat with a lug of olive oil and the spices for 15 minutes, or until starting to caramelize, stirring regularly. Stir in the flour, then the mango chutney. Pour in 800ml of boiling water and leave to blip away for 15 minutes, or until reduced to a nice sauce consistency, stirring occasionally. Taste, season and add more mango chutney, if needed.

Meanwhile, place 1 mug of rice in a medium pan. Add 2 mugs of boiling water and a good pinch of salt, then break in the creamed coconut and mix together. Bring to the boil, stir, then put the lid on and simmer for 10 minutes, or until the water has evaporated. Turn the heat off and leave with the lid on. Make a quick pickle by peeling and very finely slicing the red onion. Place in a bowl with the lemon zest and juice and a good pinch of salt. Deseed and finely slice the chilli and add to the bowl, then mix up.

Just under half fill a large sturdy pan with vegetable oil – the oil should be 8cm deep, but never fill your pan more than half full – and place on a medium to high heat. Use a thermometer to get it to 180°C, or add a piece of potato and wait until it's golden and floating. Use a slotted spoon to lower the chicken into the oil, fry for 8 minutes, or until golden and cooked through, then drain on kitchen paper.

To serve, put a quarter of the rice into a small bowl, press to compact and turn out onto a plate, then repeat with the other portions. Place the chicken next to the rice, cover with the sauce, then sprinkle over the pickle and coriander leaves.

IRRESISTIBLE

PORK BUNS

✕

× IRRESISTIBLE PORK BUNS ×

SERVES 4

6 HOURS 30 MINUTES
PLUS CHILLING & PROVING
526 CALORIES

PORK

1.2kg pork belly, bone out

sesame oil

caster sugar

BUNS

400ml semi-skimmed milk

50g unsalted butter (at room
temperature)

700g good-quality Tipo 00 flour,
plus extra for dusting

1 heaped tablespoon caster sugar

1 x 7g sachet of dried yeast

1 heaped teaspoon each baking
powder, bicarbonate of soda

PICKLES

1 cucumber

1 bunch of radishes

2 teaspoons caster sugar

6 tablespoons rice wine vinegar

TO SERVE

1 heaped tablespoon sesame seeds

4 spring onions

8 sprigs of fresh coriander

1 fresh red chilli

hoisin sauce

Recently the popularity of crispy-pork-stuffed steamed buns has gone off the scale. They're good-value, really common Korean street food, and the combination of these soft buns, sauces, pickles and pork will blow you away. I love to mix this recipe up by swapping the pork for crispy roasted duck (simply cooked at 180°C for 2 hours), or at Christmas, using roasted goose is amazing (simply cooked at 180°C for 4 hours). Have fun with it.

Start cooking the pork a day ahead. Preheat the oven to 140°C/275°F/gas 1. Carefully remove the pork skin from the belly (your butcher can do this for you) and pop into the fridge. In a large roasting tray, rub the belly with sesame oil and season with a good pinch of sea salt and sugar. Cover tightly with a double layer of tin foil and cook for 5 hours, then remove, cool and refrigerate in the same tray overnight.

The next day, by hand or in a free-standing electric mixer, combine all the bun ingredients with 1 level teaspoon of salt, then knead for 10 minutes. Place in a bowl, cover with clingfilm and prove for 1 hour. Knock the dough back and divide into 20 equal pieces. Roll into smooth balls, place on a flour-dusted tray, cover with a damp tea towel and prove for another hour. One-by-one, with a rolling pin, roll the balls into 10cm x 12cm ovals. Lay an oiled chopstick across the middle like a hinge, fold the dough in half over the top and pull the chopstick out. Place each bun on a little rectangle of greaseproof paper in bamboo steamers, in single layers, ready for steaming later.

Preheat the oven to full whack (240°C/475°F/gas 9). For the garnish bowls, I like to make quick pickles by finely slicing the cucumbers and radishes on a mandolin (use the guard!) into separate bowls. Sprinkle each with ½ a teaspoon of salt (don't worry – most will drain away), then divide the sugar and vinegar between them. Toss and pop into the fridge until needed. Lightly toast the sesame seeds and decant into another bowl. Trim the spring onions, then finely slice lengthways and pop into a bowl of ice-cold water so they curl up. Pick the coriander leaves. Finely slice the chilli. Place the pork skin on a tray, season and roast until puffy and crackled, keeping a close eye on it, then remove – once cool, smash up.

When you're ready to go, slice the pork 1cm thick, then halve each slice, return it in a single layer, to the tray it was cooked in, and roast in the oven until golden, draining away the excess fat occasionally to help it crisp up. At the same time, steam the buns over a pan of simmering water for 8 to 10 minutes, or until fluffy. Scrunch and squeeze the pickles to get rid of the excess salty liquid, then transfer to clean bowls. Take everything to the table with a bottle of hoisin and let everyone build their own.

NASI GORENG

❋

× NASI GORENG ×

SERVES 4
45 MINUTES
535 CALORIES

1 mug of basmati rice (320g)

1 onion

2 cloves of garlic

1 thumb-sized piece of ginger

1–2 fresh bird's-eye chillies

200g sugar snap peas

200g tenderstem broccoli

groundnut oil

1 tablespoon palm sugar

3 tablespoons kecap manis
   (sweet soy sauce)

fish sauce

hot chilli sauce

CUCUMBER PICKLE

1 large cucumber

1 bunch of fresh coriander (30g)

rice wine vinegar

1 lime

caster sugar

BUBBLY EGGS

4 spring onions

1–2 fresh bird's-eye chillies

4 large eggs

This twist on the Chinese technique of stir-fried rice is one of the most popular dishes of Indonesia. Historically, it came from the need to use up leftover rice at that time of no refrigerators. It should reflect what's available locally and seasonally, and by default there are thousands of different variations, though commonly it is flavoured and fried with garlic, peppers, sweet soy sauce and various condiments from fish sauce to ketchups. It's often served as breakfast, I love it for brunch, and it makes a wicked midnight munchie.

Put 1 mug of rice into a pan with a pinch of sea salt, cover with 2 mugs of boiling water and cook on a medium heat for 10 to 12 minutes, or until cooked through. Tip onto a large tray and spread out into a thin layer to steam and cool completely. Of course, you can simply use up leftover rice from the day before, which is even better.

Meanwhile, make the pickle. Peel the cucumber, then slice it ½cm thick (with a crinkle-cut knife if you've got one), and place in a bowl. Finely chop half the coriander stalks (reserving the leaves) and add to the bowl with a good few swigs of vinegar. Add the lime zest and juice, and caster sugar, then season and toss together well.

Peel the onion, garlic and ginger, deseed the chillies, then finely chop it all with the remaining coriander stalks. Finely slice the sugar snap peas at an angle, and cut the broccoli into bite-sized pieces. Place a large heavy-bottomed pan or wok on a high heat, add a lug of oil, then go in with the onion, garlic, ginger, chilli, coriander stalks and palm sugar. Stir-fry for a few minutes, then add the sugar snaps, broccoli and cooled rice and continue cooking for 3 to 4 minutes, or until the rice is hot through, tossing regularly. Stir in the kecap manis and a few shakes of fish sauce to season, then turn the heat off. Place a quarter of the rice in a small bowl, push down to compact, then turn out onto a serving plate – think sandcastles! Repeat with the remaining rice.

For the bubbly eggs, trim the spring onions and finely slice with the chillies. Place a large non-stick pan on a high heat and add ½cm of oil. Once hot, crack in the eggs and fry so the whites really bubble up and get crispy round the edges – by angling the pan you can spoon hot oil over the yolks as they cook to your liking. Remove to kitchen paper and pat off the excess oil, then use the eggs to top each portion of rice. Scatter over the spring onions, chilli and reserved coriander leaves, drizzled with some hot chilli sauce for a bit of a kick and serve with the cucumber pickle. Happy days.

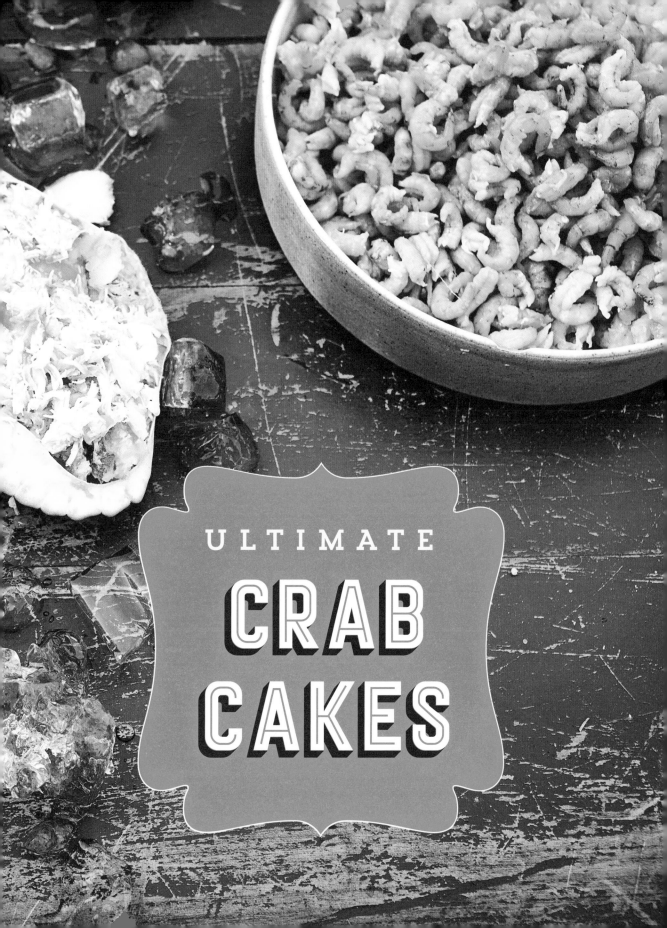

ULTIMATE
CRAB
CAKES

✕ ULTIMATE CRAB CAKES ✕

SERVES 4

1 HOUR
475 CALORIES

4 cream crackers

1 large egg yolk

½ a bunch of fresh chives (15g)

300g white crabmeat

50g brown crabmeat

1 heaped tablespoon soured
   cream, plus extra to serve

1 tablespoon Worcestershire sauce

1 fresh red chilli

1 lemon

4 heaped teaspoons plain flour,
   plus extra for dusting

sunflower oil

2 heaped teaspoons English
   mustard powder

cayenne pepper

100g small brown shrimp

SALAD PLATES

400g ripe mixed-colour tomatoes

1 small cucumber

½ a bunch of fresh flowering
   oregano (15g)

white wine vinegar

extra virgin olive oil

These beautiful crab cakes with brown shrimp are an absolute delicacy that must be enjoyed. However, they should only be made when you can get hold of wonderfully fresh picked crabmeat from a fishmonger; or, even better, if you can cook and pick the crabmeat yourself, which is a little effort but totally worth it (I've got a video to guide you through it at jamieoliver.com/how-to) – it will mean the flavour and texture of the crabmeat are even more ridiculous. Serve them up on a tomato salad plate to make it complete.

Finely crush the crackers and crumble into a bowl, then add the egg yolk. Finely slice and add the chives, along with all the crabmeat, the soured cream and Worcestershire sauce. Finely chop and add the chilli (deseed it if you like), grate in the zest of ½ a lemon, then mix it all together and divide into 4 even-sized round balls. Dust them generously with flour and place in the fridge for 20 minutes to firm up.

Meanwhile, finely slice the tomatoes into beautiful rounds. Scrape a fork down the length of the cucumber all the way round to create lovely grooves, then finely slice it into rounds too. Take a bit of care arranging the tomato and cucumber slices over four serving plates, overlapping the slices slightly to almost create a salad plate on each one. Pick over the oregano leaves, sprinkle with a little sea salt and pepper from a height, then drizzle each plate with a little vinegar and extra virgin olive oil.

Pour 2cm of sunflower oil into a large frying pan and place on a high heat with a cube of potato – when it turns golden, the oil is ready. While the oil heats up, to make a really delicious crunchy coating, mix the flour, mustard powder and a pinch or two of cayenne pepper with the juice of the zested lemon to form a thick paste, loosening with a little water if needed – you want it to be really thick and sticky. Stir the shrimps into the paste, then, one crab cake at a time, spread and stick the shrimp to the outside of each cake, flattening each one as you go from a ball into a more traditional fishcake shape. Carefully place the crab cakes in the hot oil and cook for 3 to 4 minutes on each side, or until golden. Remove to a plate lined with kitchen paper to drain, then season with salt and pepper.

Place a crab cake proudly in the centre of each salad plate. Nice served with a dollop of soured cream, a sprinkling of cayenne, and a lemon wedge for squeezing over.

HAPPINESS
IS A BACON SARNIE

Me and my dear friend Pete Begg have two very different approaches to the institution that is the perfect bacon sarnie. The only thing we agree on is that bacon ain't bacon unless it's smoked, but that's pretty much where the similarities end.

We do both use two 1½cm-thick slices of simple standard white crusty loaf, but I favour a bloomer and Pete tends to go for a tin loaf. Pete's a 3 rashers of streaky-bacon boy; I'm a back-bacon boy. He cooks it in a frying pan, starting out from cold with a little drizzle of olive oil and gradually bringing the temperature up to medium-high so the fat renders out, placing something flat and heavy on top to ensure super-even crispy bacon. I, on the other hand, put the grill on full whack, rub a tray and 3 rashers of back bacon with olive oil, then blast it until golden and crisp, which encourages the fat end of the bacon to curl up, creating a little pond of delicious bacon juice in the middle.

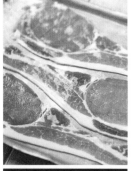

Pete butters his bread, then lays the bacon on side-by-side, like floorboards. I skip the butter, but push the bacon to the side of my tray and lay the bread in the fat for a few seconds before assembling, letting the bacon rashers sit on the bed of bread like spooning lovers. At this point, Pete goes into another gear and displays a little trick his dad taught him as a boy, sandwiching his creation together and placing it back in the pan of smoky bacon fat to lightly toast on both sides, again with a little weight on top. And it doesn't finish there – Pete stipulates that if the bacon runs north to south it must be cut east to west into 3 thin sandwiches, so you get 3 bacon soldiers in each, from which he gets 3 perfect bites. Genius. I simply cut mine diagonally from corner to corner and get it in my gob as quickly as possible .

Having been brought up in Essex I have a loyal commitment to HP sauce, but Pete pulls yet another trick out of the bag, treating his plate like an artist's palette with 60% ketchup, 30% English mustard and 10% green chilli sauce, feathered together with a knife, to ensure 9 erratic, beautiful-tasting mouthfuls. Wow.

These two sandwiches are both delicious, but most importantly, this is how I like mine and Pete likes his. How do you like yours?

2

× CHICKEN SATAY ×

SERVES 4

40 MINUTES
PLUS MARINATING
450 CALORIES

1 level teaspoon medium
  curry powder

½ level teaspoon ground cumin

1 heaped teaspoon turmeric

3–4 fresh chillies

2 cloves of garlic

1 thumb-sized piece of ginger

1 bunch of fresh coriander (30g)

6 tablespoons crunchy
  peanut butter

2 tablespoons low-salt soy sauce

6 spring onions

4 limes

8 skinless boneless chicken thighs

1 handful of shelled peanuts

groundnut oil

¼ of a watermelon (1.5kg) or
  1 ripe pineapple

Satay is one of those incredible skewered meat dishes that really hits the spot – lightly spiced, sweet and salty, it's all pulled together by that moreish peanut sauce. A fast old-school street food, this dish, which brilliantly can embrace all meats, can be found all over Malaysia and Indonesia. Its origins seem to point back to Java in Indonesia, where the concept of kebabs was brought by Muslim traders from India and Arab countries. Peanuts were introduced by Spanish and Portuguese explorers and they thrived in the tropical climate, which is why you see them used in so many garnishes and sauces there today. As a starter, a main, part of a salad spread or in a flatbread, it's always going to be good.

Gently heat the curry powder, cumin and turmeric for 1 minute in a dry pan on a medium heat. Deseed 2 chillies and peel the garlic and ginger. Place in a blender with the toasted spices and coriander (reserving a few nice leaves in a bowl of cold water for later). Add the peanut butter, soy sauce, the green parts of the spring onions, the zest of 2 limes and the juice of 3. Blitz until almost smooth, loosening with a few splashes of water, if needed, then taste and season to perfection. Cut each chicken thigh into 4 pieces and toss with half the satay sauce. Divide and thread onto 4 skewers and marinate in the fridge for at least 2 hours, but preferably overnight.

If you're using a barbecue, get it going 1 hour before you want to cook. If you're using a griddle pan, cut your wooden skewers to fit and preheat the pan.

Get a garnish plate together – drain the coriander leaves, finely slice the whites of the spring onions, finely slice the remaining chillies and wedge up the remaining lime. Toast the peanuts in a dry pan until golden, then crush and add to the plate.

When you're ready to cook, oil and lightly season the chicken on both sides, then place on your medium-hot barbecue or griddle pan. Cook for around 15 minutes, or until beautifully gnarly and golden, turning regularly. Serve on a platter with the rest of the sauce on the side. Sprinkle over the garnishes and slice up some nice ripe wedges of watermelon or pineapple to serve on the side – heavenly.

☓ BLACK COD ☓

SERVES 4

40 MINUTES
PLUS COOLING & MARINATING
254 CALORIES

COD

4 tablespoons runny honey

3 tablespoons white miso paste

3 tablespoons low-salt soy sauce

2 tablespoons sake

1 tablespoon rice wine vinegar

1 teaspoon sesame oil

4 x 150g fillets of cod, haddock,
    salmon, monkfish or pollock,
    skin on, scaled and pin-boned

extra virgin olive oil

2 sprigs of fresh coriander

PICKLE

6 radishes

1–2 fresh bird's-eye chillies

6 spring onions

4 heaped teaspoons pickled ginger,
    plus pickling liquor

1 tablespoon white wine vinegar

2 sprigs of fresh coriander

Black cod has become one of those culty restaurant dishes, made famous by the mighty Nobu Matsuhisa. This is my homage to his dish for you to enjoy at home, served with a lovely radish pickle to cut through the beautiful richness of the sauce. What makes this dish amazing is the effect the marinade has on the fish, causing it to be really tasty and flaky, and, of course, glazing it nicely. It's a brilliant, easy dish that will deliver every time.

In a small pan, mix the honey and miso with a splash of water. Boil and simmer until dark golden, stirring regularly. Remove from the heat and stir in the soy sauce, sake, rice wine vinegar and sesame oil, then leave to cool. Pour half into a large sandwich bag, add the fish, massage it in all that flavour, then squeeze the air out, seal and marinate in the fridge overnight. Reserve the remaining marinade in a dish in the fridge too.

Just before you cook the fish, with a mandolin (use the guard!) or good knife skills finely slice the radishes and chillies (deseed, if you like) and place in a bowl. Trim, finely slice and add the spring onions, finely slice the pickled ginger, then add to the bowl with 3 tablespoons of its liquor, the white wine vinegar and a good pinch of sea salt, and mix up. Lastly, finely slice and stir in a few coriander leaves.

When you're ready to cook, preheat the oven to full whack (240°C/475°F/gas 9). Put the reserved marinade into a large non-stick ovenproof frying pan and place on a high heat on the hob – once it starts to bubble, add the fish, skin-side up, and brush all over with the marinade. Transfer to the oven to roast for around 5 minutes, or until beautifully golden and a little bit caught around the edges.

Serve the fish flesh-side up, spooning over any leftover juices from the pan, with a delicate spoonful of the pickle, a little drizzle of extra virgin olive oil and a few freshly picked coriander leaves. Really nice with steamed greens – such as tenderstem broccoli, pak choi, asparagus or sugar snap peas – on the side.

× GHANAIAN GROUNDNUT STEW ×

SERVES 6
2 HOURS 10 MINUTES
PLUS MARINATING
382 CALORIES

1 x 1.6kg whole chicken

2 teaspoons ground coriander

2 heaped teaspoons sweet
    smoked paprika

1 level teaspoon cayenne pepper

olive oil

2 medium onions

1 fresh Scotch bonnet chilli

2 large aubergines

1 tablespoon tomato purée

800g ripe tomatoes

750ml fresh chicken stock

1 heaped tablespoon smooth
    peanut butter

300g okra

SUPER-HOT QUICK PICKLE

1 red onion

1–2 fresh Scotch bonnet chillies

4 fresh bay leaves

1 heaped teaspoon golden
    caster sugar

8 tablespoons red wine vinegar

Last year I was due to film with incredible actor Idris Elba, and we were going to celebrate a special comfort food dish that has a particular meaning to him. This amazing groundnut stew was his mother's recipe and has wonderful Ghanaian roots – I've tweaked it a little here, but the heart and soul are the same. Sadly Idris didn't make it onto the show as his dear father passed away, so I felt this was the perfect opportunity to dedicate this recipe to his dad, Winston, who also adored this delicious dish. Be sure to give this one a go.

With a large knife, hack up the chicken into thighs, drumsticks, wings and manageable chunks of breast, all kept on the bone with the skin on for maximum flavour. Place in a bowl, sprinkle over the ground coriander, paprika, cayenne and a pinch of sea salt and black pepper, drizzle with oil, then toss to coat. Cover with clingfilm and place in the fridge for 2 hours, but preferably overnight.

Preheat the oven to 200°C/400°F/gas 6. Arrange the chicken pieces in a roasting tray in a single layer and roast for around 45 minutes, or until golden. Meanwhile, peel and roughly chop the onions, halve, deseed and finely chop the Scotch bonnet (be careful!), and cut the aubergines into big chunks. Place a large casserole pan on a medium heat, add a good lug of oil and the chopped veg and cook for 30 minutes, stirring regularly. Stir in the tomato purée, followed by the chicken. Add a splash of water to the empty chicken tray and scrape up all the sticky goodness from the bottom, then add to the pan. Erratically chop up and add the tomatoes, pour in the stock, bring to the boil, then simmer gently with the lid off for just over 1 hour, or until the chicken is tender and the sauce has thickened slightly. With 30 minutes to go, dollop the peanut butter into the centre of the stew, and let it melt in as it finishes cooking. Idris likes 1 spoonful of peanut butter, but his mum said you can add a little more to taste, if you like.

Meanwhile, make the super-hot quick pickle. Peel and finely slice the red onion, deseed and very finely slice the Scotch bonnets, put into a bowl with the remaining pickle ingredients and 1 teaspoon of salt, and stir until the sugar has dissolved.

Trim the okra and char on a hot griddle pan. When it's ready, season the stew to perfection, then serve with the pickle, griddled okra, and either traditionally with little fufu (dumplings), flatbreads or, as I like it, with fluffy rice (Idris loves to slice just 4 okra and add them into his rice while it cooks, which is a lovely tip).

BEST CORNBREAD & CHIPOTLE BUTTER

× BEST CORNBREAD & CHIPOTLE BUTTER ×

SERVES 12
1 HOUR 35 MINUTES
PLUS CHILLING & COOLING
282 CALORIES

CHIPOTLE BUTTER

4 dried smoked chipotle chillies
   (smoked ancho chillies
   are good too)

4 cloves of garlic

2 fresh red chillies

500g unsalted butter
   (at room temperature)

CORNBREAD

2 fresh jalapeño chillies

2 tablespoons cider vinegar

325g coarse cornmeal or polenta

100g plain flour

1 teaspoon baking powder

250ml whole milk

4 large eggs

2 corn on the cob

150g Cheddar cheese

2 tablespoons cottage cheese

I love making cornbread. This is a particularly strong recipe, with tempting little smacks of jalapeño, Cheddar cheese and corn inside the bread. While it's still warm, hit it up with some smoky chipotle butter – come on, you know that's good. Great as a base for breakfast or brunch and brilliant as a side with any roasted or pulled meats.

If you're going to make chipotle butter, make it for the year – it's genius; you can use it in all sorts of cooking. Pop the dried chipotle chillies into a small bowl, just cover with boiling water and leave to rehydrate for 20 minutes. Peel the garlic, deseed the fresh chillies (every chilli has a different heat, so always taste a little bit and gauge whether you want to use more or less than I've recommended here), put them into a food processor with the chipotle chillies (discarding the soaking water) and a pinch of sea salt and black pepper, then blitz until finely chopped. Dice up the butter, add to the processor and pulse until combined. Divide between a couple of sheets of greaseproof paper, roll up into logs, twist the ends like Christmas crackers and pop into the freezer. After 30 minutes, get the butters out and slice them up to pre-portion, then re-roll and return to the freezer until needed.

Preheat the oven to 200°C/400°F/gas 6. Grease a deep baking tray (20cm x 25cm) and line with greaseproof paper. Finely slice the jalapeño chillies, mix with the vinegar and a pinch of salt in a small bowl, and leave to pickle while you put the cornmeal or polenta, flour, baking powder, milk, eggs and a good pinch of salt into a large bowl. Holding the cobs upright, carefully cut off the corn kernels and add them to the large bowl. Crumble in little bombs of Cheddar, add the cottage cheese, scoop up and add the chillies (saving the vinegar for a dressing another day), then mix until combined. Pour into the lined tin and bake for 35 minutes, or until golden and smelling wonderful. Leave in the tin for 10 minutes, then turn out onto a wire rack to cool.

For the most epic breakfast or brunch, simply slice the cornbread 2cm thick, toast on a hot griddle pan and spread with some chipotle butter. Amazing with slices of ripe tomato and wedges of ripe avocado, all seasoned and dressed with a little lime juice, as well as crispy smoked streaky bacon, a few extra slices of fresh chilli if you're feeling the urge, and a few fresh mint or coriander leaves sprinkled over.

× BEEF WELLINGTON ×

SERVES 6

1 HOUR 30 MINUTES
835 CALORIES

1kg centre fillet of beef, trimmed
(the timings below work perfectly
for a fillet of roughly 10cm in
diameter)

olive oil

2 large knobs of unsalted butter

3 sprigs of fresh rosemary

1 red onion

2 cloves of garlic

600g mixed mushrooms

100g chicken livers (cleaned)

1 tablespoon Worcestershire sauce

optional: ½ teaspoon truffle oil

50g fresh breadcrumbs

1 x 500g block of puff pastry

1 large egg

GRAVY

2 onions

4 sprigs of fresh thyme

1 heaped teaspoon
blackcurrant jam

100ml Madeira wine

1 heaped teaspoon English mustard

2 heaped tablespoons plain flour,
plus extra for dusting

600ml beef stock (hot)

Beef Wellington celebrates the luxurious and very tender fillet of beef and is one of those ultimate blowout dishes that hits the right spot several times in one meal. When you've made this once, you'll get a sense of how you can perfect it in your oven and make it work for parties and special occasions; once prepared it's super-easy to cook and serve.

Preheat a large frying pan on a high heat. Rub the beef all over with sea salt and black pepper. Pour a good lug of oil into the pan, then add the beef, 1 knob of butter and 1 sprig of rosemary. Sear the beef for 4 minutes in total, turning regularly with tongs, then remove to a plate. Wipe out the pan and return to a medium heat. Peel the onion and garlic, then very finely chop with the mushrooms and put into the pan with the remaining knob of butter and another lug of oil. Strip in the rest of the rosemary leaves and cook for 15 minutes, or until soft and starting to caramelize, stirring regularly. Toss the livers and Worcestershire sauce into the pan and cook for another few minutes, then tip the contents onto a large board and drizzle with the truffle oil (if using). Finely chop it all by hand with a big knife, to a rustic, spreadable consistency. Taste and season to perfection, then stir in the breadcrumbs (you can use pancakes to line the pastry and absorb the juices, but I prefer using breadcrumbs like this).

Preheat the oven to 210°C/425°F/gas 7. On a flour-dusted surface, roll out the pastry to 30cm x 40cm. With one of the longer edges in front of you, follow the step-by-step pictures (page 132) and spread the mushroom pâté over the pastry, leaving a 5cm gap at either end and at the edge furthest away from you – eggwash these edges. Sit the beef on the pâté, then, starting with the edge nearest you, snugly wrap the pastry around the beef, pinching the ends to seal. Transfer the Wellington to a large baking tray lined with greaseproof paper, with the pastry seal at the base, and brush all over with eggwash (you can prep to this stage, then refrigerate until needed – just get it out 1½ hours before cooking so it's not fridge-cold). When you're ready to cook, heat the tray on the hob for a couple of minutes to start crisping up the base, then transfer to the oven and cook for 40 minutes for blushing, juicy beef – the two end portions will be more cooked but usually some people prefer that.

Meanwhile, for the gravy, peel and roughly chop the onions and put into a large pan on a medium heat with a lug of oil and the thyme leaves. Cook for 20 minutes, stirring occasionally, then stir in the jam and simmer until shiny and quite dark. Add the Madeira, flame with a match, cook away, then stir in the mustard and flour, gradually followed by the stock. Simmer to the consistency you like, then blend with a stick blender and pass through a sieve, or leave chunky. Once cooked, rest the Wellington for 5 minutes, then serve in 2cm-thick slices with the gravy and steamed greens.

✕ DIVINE DOSA ✕

SERVES 8–10
1 HOUR 45 MINUTES
299 CALORIES

2 baking potatoes (500g)

3 sweet potatoes (750g)

400g mixed-colour heritage carrots

olive oil

1cm piece of ginger

1 dried red chilli

1 fresh red chilli

2 teaspoons black mustard seeds

1 level teaspoon turmeric

4 spring onions

½ a bunch of fresh coriander (15g)

1 lime

MINTY YOGHURT

6 sprigs of fresh mint

250g natural yoghurt

1 heaped tablespoon creamed
  coconut

mango chutney

DOSA BATTER

250g gram (chickpea) flour

1 level teaspoon bicarbonate
  of soda

2 teaspoons black mustard seeds

I love making dosa – the gorgeous flavours, and the contrast of the crisp pancake wrapped around the spicy smashed roasted veg, are unbelievable. Throw in a tasty dip on the side, and you've got a brand new comfort food classic. Simple, tasty, and guaranteed to please.

Preheat the oven to 190°C/375°F/gas 5. Scrub the potatoes, sweet potatoes and carrots, place in a roasting tray and toss with a drizzle of oil and a pinch of sea salt and black pepper. Roast for around 1 hour, or until soft and cooked through, then remove. As soon as they're cool enough to handle, crudely smash up the sweet potatoes and carrots, then halve the baking potatoes and scoop out the flesh (you could chop up the baking potato skins and use those too, if you like, for a bit of added texture).

Peel the ginger, then finely slice with both the chillies and put into a large frying pan on a medium heat with a lug of oil, the mustard seeds, turmeric and a good pinch of salt and pepper. Cook, shaking the pan frequently, until it smells amazing and the seeds start to pop, then add all the roasted veg. Ensure that they get tossed in all that lovely flavour, but don't move them around too much – you want the veg to stay crudely smashed. Just let them catch on the bottom, then turn the heat off. Trim, finely slice and add the spring onions, pick over most of the coriander leaves, squeeze over the lime juice, then gently fold together. Have a taste, and tweak the seasoning, if needed.

For the minty yoghurt, pick and finely chop the mint leaves, then, in a small bowl, stir them into the yoghurt with the creamed coconut. Taste, and season to perfection.

For the dosa, sift the flour into a bowl with the bicarbonate of soda, mustard seeds and a good pinch of salt. Gradually whisk in about 600ml of water, until you have a nice loose smooth batter. Put a splash of oil into a 26cm non-stick frying pan on a medium-high heat and carefully wipe it around with a ball of kitchen paper. Use a ladle to add enough batter to lightly coat the base of the pan, swirling it around a couple of times to give you a thin dosa and pouring any excess back into the bowl. When you can see it's getting golden underneath and bubbles appear on the surface, use a fish slice to carefully prise the dosa away from the sides, then add a portion of your filling down the centre. Carefully fold and roll up the sides so you have a large cigar shape, then, to make it really crispy on the outside, simply keep turning for a few minutes. Serve with the minty yoghurt swirled with chutney, and with the rest of the coriander leaves on top. If you want to serve everyone's at the same time, keep each dosa crispy in the oven or in another pan until they're all done. Delicious.

× HOT SMOKED SALMON CLUB SANDWICH ×

SERVES 2
1 HOUR
732 CALORIES

200g piece of salmon, skin on,
  scaled and pin-boned

½ x basic mayo with basil
  (page 258)

4 sprigs of fresh rosemary

4 slices of smoked streaky bacon

4 slices of nice bread

1 large ripe tomato

1 small ripe avocado

1 punnet of cress

1 handful of round lettuce leaves

1 lemon

12 good-quality salted crisps

If anything, the infamous club sandwich has almost become too famous, to the point where a lot of hotels on the planet have a fairly bad expression sitting on their room service menu. After all, it is just a sandwich, so to make it truly incredible, you need to put love and care into every little detail. An edge of surprise is also good, which is why I've come up with this hot smoked salmon club sandwich, which people just love to eat. It's super-easy to do, even though I do recommend that you smoke your own salmon – it might seem daunting, but it's easy, fun, totally rewarding and will impress your buddies.

Season the salmon with sea salt and black pepper, place in the fridge and leave for 20 minutes to draw out the moisture. Meanwhile, make up a batch of basil mayo and pop it into the fridge until needed (any leftovers will be delicious used for salads, sandwiches or even as a dip in the days that follow).

Get yourself a biscuit tin without paint or coating on the inside. Carefully punch 10 holes in the lid using a hammer and nail. Cover the base with a thin layer of wood chips (try hickory or oak, or you could even use hay) and lay the rosemary sprigs on top. Carefully cut yourself a piece of chicken wire and place it in the tin – use your common sense and work safely – then put the tin over a medium heat and leave until the wood chips start smouldering. I do this in the kitchen with the fan on, but it can get smoky so feel free to do it outside on a portable gas hob or barbecue, if you prefer. At this point, pat the salmon dry with kitchen paper and place skin-side down on the chicken wire. Pop the lid on, reduce to a medium-low heat and smoke nice and evenly for 15 to 20 minutes, or until the salmon is cooked through and easy to flake apart, then remove to a board, discarding the skin, and flake it up a bit.

While the salmon is smoking, cook the bacon in a large frying pan on a medium heat until golden and crispy on both sides, then remove from the pan, leaving the fat behind. Swirl the pan to spread the fat out, then toast the slices of bread so they suck up all that wonderful flavour. Slice the tomato, then peel, destone and slice the avocado.

To make these epic sandwiches, start with a couple of slices of toast spread with basil mayo, then layer up the crispy bacon, slices of tomato and avocado, salmon, cress, lettuce, a squeeze of lemon juice and a few cheeky crisps. Put the other slices of toast on top, press down, secure with cocktail sticks, then devour.

GNOCCHI

& SQUASH SAUCE

× GNOCCHI & SQUASH SAUCE ×

SERVES 6–8

<u>2 HOURS</u>
<u>312 CALORIES</u>

1.5kg King Edward or Maris
   Piper potatoes

2 large egg yolks

150g good-quality Tipo 00 flour,
   plus extra for dusting

1 whole nutmeg, for grating

SQUASH SAUCE

1 butternut squash (1.2kg)

4 cloves of garlic

1 fresh red chilli

4 sprigs of fresh rosemary

olive oil

1 vegetable stock cube

Parmesan cheese

×

*For a fresh finishing touch,
try finely grating just a little
lemon or orange zest over
the top before serving.*

Mastering the art of the humble and very affordable gnocchi is a great skill to have. These lovely little potato dumplings are Gennaro's favourite comfort food, and if made correctly are light in texture, look beautiful and can, like pasta, be used with so many different sauces, and reflect the seasons, any day of the year. Get stuck in and have a go.

Preheat the oven to 200°C/400°F/gas 6. Wash the potatoes, place in a large baking tray and bake for 1 hour, or until cooked through. Allow to cool slightly, then cut them in half and scrape out all the soft potato from the centre (keep the skins to make cheesy potato skins, if you like). Mash the potatoes really well and put aside.

For the sauce, peel the squash, carefully cut it in half lengthways and deseed, then slice ½cm thick. Peel the garlic, then finely chop it with the chilli and rosemary leaves and put into a large casserole pan on a medium heat with a lug of oil to fry for 1 minute. Add the squash, crumble in the stock cube and cover with 500ml of boiling water. Simmer with the lid on for 25 to 30 minutes, or until the squash breaks up and you have a lovely, thick sauce consistency, stirring occasionally, then season to perfection.

Meanwhile, put a large pan of water onto boil. Pile your mash on a large board and make a well in the centre. Add the yolks and flour to the well with a good pinch of sea salt, finely grate over a quarter of the nutmeg, then use your hands to gently fold and mix it all together. Don't overwork it or you'll need to add extra flour, which you don't want to do – as Gennaro says, 'you want to taste potato, not flour'. Now for the fun bit – a quarter at a time, roll out the mixture into 2cm-thick logs, then chop up into 2–3cm lengths, dusting very lightly with flour as you go. You can either run them down a fork or a wooden gnocchi board (like you see in the picture) to create grooves that will pick up extra sauce, or you can simply pinch each one in the middle – every region of Italy has its own way of shaping gnocchi, so do what feels right to you.

Gnocchi only takes 2 minutes to cook in boiling water – simply wait for the gnocchi to float to the surface. I like to cook two-portion batches at a time, to ensure the gnocchi don't bash each other up, so transfer a quarter of the sauce to a small pan on a low heat, then use a slotted spoon to scoop the gnocchi straight from the water into that pan with a good grating of Parmesan. Gently toss together, loosening with a little cooking water, if needed. Divide between warm bowls, grate over a little more Parmesan and serve right away, while you get on with the next batch.

× TOP QUESADILLAS ×

SERVES 4

50 MINUTES

490 CALORIES

2 red onions

250g Brussels sprouts

1 small knob of unsalted butter

½ teaspoon cumin seeds

¼ teaspoon smoked paprika

a few sprigs of fresh thyme

1 lime

4 flour tortillas
  (or see recipe below)

150g pecorino cheese

4 tablespoons natural yoghurt
  or soured cream

Cholula hot sauce

QUINOA TORTILLAS

300g quinoa

1 tablespoon olive oil

1 heaped teaspoon fennel seeds

1 level teaspoon baking powder

Brussels sprouts, kale and more unusual brassicas seem to be quite trendy these days in cool restaurants all around the world. And hey, I could think of worse things to become fashionable – I really love the fact that people are finding great ways to make veg taste even more amazing, so this page is all about celebrating the humble Brussels sprout. In this recipe I've also given you the method for making your own delicious healthier tortillas with blitzed-up quinoa, but regular flour tortillas are fine too if you prefer.

Peel the onions and finely slice them with the sprouts (you can do this in a food processor). Place in a large frying pan on a medium heat with the butter, cumin seeds and paprika. Pick in the thyme leaves, then pop the lid on and fry for 10 minutes, stirring occasionally. After this time, remove the lid and fry for a further 10 minutes to get everything nicely golden and caramelized, then stir in a good squeeze of lime juice.

Now for me, this dish is about having something in the middle of the table to share, not having an individual plate. So, get your tortillas, or make your own (see below), and lay them on a flat surface. Use half the cheese to add a good grating to just half of each tortilla. Sprinkle the sprout filling on top of the cheese, then grate over the rest of it. Fold the tortillas in half and press together. Cook two at a time in a large non-stick frying pan on a medium heat until golden and crisp on both sides and the cheese has melted. Place on a board, cool for 1 minute (otherwise they just ooze everywhere!), then slice up and serve with a little yoghurt or soured cream spiked with hot sauce, plus wedges of lime for squeezing over. Yum.

QUINOA TORTILLAS

To make 4 tortillas, simply whiz all the ingredients in a blender until fine, shaking regularly to ensure everything gets blitzed. Once you have a fairly fine flour, remove a couple of heaped tablespoons for dusting, then tip the rest into a bowl. Slowly add enough water to turn it into a firm-ish dough, knead for 1 minute then divide into 4 equal-sized balls. Use the reserved flour to generously dust a clean surface, then press out a piece of the dough with your hand. Dust the top with some of the reserved flour, then gently roll out to the thickness of a beer mat. This dough hasn't got gluten in it, so it won't be stretchy and may well crack, but you can easily pull a bit from the side to patch up any holes. Use a 20cm cake tin, lid or plate to cut out each perfect round, then cook in a hot dry pan as and when they're rolled for 1 minute on each side. Place on a clean tea towel and cover until needed.

✕ GREEK EGG & CHIPS ✕

SERVES 4
50 MINUTES
479 CALORIES

800g Maris Piper potatoes

1 knob of unsalted butter

2 onions

vegetable oil

6 large eggs

malt or any nice vinegar

½ a bunch of fresh flat-leaf
   parsley (15g)

This filthy little pile of heaven is the child/adulthood comfort food of my Greek sister Georgina, and all of her family swear by it. Georgie and her family are fantastic cooks, and although it's humble and simple, this concoction is very much a Greek-Cypriot comfort food. We cooked it together and it was devoured within minutes. Boy is it good. It's a lovely lunch to complement a nice salad, or can be enjoyed as a wicked side dish.

Peel the potatoes and cut into thumb-sized chips. Parboil in a pan of boiling salted water for 8 minutes, so they hold their shape but have softened, and drain. Meanwhile, melt the butter in a large non-stick frying pan on a medium-low heat while you peel and finely slice the onions. Add them to the pan with a pinch of sea salt and cook for 15 minutes to soften, stirring occasionally, then turn the heat up for a further 5 minutes to get them a bit crispy and brown at the edges.

Just under half fill a large sturdy pan with oil – the oil should be 8cm deep, but never fill your pan more than half full – and place on a medium to high heat. Use a thermometer to get it to 180°C, or add a raw chip as it's heating up and when it's golden and floating you'll be about right. Use a large metal sieve to gently lower the rest of the chips into the pan and cook for 12 to 14 minutes, or until perfectly golden, crisp and soft in the middle. Remove to a plate lined with kitchen paper, shake around a bit and sprinkle with salt.

At this point, toss the chips into the onion pan. In a bowl, whisk the eggs well with a pinch of salt and pepper, then, working quickly on a high heat, pour the eggs into the pan and gently mix and scramble them in with the chips and onions, until nice and silky and everything is coated. Now stop moving it and let it just catch on the bottom for 30 seconds only, then remove from the heat. Finish with a generous few dashes of vinegar, to taste, and a scattering of chopped parsley leaves, and enjoy.

× PULLED PORK & SWEET POTATO HASH ×

SERVES 4

1 HOUR 25 MINUTES
PLUS CHILLING
502 CALORIES

1 onion

1 carrot

1 large sweet potato

olive oil

2 sprigs of fresh rosemary

250g leftover pulled pork

1 spring onion

8 quail eggs or 4 large
    chicken eggs

sunflower oil

1 fresh red or green chilli

SALAD

4 tablespoons extra virgin olive oil

2 tablespoons cider vinegar

1 tablespoon runny honey

2 red or green chicory

4 handfuls of mixed leaves, such
    as lamb's lettuce, spinach, chervil

Meat hash, or stovies as they call it in Scotland, is a nice comfort food expression that utilizes leftover cheap cuts of cooked meat to great effect. The word 'hash' implies that something is mixed up or uneven, which is fair, as no hash is ever the same and you'll always find a varying mixture and ratio of veggies, spices and herbs. During and after the Second World War, many people in Europe grew up eating hash of some description, and now it's come back into fashion, especially for breakfast or brunch. This tasty combination was put together after a couple of my mates came back from New York and were describing it – it sounded really good, so I had a go at recreating it. You'll love it.

Peel the onion and carrot and scrub the sweet potato clean, then chop them all into ½cm chunks. Put a large frying pan on a medium heat with a lug of olive oil and strip in the rosemary leaves. Fry for a couple of minutes, then go in with the chopped veg and a pinch of sea salt and cook for around 20 minutes, or until soft, sweet and lightly golden, stirring occasionally. Roughly mash three-quarters of the veg in the pan, then stir that mash back through the chunky veg, tip into a bowl and leave to cool.

Meanwhile, in a salad bowl, mix the extra virgin olive oil, vinegar and honey with a pinch of salt and pepper to make a dressing. Trim the chicory bases, then click apart the leaves and place on top of the dressing. Pick through the mixed leaves and add to the bowl, tossing the salad in the dressing only seconds before serving. Chop your leftover meat into 1cm chunks, and trim and finely slice the spring onion. Once the veg are cool, add the meat and spring onion to the bowl and mix everything together. Use your hands to divide the mixture into 4 equal parts, roll each one into a ball, then pat and press into patties about 2cm thick and firm up in the fridge for 30 minutes.

Wipe out the empty veg pan, return it to a medium-low heat, and add a lug of olive oil, then the hashes. Cook for around 6 minutes on each side, or until nicely golden. Be gentle and don't move them until you're ready to flip, then flip confidently – if they break, just pat them back into a pattie (I could have added egg to help them stick together, but I really like the light texture of these hashes and I think you will too). Once cooked, transfer to four plates and fry the eggs to your liking. The secret to sunny-side-up eggs is to cook them in about ½cm of sunflower oil, then to spoon over some hot oil to help them cook through more evenly. Place the eggs on top of the hashes, dress and divide the salad between the plates beside them, then finely slice and scatter over the chilli. Absolute perfection.

× BLOODY MARY BEEF ×

SERVES 8
5½–6½ HOURS
567 CALORIES

1 x 1kg piece of brisket

olive oil

1 head of celery

4 small red onions

½ a bunch of fresh rosemary (15g)

2 fresh bay leaves

BLOODY MARY MIX

1 lemon

1 x 700g jar of passata

2 tablespoons
 Worcestershire sauce

a few drops of Tabasco sauce

3 tablespoons vodka

1 tablespoon port

MASH

1.6kg Maris Piper potatoes

50g unsalted butter

1–2 heaped tablespoons jarred
 grated horseradish

semi-skimmed milk

KALE

400g curly kale

extra virgin olive oil

There's something very fulfilling about a good bloody Mary, especially when you've got a little hangover. Combining this classic drink with brisket – a beautiful cut of beef that slow-cooks in a wonderful way so both beef and sauce become rich and comfort personified – makes for a stunning dish. It's great with seasonal greens on those winter days when you've been out for a long walk and the nights are drawing in, but equally good in the summer served with lovely peas, broad beans and asparagus to freshen it up.

Preheat the oven to 130°C/250°F/gas ½. Place a casserole pan (25cm in diameter and 10cm high) over a high heat. Season the brisket all over with sea salt and pepper, then put into the pan (it should fit inside fairly snugly) with a splash of olive oil and cook for 10 minutes, turning until browned all over. Meanwhile, trim the celery and chop into 5cm chunks, then peel and quarter the onions. Add both to the pan, reduce to a low heat and cook gently for 5 to 10 minutes, or until slightly softened.

Squeeze the lemon juice into a large jug and mix with all the rest of the bloody Mary ingredients. Pour into the pan with 500ml of cold water and a good pinch of salt and pepper. Tie the rosemary and bay together and add to the pan. Bring everything to the boil, then turn off the heat, cover the pan with damp greaseproof paper and tin foil and cook in the oven for 5 to 6 hours, or until the beef is tender and falling apart.

With about 20 minutes to go, peel and roughly chop the potatoes and cook in a pan of boiling salted water for 15 minutes, or until tender. Remove any tough stalks from the curly kale, put into a pan of boiling water for 1 to 2 minutes, or until tender, then drain and drizzle with a little extra virgin olive oil. Drain the potatoes in a colander and leave to steam dry, then return to the pan and mash well with the butter, horseradish and a splash of milk, then season to perfection. Pull the beef apart with two forks, toss through the bloody Mary sauce (discarding the herb bunch), then serve with the horseradish mash and curly kale.

×

Keep your eye out for fresh horseradish root when you're shopping – it's even more delicious. Peel it, finely grate it, and use it instead of jarred for your mash.

GORGEOUS FOOD TO
RAISE YOUR SPIRITS

PICK ME UPS

BEST
BUN CHA
BOWLS

× BEST BUN CHA BOWLS ×

SERVES 4
50 MINUTES
539 CALORIES

1 large handful of shelled
   unsalted peanuts

¼ of a white cabbage

1 bunch of fresh mint (30g)

½ a bunch of fresh basil (15g)

4 spring onions

½ an iceberg lettuce

200g beansprouts (ready to eat)

½ a cucumber

2 carrots

150g vermicelli rice noodles

8 large raw shell-on king prawns

200g pork belly, skin removed

1 onion

4 tablespoons hoisin sauce

DRESSING

3 fresh red chillies

2 heaped tablespoons golden
   caster sugar

2 tablespoons white wine vinegar

4 tablespoons fish sauce

2 limes

This is a Vietnamese classic from Hanoi – 'bun' means fine noodle, 'cha' means fatty pork, and it's often served in markets at lunchtime when you're allowed to grill on the street. It's served cold in summer and hot in winter, so it's a real all-year-round dish. The idea is to build your own bowl, choosing the combination of meat, herbs and veg that you fancy. I've paired pork belly with delicious sticky prawns here, to give this version an extra edge.

What we're going to do is assemble a load of little bowls and plates of garnishes, but we'll kick off by making a big jam jar dressing. Finely chop 2 chillies and place in a large clean jar with the sugar, vinegar, fish sauce, lime juice and 100ml of boiling water. Secure the lid and shake well until dissolved.

Toast the peanuts in a frying pan, smash them up in a pestle and mortar and place in a bowl. Very finely slice the cabbage (ideally on a mandolin – use the guard!) and scrunch well with 4 tablespoons of the dressing and an extra swig of vinegar in a bowl. Pick the mint and basil leaves into bowls of cold water. Trim and finely slice the spring onions and the remaining chilli, shred the iceberg lettuce and put it all on a little plate with the beansprouts. Halve the cucumber lengthways and deseed with a teaspoon, then finely slice (I like to use a crinkle-cut knife). Peel the carrots and grate into another bowl. Pour boiling water over the noodles, cover and leave to soak for 5 minutes, or until soft, then drain and refresh under cold water.

Peel the prawns, leaving the tails on, run your knife down the back and pull out the veins, then run the knife down again to butterfly them. Chop the pork belly quite finely and fry in a hot pan until golden while you peel and finely slice the onion, then add it to the pan. Stir-fry for 5 minutes, then throw in the prawns. Cook for a final couple of minutes, add the hoisin to glaze everything and tip onto a plate.

Place all your garnishes in the middle of the table with the jam jar dressing and four large serving bowls, and let everyone build their own exciting bun cha bowl.

×

Embrace the spirit of this recipe and tweak the ingredients to your liking. Griddled squid would be delicious, as would slices of perfectly cooked steak. It's also a great opportunity to embrace any seasonal veg you can get your hands on.

× SPINACH, BACON & PINE NUT SALAD ×

SERVES 4
20 MINUTES
309 CALORIES

6 thick rashers of smoked
  streaky bacon

olive oil

2 heaped tablespoons pine nuts

12 x 1cm-thick slices of
  French bread

6 medium pickled onions, plus
  2 tablespoons pickling liquor

2 teaspoons Dijon mustard

4 tablespoons quality extra
  virgin olive oil

4 large handfuls of baby spinach

1 handful of seasonal salad leaves

Classic, comforting and simple, this salad is all about getting those little details spot on – the freshness of the spinach and salad leaves, the crispness of the smoky bacon, a delicious bright smooth dressing made with mustard, good oil and pickled onion juice for an extra bang, and of course those bacon-fat crispy bread croutons. This is hard to beat. And, without sounding too geeky, spinach is really easy to grow, and you haven't truly tasted spinach until you've grown and cut, then eaten your own – please give it a go.

Slice the bacon into thin lardons and put into a large frying pan on a medium heat with a good drizzle of olive oil. Fry until golden, adding the pine nuts for the last minute, then scoop out with a slotted spoon onto a plate, leaving the bacon fat behind in the pan. Toast the slices of bread in the fat until beautifully golden on both sides.

Meanwhile, finely slice the pickled onions. In a large bowl, mix the pickled onion liquor with the mustard, extra virgin olive oil and a pinch of black pepper. Gently pile the spinach and salad leaves on top, add the crispy bacon, pine nuts and pickled onions, then lightly toss everything together with your fingertips, picking the salad up and sprinkling it back down from a height a few times – doing it this way means the salad is perfectly dressed but you avoid bruising the leaves. Add the crispy toast croutons and tuck straight in.

×

A couple of ideas to tweak this salad: a tiny amount of crumbled blue cheese or feta would be very nice, but you don't need to add much to make a difference. Similarly, some matchsticks of seasonal orchard fruit such as apple or pear would be a joy.

✕ HUEVOS RANCHEROS ✕

SERVES 4
30 MINUTES
476 CALORIES

4 flour tortillas

olive oil

1 pinch of cumin seeds

1 x 400g tin of black beans

50g sliced pickled jalapeños,
  plus pickling liquor

½ a bunch of fresh coriander (15g)

2 ripe avocados

1 large ripe beef tomato

2 sprigs of fresh oregano

1 lime

6 large eggs

50g good Cheddar cheese

Cholula hot sauce or Tabasco sauce

Huevos rancheros or ranch-style eggs has to be one of my favourite breakfasts, and as the term is quite general, it means that every place you eat them, they'll be slightly different, which I love. It's pretty standard that you'll get guacamole, grilled or fried tortillas, eggs of some description – my preference is scrambled – beans and/or rice, tomatoes and various chilli sauces, but the make-up and ratios differ and that really keeps things interesting. It's definite comfort food and will give you energy for a hard morning's work!

Put a large frying pan on a medium-high heat and, one by one, rub one side of each tortilla with a tiny drizzle of oil, then toast until nicely golden on that side only. As you take each one out of the pan, carefully fold and push the soft side down into a mug, and after a couple of minutes they'll crispen beautifully. Transfer them to your plates. Pour a good lug of oil into the frying pan and add the cumin seeds. Drain the beans, then add to the pan and let them crack, pop and sizzle, then turn the heat off.

Meanwhile, empty the jalapeños into a blender with most of the coriander, then blitz until super-smooth and delicious, adding enough jalapeño pickling liquor to bring it all together into a thick sauce. Halve, destone and peel the avocados, then slice ½cm thick, along with the tomato, and divide between your plates. Sprinkle over the oregano leaves and a pinch of sea salt and pepper. Cut the lime into wedges.

In a bowl, whisk the eggs with a pinch of salt and pepper while you pop a pan on a medium-low heat to get hot. Add a lug of oil to the pan, then pour in the eggs. Using a spatula, as a thin layer of egg cooks and sets on the bottom of the pan, slowly stir the cooked delicate sheets of egg, allowing the uncooked eggs to replace them, then leave to set again before doing the same again – at this point, break in the Cheddar in nuggets. Your scrambled eggs should be a lovely mixture of soft, custardy egg and cooked sheets of egg, and remember you need to slightly undercook them in the pan because they'll carry on cooking and you want to achieve perfection on the plate.

Divide up your silky eggs and spoon over the crispy popped beans. Drizzle with the jalapeño sauce and a few drips of hot sauce or Tabasco. Pick over the remaining coriander leaves, and serve with the lime wedges for squeezing over. Yum.

× ULTIMATE ×
BLACK
DAAL

An amazing, delicious daal should be a recipe in every good modern-day cook's repertoire. I say this, because in a time when we have so much access to protein and fresh vegetables, it's nice to go back to the simplicity of taking dried daal, lentils or beans, soaking them, then slow-cooking and flavouring them – it seems like a real rite of passage, and come dinner time, you'll be greeted with the fantastic aroma and incredible taste of this amazing daal. Enjoy on its own, or as part of a bigger spread.

✕ ULTIMATE BLACK DAAL ✕

SERVES 8

6 HOURS 45 MINUTES
PLUS SOAKING
291 CALORIES

350g urad daal (whole black lentils)

2 onions

6 cloves of garlic

100g ginger

unsalted butter

2 tablespoons garam masala

1 teaspoon ground coriander

1 teaspoon cumin seeds

½ teaspoon ground cinnamon

1 tablespoon tomato purée

1 vegetable stock cube

1 x 400g tin of plum tomatoes

75ml single cream, plus extra
   to serve

optional: 1 handful of cloves

½ a bunch of fresh coriander (15g)

TEMPER

3 tablespoons groundnut oil

8 fresh bird's-eye chillies

6 cloves of garlic

1 teaspoon each cumin seeds,
   fennel seeds, mustard seeds

Soak the lentils overnight in plenty of cold water, to let them soften and expand. The next morning, preheat the oven to 150°C/300°F/gas 2. Peel the onions, garlic and ginger, then blitz to a paste in a food processor. Melt 25g of butter in a large saucepan on a medium heat. Add all the spices, fry for 1 minute, then stir in the blitzed onion paste. Cook down for 20 minutes, or until softened and golden brown, stirring regularly with a splash of water to pick up the sticky goodness from the bottom of the pan. Stir in the tomato purée and crumble in the stock cube, then after a couple of minutes, squash in the tinned tomatoes, add the drained lentils and pour in 1.5 litres of water. Bring to the boil, season and cover with a scrunched-up sheet of damp greaseproof paper, then with a lid or tin foil. Place in the oven for around 6 hours and be patient! Halfway through, check it, stir and top up with 500ml of boiling water.

When the time's up, stir in the cream, getting right into the edges, then season beautifully to taste. Now you have a decision to make – do you want to go the extra mile? This is an optional extra that requires you to find a couple of pieces of charcoal from a fire or barbecue, or you can even start one piece off on your hob, holding it over the flame with tongs. Either way, pop the screaming-hot coal into a small metal bowl, float the bowl in your daal, and sprinkle the hot coal with a handful of cloves and a knob of butter. Pop the lid on for another 30 minutes and place over the lowest heat, and your daal will develop an incredible and unique smoky flavour.

So now we have a delicious, oozy daal with a great base and mid-tone flavours, but I'm not happy just yet – it needs a temper (a flavoured, perfumed oil with crispy bits!). Simply put the groundnut oil into a small frying pan. Run your knife halfway down the length of each chilli to keep them intact but allow you to scrape out and discard the seeds. Add the chillies to the pan and place on a medium-low heat to warm up. Peel and finely slice the garlic and add to the pan with all the spices. Fry until the garlic is golden and crispy, the spices smell amazing and the chillies have softened, stirring regularly. Pour the daal over a hot serving platter, drizzle over a tiny bit of extra cream, if you like, spoon over the temper, then tear over the coriander leaves. Serve with fluffy basmati rice or chapatis and a simple lemon-dressed salad.

× STEAMING RAMEN ×

SERVES 8

4 HOURS
PLUS MARINATING
914 CALORIES

8 chicken wings

1 handful of pork bones
   (ask your butcher)

750g pork belly
   (skin removed and reserved)

2 thumb-sized pieces of ginger

5 cloves of garlic

sesame oil

1 heaped tablespoon miso paste

400g baby spinach

500g dried soba or ramen noodles

8 small handfuls of beansprouts
   (ready to eat)

8 spring onions

1–2 fresh red chillies

2 sheets of wakame seaweed

8 tablespoons kimchee

chilli oil

SOY SAUCE EGGS

4 large eggs

200ml low-salt soy sauce

1 splash of mirin

4 star anise

1 thumb-sized piece of ginger

2 cloves of garlic

Ramen is all about investing time to make an incredible steamy broth, using cheaper cuts of meat and bones for maximum flavour. Like many humble foods, the original Chinese ramen (meaning noodle) really evolved with its introduction to Japan and Western culture, which allows us to have a bit of fun with it, aka contrasting flavours, pickles and garnishes. Feel free to bend this recipe seasonally – that's the spirit of it. Kimchee is a fermented cabbage that tastes great – hunt it out in good supermarkets.

To make the soy sauce eggs, boil the eggs for 5 minutes, then refresh in cold water and peel. Pour the soy sauce and 250ml of water into a small pan with the mirin and star anise. Peel, slice and add the ginger and garlic, then bring to the boil, remove from the heat, leave to cool and pour into a sandwich bag with the eggs. Squeeze out the air, seal, and pop into the fridge for 6 hours, then drain (this is important).

Preheat the oven to 200°C/400°F/gas 6. Put the chicken wings and pork bones into a large casserole pan. Bash and add the unpeeled ginger and garlic, then toss with a good drizzle of sesame oil. Put the pork skin on a baking tray and place both tray and casserole pan in the oven for around 40 minutes, or until the skin is perfectly crackled, then remove for garnish. This is also the perfect time to transfer the casserole pan to the hob, adding in the pork belly and miso. Cover with 3 litres of water, bring to the boil, then simmer gently on a low heat for around 3 hours, or simply until the pork belly is beautifully tender, skimming the surface occasionally.

Lift the pork belly onto a tray and put aside, then sieve the broth and pour back into the pan. Return to the heat and reduce the liquid down to around 2.5 litres. While doing this, put a large colander over the pan and steam the spinach until it's wilted. Let it cool, then squeeze out the excess moisture and divide into 8. In a separate pan, cook the noodles according to packet instructions, then drain and divide between 8 large warm bowls with the beansprouts and spinach. Slice and divide up the pork, then halve the eggs and place around the bowls. Trim the spring onions, finely slice with the chilli, and sprinkle between the bowls. Taste the broth and season with soy sauce, then ladle the steaming broth over everything. Tear over the seaweed and divide up the kimchee. Drizzle with chilli oil, then break over the crackling. Slurp away!

× POLISH PIEROGI ×

SERVES 8–10

1 HOUR 40 MINUTES
457 CALORIES

DOUGH

2 large eggs

400g soured cream

350g plain flour, plus extra
  for dusting

½ teaspoon baking powder

FILLING

¼ of a white cabbage (250g)

2 tablespoons white wine vinegar

500g Maris Piper potatoes

2 teaspoons caraway seeds

2 onions

olive oil

unsalted butter

120g mature Cheddar cheese

white pepper

TO SERVE

1 bunch of fresh chives (30g)

1 lemon

I'm a great lover of a good pierogi. It's basically a Polish boiled dumpling that gets fried or baked to give it a contrasting texture. It's really flexible and exciting as a starter or snack, and can be made with a massive range of flavours. The veggie version is the more famous variety and would be eaten on Christmas Eve, and this recipe dates back to the thirteenth century! The thing I love about pierogi is that they were almost always made for a special occasion or wedding, and a massive emphasis was put on the joy of family and friends sitting down together to make them, just as much as the joy of eating them.

To make the dough, beat the eggs with 150g of soured cream. Sift in the flour, baking powder and ½ a teaspoon of sea salt, then mix until the dough comes together. Knead on a flour-dusted surface until smooth, then wrap in clingfilm and pop into the fridge.

Coarsely grate the cabbage into a bowl, scrunch and toss with the vinegar and a pinch of salt and leave to lightly pickle. Peel the potatoes, roughly chop, and cook in a pan of boiling salted water for 10 to 12 minutes, or until tender. Drain and steam dry. Put the caraway seeds into a cold frying pan, place on a medium-low heat and toast for a few minutes while you peel and finely chop the onions, then add to the pan with a good lug of oil. Cook for 5 to 8 minutes, until lightly golden, stirring occasionally, then add the cabbage and a knob of butter for 5 minutes, before mashing in the potatoes. Coarsely grate in the cheese, add a generous pinch of white pepper and mix. Have a taste and season to perfection, then leave to cool. Meanwhile, very finely chop the chives and mix in a bowl with the remaining soured cream and the lemon zest and juice. Taste, season to perfection and decant onto a large platter in the fridge.

On a clean, flour-dusted surface, divide the dough in half, then, one at a time, roll each half out to 2mm thick, dusting with flour as you go. Cut out as many circles as you can with a 9cm cutter. Divide the filling into heaped teaspoon portions on a tray, then roll by hand into little balls. Place a pastry circle in the palm of your hand, put a ball of filling into the middle, then gently fold in half, pinching all the way round the half-moon shape, and place on a flour-dusted surface. Take them all to this stage, then with a fork dipped in flour, seal and stamp around the outer edge. Place on a flour-dusted tray until ready to cook – you'll feel really proud of yourself.

In batches, cook a few pierogi at a time in a large pan of boiling salted water for around 4 minutes, until they rise to the surface, then carefully scoop out, put them into a large medium-hot non-stick pan with a knob of foaming butter, and fry until golden on one side only. Serve them on top of the chive soured cream for dipping.

× SUPERFOOD SALAD ×

SERVES 4
40 MINUTES
520 CALORIES

200g quinoa

2 tablespoons sunflower seeds

2 tablespoons pumpkin seeds

3 medium blood oranges
or clementines

2 ripe avocados

100g purple kale, swiss chard
or any nice seasonal greens

50g alfalfa, radish or pea shoots

½ a bunch of fresh mint (15g)

2 large handfuls of seasonal
salad leaves

60g feta cheese

1 pomegranate

DRESSING

½ a clove of garlic

1 clementine

1 lime

60ml cold-pressed extra
virgin olive oil

I want to show you how to celebrate a really invigorating salad that will fulfil you, tickle your taste buds and only be a positive addition to your diet. My nutrition team aren't keen on the term 'superfood' as it's so litigious and requires you to prove what each ingredient does, but let's be honest, you all know what you're going to get from this salad – lots of healthy, nutritious ingredients. It won't make you run faster or give you the ability to fly; it's about a beautiful dish that feels good to eat and won't be too heavy on your tummy.

Cook the quinoa according to packet instructions, then drain well and put aside to cool. Toast the seeds in a dry pan on a medium heat for a few minutes, or until lightly golden, tossing occasionally, then lightly crush in a pestle and mortar. To make the dressing, rub the cut-side of the garlic clove fairly aggressively around the inside of a large salad bowl, then sprinkle with a pinch of sea salt – this will give off just enough flavour to perfume your dressing (discard the garlic when you're done). Squeeze in the clementine and lime juice, add the extra virgin olive oil, whisk and season to taste.

Peel and finely slice 2 of the blood oranges or clementines into rounds, picking out any pips and adding any escaped juice to the dressing. Halve the avocados and remove the stones, then pick through your kale or seasonal greens, make sure they're clean, and take pride in delicately tearing them up. Sometimes you'll find tough stalks, so finely slice those, have a chomp, and if they're delicious, use them. These greens are really nice raw, but if you put them into a colander and pour over a kettle of boiling water it will loosen them up a bit without losing too much nutritional value. Drain well and add to the salad bowl with the quinoa and sprouts. Pick, finely chop and add the mint leaves. Toss and dress with your fingertips to evenly distribute the flavour, then add the salad leaves and use a teaspoon to scoop out curls of avocado. Delicately toss one last time, then either serve in one large bowl or divide onto four plates. Scatter with the orange or clementine slices, sprinkle with the crushed seeds and crumble over the feta. Finish by holding a pomegranate half cut-side down in your palm and bashing the back of it with a spoon, so that all those jewels tumble over the salad. Squeeze over the juice from the remaining blood orange or clementine, and serve.

×

This tasty superfood salad should be thought of as a principle – it demonstrates that there are so many more ingredients than you might think that can be used in a salad. Be agile, mix things up and, importantly, embrace the seasons, all of which will help you take your salads to the next level, for you and your family.

✕ MASALA EGGS ✕

SERVES 2

30 MINUTES

655 CALORIES

TOMATOES

12 cherry tomatoes (on the vine)

olive oil

FLATBREAD

125g self-raising flour, plus extra
  for dusting

125g natural yoghurt

1 heaped tablespoon sesame seeds

1 small knob of unsalted butter
  (at room temperature)

EGGS

½ a bunch of fresh coriander (15g)

1 fresh green chilli

6 spring onions

1 small knob of unsalted butter

1 teaspoon cumin seeds

1 level teaspoon garam masala

4 large eggs

20g feta cheese

medium curry powder

Inspired by the fast street food of Mumbai, where they serve egg bhurji and pav, a Portuguese-inspired bread (so basically a turbo-charged egg sandwich), this dish is a fantastic breakfast or brunch. The use of light spice, sweet onions and tomatoes pushes these fluffy scrambled eggs into a whole new stratosphere, making them a total joy to eat.

Preheat the oven to 170°C/325°F/gas 3. In a roasting tray, leaving the tomatoes on the vine, drizzle them with oil, sprinkle over a small pinch of sea salt, then roast for 20 minutes. Meanwhile, to make the flatbread, mix the flour, yoghurt, sesame seeds and a pinch of salt together in a bowl, using your hands once it starts to come together. Knead for a few minutes on a flour-dusted surface while you put a griddle pan on a medium heat. Roll the dough out 1cm thick and cook on the hot dry griddle for 3 minutes on each side, or until nicely charred and golden, then brush with the butter.

To make the eggs, finely chop the coriander stalks (reserving the leaves) and chilli (deseed if you like), then trim and finely slice the spring onions. Put it all in a frying pan on a medium-low heat with the butter, cumin and garam masala and fry for 4 minutes, or until the veg have softened. Whisk the eggs in a bowl, then pour into the pan and scramble, stirring gently with a spatula – every time a delicate layer lightly sets, use the spatula to scrape it up through the rest of the eggs to create silky sheets. It's important to slightly undercook them – because eggs cook at a very low temperature and the pan won't immediately cool down when you take it off the heat, the eggs will continue cooking, so you want to stop just before they're perfect to reach true perfection when they hit your plate. The ultimate scrambled eggs should be made up of fine, silky layers of cooked egg, surrounded by softer custardy egg. Of course, cook them to your liking – and if you get them right, scrambled eggs are delicious, fulfilling and up there with some of the finest foods on the planet.

Spoon the eggs between two plates, arrange the vines of roasted tomatoes on top, then crumble over the feta and sprinkle with the coriander leaves. Finish with a pinch of curry powder scattered over from a height and serve with the sesame flatbread.

BLUSHING SPAGHETTI

VONGOLE

× BLUSHING SPAGHETTI VONGOLE ×

SERVES 2
25 MINUTES
584 CALORIES

2 cloves of garlic

8 ripe cherry tomatoes

½ a dried red chilli

½ a bunch of fresh flat-leaf
   parsley (15g)

160g dried spaghetti

olive oil

2 tablespoons sun-dried
   tomato paste

300g clams or cockles
   (washed and debearded)

1 glass of Venetian Pinot
   Grigio blush

extra virgin olive oil

Vongole is a dish much loved by people all around the world. Ultimately, it's a very simple pasta that celebrates the juice and flavour of clams, and if you cook it right, it's a very delicious, classy, comforting pasta that hits the spot, every time. I've gone for a subtle variation on the classic here, by adding fresh tomatoes and sun-dried tomato paste, then using rosé instead of white wine, to give you a beautiful blushing dish, but of course you can revert to the original, if you prefer – they're both equally brilliant.

The key to success with vongole is to have everything prepped before you start cooking, because the whole thing will be ready in just a matter of minutes once you get going. We want perfectly cooked pasta, just-opened shellfish and spot-on seasoning – it sounds easy, but to achieve this you do need to focus.

So, to start, peel and finely slice the garlic, quarter the tomatoes, then break apart the dried chilli, shake out and remove the seeds, and finely chop or crumble it (it's your responsibility to check the heat of the chilli, because they're all different). Very finely slice the parsley stalks, then roughly chop the leaves and put them aside for later.

Cook the spaghetti in boiling salted water according to packet instructions. Around 5 minutes before it's ready, place a large frying pan on a high heat. After 2 minutes, add a generous swig of olive oil, quickly followed by the garlic, tomatoes, chilli, parsley stalks and sun-dried tomato paste. Shake around, then add the clams or cockles (remembering to tap any that are open and if they don't close, throw those ones away) and, after 30 seconds, add the wine. Pop the lid on for 1 minute, then remove so you can watch the clams or cockles open and the wine evaporate. If you've got your timings right, as most of the shellfish pops open (throw away any that remain closed) you'll be ready to drain your pasta and throw it on top with the chopped parsley leaves and a drizzle of extra virgin olive oil. Give it all a good toss together, then taste the sauce – it shouldn't need seasoning because of the clams but it's always wise to check. Divide the pasta between two warm bowls, followed by the clams or cockles and all those wonderful juices, and tuck straight in.

✕ PHO SURE, IT'S GOOD ✕

SERVES 6

4 HOURS 15 MINUTES
718 CALORIES

300g ginger

2kg beef bones (ask your butcher)

½ a cinnamon stick

6 cloves

6 star anise

sesame oil

2 sticks of lemongrass

4 tablespoons low-salt soy sauce

2 tablespoons fish sauce

600g thick rice noodles (8mm)

1 bunch of fresh mint (30g)

1 bunch of fresh coriander (30g)

4 spring onions

1 onion

1–2 fresh red chillies

2 limes

300g beansprouts (ready to eat)

600g skirt steak

groundnut oil

hot chilli sauce

BRINED GARLIC

4 cloves of garlic

1 heaped teaspoon golden
  caster sugar

2 tablespoons white wine vinegar

Pho is a celebrated Vietnamese broth made from roasted bones, which is well flavoured and therapeutic to slurp. I'm serving mine with seared skirt steak, brined garlic slices, lots of fresh herbs, sprouts and rice noodles. The soup was first recorded in the early 1900s, when French colonies were settling in Vietnam. Some say that 'pho' comes from the French 'pot-au-feu', while others think it was Chinese vendors yelling out 'meat and noodles', elongating the last word, 'phan', which sounded like pho. Ultimately, it's all about depth of flavour from the broth, embellished with lots of fresh goodies.

Preheat the oven to 180°C/350°F/gas 4. Bash and crack the ginger and place in a very large casserole pan with the beef bones, cinnamon, cloves and star anise. Drizzle with sesame oil and roast for 2 hours, then transfer the pan to the hob over a medium heat and cover the bones with 3.5 litres of water. Bash the lemongrass and add along with the soy and fish sauces, then simmer on a low heat for 2 hours. Skim off any fat from the surface and discard (if you make the broth in advance and let it cool, the fat will solidify on the top and will be super-easy to remove).

Meanwhile, to make the brined garlic, simply peel and finely slice the garlic and put into a little dish with the sugar and a good pinch of sea salt. Stir in a couple of splashes of boiling water from the kettle, followed by the vinegar. It's a nice condiment to spoon over the steak, and adds an extra edge to the broth.

Cook the rice noodles according to packet instructions and divide between six bowls. Pick the mint and coriander leaves, then trim the spring onions, peel the onion and finely slice both with the chillies. Cut the limes into wedges. Place it all on a big serving platter with the beansprouts and take to the table with the noodle bowls.

Place a frying pan on a high heat and, once screaming hot, season the skirt steak, pat with groundnut oil, then sear, turning every minute, for 6 to 8 minutes, or until medium-rare (depending on the thickness of your steak). You want it medium-rare, because when you pour the hot broth over the top it will gently cook it through, should you want it to. Remove to a board to rest, then slice up finely and take to the table along with the pan of broth. Get everyone to pimp their own bowls with all the bits and pieces, then pour over some ladlefuls of hot broth. Serve with bottles of hot chilli sauce, fish sauce and soy sauce on the side to perfect the broth to taste.

✕ MASSAMAN CURRY ✕

SERVES 8

<u>1 HOUR 20 MINUTES</u>
<u>442 CALORIES</u>

<u>CURRY</u>

2 large onion squash (1.2kg)

olive oil

150g shelled unsalted peanuts

4 fresh bay leaves

1 large onion

500g baby new potatoes

2 x 400g tins of light coconut milk

4 tablespoons palm sugar

2 tablespoons tamarind paste

2 tablespoons fish sauce

350g silken tofu

400g sugar snap peas

<u>PASTE</u>

1 heaped teaspoon each fennel
    seeds, coriander seeds,
    cardamom pods, whole cloves,
    black peppercorns, dried chilli
    flakes, turmeric, ground cinnamon

6 cloves of garlic

1 thumb-sized piece of ginger

1 red onion

2 sticks of lemongrass

½ a bunch of fresh coriander (15g)

1 lime

vegetable oil

This is an astonishingly beautiful, floral curry that you must try! I was taught to make it by a fantastic Thai cook, Khun Saiyuud Diwong, who runs a great cooking school and is actively involved with the Helping Hands project in the largest slum in Bangkok – look her up, she's an inspirational woman. I've evolved her principles into this incredible vegetable massaman that you'll love, but you can easily add meat, if you want to.

Preheat the oven to 180°C/350°F/gas 4. Carefully halve the squash, deseed and chop into 5cm boats (use butternut squash instead, if you prefer), then toss in a large roasting tray with a good drizzle of olive oil and a pinch of sea salt and pepper. Roast for 1 hour, or until beautifully golden and caramelized at the edges.

Meanwhile, for the paste, put the fennel and coriander seeds, cardamom pods, cloves, peppercorns and chilli flakes into a dry pan and toast on a medium heat until they just start to colour and smell amazing. Pour into a pestle and mortar, crush the cardamom pods and remove the seeds, adding them to the mortar and discarding the pods, then pound it all up until very fine. Peel the garlic, ginger, onion and lemongrass, then roughly chop. Put it all into the dry pan for 4 minutes to soften slightly, moving regularly, then tip into a food processor. Add the ground spice mixture, the turmeric, cinnamon, coriander stalks (reserving the leaves), lime zest and a good few lugs of vegetable oil. Blitz to a fine paste, pausing halfway to scrape down the sides, if needed.

Toast the peanuts in a large dry casserole pan on a medium heat for 5 minutes, tossing regularly, then add half the paste (freeze the rest for another day), along with a lug of vegetable oil and the bay leaves. Stir regularly while you peel, chop and add the onion, and wash, quarter and add the new potatoes (this would be the stage to add any raw or cooked meat). Pour in the coconut milk and 1½ tins' worth of water, add the palm sugar, tamarind paste and fish sauce, bring to the boil, then simmer for 25 to 30 minutes, or until the potatoes are cooked. Drain the tofu and cut into 2cm dice. Stir the sugar snap peas into the curry – they'll only need 2 minutes – then sprinkle over the tofu. Squeeze in the lime juice, then taste the sauce and tweak with fish sauce for saltiness, tamarind paste for sourness, and adjust the consistency with a little water, if required. Divide the roasted squash between warm bowls, spoon over the curry and sprinkle with the coriander leaves. Serve with rice, bread or noodles.

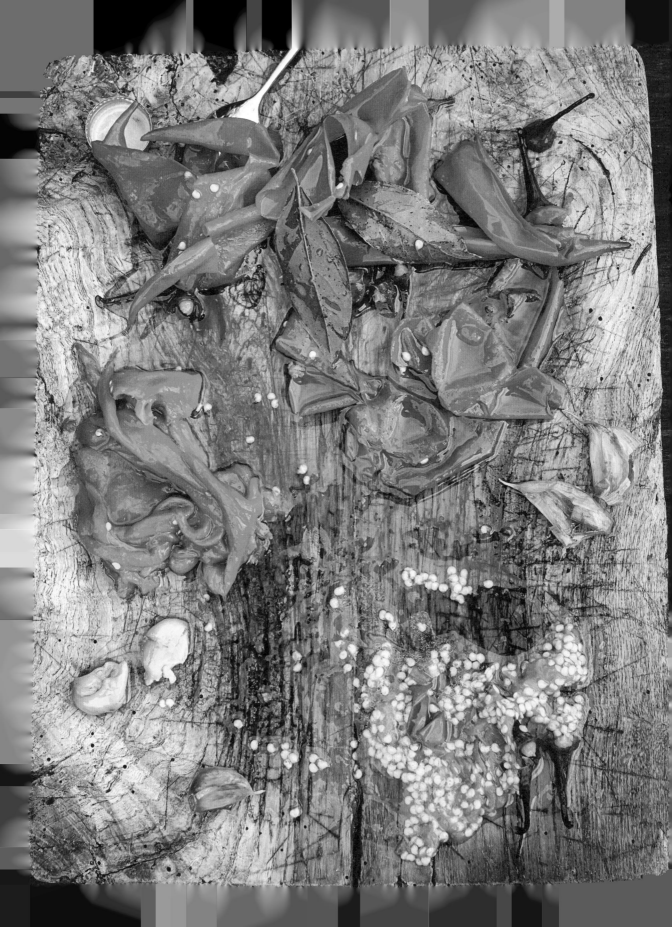

× ULTIMATE ARRABBIATA ×

SERVES 4

<u>1 HOUR 15 MINUTES</u>
<u>414 CALORIES</u>

<u>CHILLI OIL & CONFIT</u>

10 long fresh red chillies

3 fresh bay leaves

1 bulb of garlic

olive oil (500ml)

red or white wine vinegar

<u>SPAGHETTI ARRABBIATA</u>

chilli oil (see above)

1 clove of garlic

1 dried chilli

1 tablespoon fennel seeds

confit chilli and garlic (see above)

1 x 400g tin of quality
   plum tomatoes

320g dried spaghetti

½ a bunch of fresh flat-leaf
   parsley (15g)

extra virgin olive oil

Arrabbiata sauce is such a classic – just garlic, olive oil, chilli and tomatoes, and get on with it. It can be that simple, and good, but this recipe's not about that – this is the ultimate mumma of arrabbiata recipes. It'll give you the best sauce on the planet, no questions asked, but the by-product of making it will also give you the most incredible-tasting chilli oil you ever did drizzle on anything lucky enough to receive it, as well as a kind of confit-chilli-come-harissa in a jar, which you can keep in the fridge for up to a week to subtly grace any possible dish with a lovely slap of warmth.

To make the chilli oil, prick the fresh chillies with a knife (to prevent them from exploding) and place them in a snug-fitting pan with the bay leaves. Break apart and add the garlic cloves, leaving the skin on, then just cover with olive oil and place on a very low heat. Leave to tick away gently for 40 to 45 minutes, or until the garlic and chillies have softened. Allow to cool, then, shaking off the excess oil, remove the chillies to a board. Remove and discard the stalks and skin, then deseed and roughly chop the flesh and scrape it into a clean jam jar. Squeeze the soft garlic out of the skins and into the jar. Add a pinch of salt and pepper and a swig of vinegar, then cover with 2cm of the chilli oil – this is the confit. Use a funnel to pour the rest of the cool chilli oil into a bottle, or decant it into smaller bottles, seal, and give them away as wonderful gifts.

For the spaghetti arrabbiata, pour 2 tablespoons of chilli oil into a large cold pan and place on a medium heat. Peel, finely slice and add the garlic, crumble in the dried chilli and crush and add the fennel seeds. When the garlic starts to lightly colour, add 2 heaped teaspoons of the confit chilli and garlic. Fry gently for a few minutes, then tip in the tomatoes and half a tin's worth of water. Mash and simmer to the consistency you desire, while you cook the spaghetti in boiling salted water according to packet instructions, then drain, reserving a cupful of cooking water. Season the sauce to perfection, then toss the spaghetti through it, loosening with a splash of cooking water, if needed. Finely chop and scatter over the parsley leaves, drizzle with a little extra virgin olive oil, then find a cosy corner, curl up and prepare yourself for the endorphin release that this incredible chilli sauce will give you – it'll be the best sauce you've ever had.

× CHICKEN BROTH, VEG & PESTO ×

SERVES 6
2 HOURS
494 CALORIES

1 x 1.6kg whole chicken

2 bulbs of fennel

1 celery heart

6 carrots

6 baby turnips

2 large handfuls of seasonal greens
(any combination of Swiss chard,
kale, cabbage, Brussels tops,
spinach, spring greens)

1 bunch of mixed fresh herbs,
such as flat-leaf parsley, mint,
thyme (30g)

PESTO

1 clove of garlic

1 handful of shelled walnuts

1 bunch of fresh flat-leaf parsley
and tarragon (30g)

50g Cheddar cheese

1 tablespoon jarred or
fresh grated horseradish

1 tablespoon cider vinegar

6 tablespoons extra virgin
olive oil

This dish always feels like such a celebration of food – a real harvest festival – but it couldn't be any simpler to make. Whole chicken, chunky veg, and an hour and a half of slow poaching creates a wonderful clean pick-me-up broth. It's the perfect dish to help you reflect the seasons, but always remains exciting, delicious and healthy. With a dollop of homemade walnut pesto on the side, you've got an incredibly, satisfying bowl of food.

Put the chicken into a large deep casserole pan. Trim and halve the fennel bulbs and celery heart, peel the carrots, trim the turnips and add to the pan. Pour in enough cold water to cover everything and add 1 teaspoon of sea salt. Place on a medium-high heat and bring to a simmer – this will take about 15 minutes – then reduce to a low heat and leave to tick away for 1 hour 15 minutes, skimming the surface when necessary. Bringing it to a simmer from cold gives you nice clarity in your broth, and by not boiling, but simmering, you ensure the meat is really tender and juicy.

Meanwhile, to make the pesto, peel the garlic and smash up with the walnuts in a pestle and mortar. Pick and finely chop or bash the parsley and tarragon leaves, grate the cheese, add both to the mortar with the horseradish, vinegar and extra virgin olive oil, then muddle and mix together, and season to taste.

When your broth is ready, add the seasonal greens and cook for 5 to 10 minutes, until they're done. Now I've got a really exciting way for you to perfect the flavour with all the delicate, light perfume of fresh herbs. First of all, tie up your bunch of mixed herbs. Have a slurp of the broth, think about it, then dip the herb bunch in for 10 seconds, remove it and taste again. Keep repeating this process until the broth is flavoured to your liking (just like dunking a teabag). The mix of herbs and the size of the bunch will of course affect the flavour, so by removing it every 10 seconds you're in control of how perfumed or intense you make it. Adjust the seasoning if required.

To serve, carefully lift the chicken (don't worry if it falls apart) and veg out of the broth into a large warm bowl. Using a little board and a knife, cut the larger veg up into chunks and distribute between warm bowls, followed by the leafy greens. Use tongs to tear away chunks of meat and add to the bowls, discarding the skin. Ladle over the hot, delicious broth and finish each portion with a generous dollop of walnut pesto. This is delicious served with a pot of mustard and a loaf of crusty bread on the side.

× KUSHARI AL FORNO ×

SERVES 8–10
1 HOUR 30 MINUTES
644 CALORIES

6 red onions

4 cloves of garlic

2 fresh red chillies

1 bunch of fresh flat-leaf
parsley (30g)

olive oil

2 teaspoons ground cumin

1 teaspoon sun-dried
tomato paste

3 x 400g tins of plum tomatoes

1 vegetable or chicken stock cube

red wine vinegar

1 x 400g tin of chickpeas

300g basmati rice

500g dried mixed pasta

1 x 400g tin of Puy lentils

200g feta cheese

½ a bunch of fresh mint (15g)

2 large eggs

1 litre vegetable oil

1 heaped teaspoon fennel seeds

1 heaped teaspoon cumin seeds

plain flour

Tasty, super-comforting and super-cheap to make, this dish has been a massive hit with me and my food team. Originating from Egypt, kushari came up time and time again on social media when I reached out for your favourite comfort food dishes. Kushari is ultimately a carb fest, served with a spoonful of tomato sauce with Egyptian attitude and some delicate crispy onion rings. All that is delicious, but I really wanted to move it on, so I've treated it more like an Italian pasta al forno and freshened it up with some soft herbs.

Peel 4 onions and all the garlic, then finely chop with the chillies and parsley stalks (reserving the leaves). Put into a large pan on a medium heat with a lug of olive oil and the ground cumin and cook for 15 minutes, or until soft and sticky but not coloured, stirring regularly and adding a splash of water if it starts to stick. Stir in the tomato paste for 1 minute, then add the tinned tomatoes, breaking them up with a wooden spoon. Crumble in the stock cube, then add 1 tablespoon of vinegar, the chickpeas and their juice and 1 tin's worth of boiling water. Bring to the boil, simmer for 30 minutes, then season to taste.

Preheat the oven to 180°C/350°F/gas 4. Cook the rice and pasta together in a large pan of boiling salted water, according to packet instructions, then drain and return to the pan. Drain, rinse and add the lentils. Pour over the tomato sauce, then crumble in one-third of the feta in 1cm chunks. Roughly chop most of the parsley and mint leaves and add those too, crack in the eggs, then mix together. Season to taste, then decant into a large earthenware dish (30cm x 35cm), crumble over another third of the feta and bake on the bottom shelf of the oven for 30 to 35 minutes, or until golden.

Meanwhile, half fill a pan with the vegetable oil and place on a medium to high heat – add a cube of potato and when it turns golden (180°C), the oil is ready. Peel the remaining 2 onions and cut into ½cm rounds, toss in a good splash of vinegar and a pinch of salt, leave to pickle for a few minutes, then sprinkle over the fennel and cumin seeds and enough plain flour to make them go sticky and lightly coat them. When the oil is hot enough, deep-fry the onion rings in batches (to prevent them sticking together), transferring them to a plate lined with kitchen paper as you go.

Serve the kushari al forno scattered with the crispy onion rings and the remaining parsley and mint leaves, then finely crumble the remaining feta over the top. This is delicious with a fresh crunchy salad on the side and a nice bottle of cold white wine.

BELLINI

SERVES 1
<u>10 MINUTES</u>
<u>84 CALORIES</u>

When peaches are in season and outrageously delicious, halve, destone and blitz their flesh in a blender until puréed, then pass through a fine sieve. Put 2.5cm of this beautiful purée into a tall, chilled Champagne glass. Pour in chilled Prosecco, not quite to the top, carefully mix with a long spoon, then fill to the brim with more bubbles, and enjoy. Of course, you can easily go from a Bellini to a Rossini by using strawberry purée with Prosecco instead of peach.

MOJITO

SERVES 1
<u>5 MINUTES</u>
<u>165 CALORIES</u>

Cut ½ a lime into 4 wedges and put into a tall glass with 2 heaped teaspoons of golden caster sugar. Briefly muddle together, then twist 12 fresh mint leaves once and spank to release the aroma. Rub around the rim of the glass, then drop them into it and use a muddler to gently push and mash them down into the lime. Half fill the glass with crushed ice, pour in 50ml of Bacardi Superior, muddle until the sugar dissolves, then top up with crushed ice and a splash of soda water.

TOM COLLINS

SERVES 1
5 MINUTES
157 CALORIES

First of all, get a nice tall glass filled with ice so it starts to frost up. Make some cool retro skewers of 2 glacé cherries sandwiched with a delicate wedge of unwaxed lemon. Into a cocktail shaker, put 50ml of Bombay Sapphire gin, the juice of ½ a lemon, 1 heaped teaspoon of caster sugar and 100ml of soda water. Shake hard with plenty of ice for 20 seconds to make it really nice and cold. Strain over the ice in your prepared glass and top with your retro skewer.

SMOKIN' BLOODY MARY

SERVES 1
5 MINUTES
192 CALORIES

Put 50ml of Grey Goose vodka into a cocktail shaker, with 200ml of organic tomato juice, the juice from ¼ of a lemon, 1 teaspoon of Worcestershire sauce, 1 level tablespoon of BBQ sauce, 1 pinch of celery salt and pepper, and ½ a teaspoon of jarred horseradish or, ideally, 1 heaped teaspoon of freshly grated horseradish. Mix, taste, correct the seasoning, then shake over ice and serve in a large tumbler with a stick of celery and a mini kebab of gherkin, chilli, olive and crispy bacon.

TRUE COMFORT IS
IN THE MAKING

♡

RITUAL

WINTER NIGHTS CHILLI

When the weather's closing in, it's really great to tuck into a full-flavoured, hearty dish, and for me, a proper, rustic chilli rocks. The meat will fall apart and melt in your mouth. It's moreish, spicy and with a clever contrasting salsa is a total joy.

× WINTER NIGHTS CHILLI ×

SERVES 12
6 HOURS
553 CALORIES

CHILLI

20g dried porcini mushrooms

2 tablespoons each fennel seeds,
  coriander seeds, smoked paprika

1 butternut squash (1.2kg)

olive oil

1kg pork belly, skin removed
  and bone out

1kg brisket

2 large onions

2 teaspoons soft light brown sugar

150ml balsamic vinegar

2 x 400g tins of cannellini beans
  or chickpeas

2 x 400g tins of plum tomatoes

2 red peppers

2 yellow peppers

2–3 fresh red chillies

1 bunch of fresh coriander (30g)

SALSA

1 red onion

2 crisp eating apples

3 tablespoons cider vinegar

3 tablespoons extra virgin olive oil

Preheat the oven to 190°C/375°F/gas 5. Pop the mushrooms into a small bowl and just cover with boiling water. Bash the fennel and coriander seeds, paprika and 1 teaspoon each of sea salt and black pepper in a pestle and mortar. Carefully cut the squash in half lengthways, deseed, then chop into 4cm chunks. Toss with half the spice mixture and a drizzle of olive oil on a baking tray. Roast for 50 minutes, or until golden, then remove from the oven and reduce the temperature to 150°C/300°F/gas 2.

Meanwhile, drizzle both cuts of meat with olive oil and rub with the remaining spice mixture, then place a large casserole pan (at least 30cm wide, 8cm deep) on a medium-high heat. Place the pork and the brisket in the pan fat-side down and brown on all sides for around 15 minutes in total, then peel and roughly chop the onions. Remove both meats to a plate, reduce the heat to medium, add the onions and sugar to the fat and fry for 10 minutes, stirring regularly until lightly caramelized. Add the balsamic vinegar and most of the mushroom liquid (discarding any gritty bits). Roughly chop and add the mushrooms, followed by the beans or chickpeas, liquid and all, and the tomatoes, breaking them up with a spoon, then return both meats to the pan. Loosen with a splash of water if needed, then bring to the boil, season, and pop a layer of damp greaseproof paper directly on the surface. Cover with tin foil and cook in the oven for around 5 hours, or until the meat is tender.

Prick the peppers and chillies, then blacken all over on a barbecue or in a griddle pan. Place in a bowl, cover with clingfilm and leave to cool, then peel and deseed them, keeping as much juice as you can for extra flavour. Roughly chop with half the coriander, and toss with a little salt and pepper. When the meat is tender, remove from the oven, break up the meat, then stir in the squash, peppers and chillies. Adjust the consistency with water if needed, taste and season to perfection, then keep warm.

To finish, peel the onion, then finely chop with the apples (core and all) and the remaining coriander. Dress with the cider vinegar and extra virgin olive oil and season to perfection. Serve the chilli with the salsa, bread or rice, and a dollop of yoghurt.

× GYOZA WITH CRISPY WINGS ×

SERVES 6–10
1 HOUR 30 MINUTES
279 CALORIES

DOUGH

300g good-quality Tipo 00
  flour, plus extra for dusting
  and the wings

groundnut oil

FILLING

¼ of a green cabbage (250g)

200g pork belly, skin removed
  and bone out

2 cloves of garlic

1 thumb-sized piece of ginger

4 spring onions

1 teaspoon miso paste

1 teaspoon sesame oil

1 fresh red chilli

TO SERVE

low-salt soy sauce

rice wine vinegar

English mustard

Worcestershire sauce

Tabasco sauce

I fell in love with gyoza when I worked in Japan for a few years. We used to hang out in gyoza bars, which were often downscale shabby restaurants serving many different varieties of gyoza, interestingly always with some English condiments on the side, just like I've done here. They're super-delicious, and recently I've been introduced to gyoza with wings, totally taking the gyoza experience to another level. Give them a go.

To make the dough, mix the flour and a few pinches of sea salt with 170ml of boiling water in a bowl until it starts to come together. As soon as it's cool enough to handle, knead for 5 minutes, or until you have a smooth elastic dough. Cover with clingfilm.

To make the filling, cut the cabbage and pork belly into rough chunks and place in a food processor. Peel and add the garlic and ginger and the green tops from the spring onions, along with the miso paste, sesame oil and chilli, and pulse until well combined. Pop into the fridge until needed.

On a flour-dusted surface, split the dough into two and roll one piece out as thinly as you can. Use a flat 8cm cutter to stamp out about 20 circles – try to get as many as you can from the first roll, as if you re-roll too many times the dough will get tough. One by one, dot a heaped teaspoon of filling onto each round, then fold the dough in half over the filling. Working from the middle to each end, make pleats on one side only, pinching each one against the flat side (see pictures right). Repeat both processes until you've made all your gyoza. You'll be a bit slow on the first five, but, frankly, as long as you seal the dumplings it's happy days, however they look.

To cook, arrange half the gyoza in a very large non-stick frying pan oiled with groundnut oil and fry on a medium heat until golden on the bottom. Meanwhile, whisk 2 heaped teaspoons of flour with 400ml of water. Once the gyoza bottoms are golden, pour in half the floury water. Cover with a tight-fitting lid or tin foil and simmer for 10 minutes, then remove the lid until it begins to fry again – you'll notice a delicate kinda pancake starting to form and encase the dumplings. When it's nicely golden, confidently bang it out onto a serving board. Finely slice and sprinkle over the whites of the spring onions, and serve with soy sauce, rice wine vinegar, English mustard, Worcestershire sauce, or even Tabasco – anything goes! Repeat with the remaining gyoza and floury water.

✕ CASSOULET DE ESSEX ✕

SERVES 8

3 HOURS 20 MINUTES
PLUS MARINATING
755 CALORIES

20g coarse sea salt

8 sprigs of fresh thyme

8 cloves

8 juniper berries

12 fresh bay leaves

5 cloves of garlic

1 orange

1 whole nutmeg, for grating

3 duck legs

600g lamb breast

500g pork belly, skin removed

3 Toulouse sausages

1 large onion

2 sticks of celery

1 large leek

6 sprigs of fresh rosemary

2 x 400g tins of plum tomatoes

1 good splash of Merlot or Malbec

1 x 660g jar of cannellini beans

200g fresh breadcrumbs

olive oil

½ a lemon

The Essex cassoulet will raise your spirits, pleasure your taste buds and probably cause you to require a siesta afterwards. Cassoulet is a wonderful concept where different types of meat and cheaper cuts are put on an equal playing field alongside humble veg, beans and bread to make one beautiful dish of happiness. You'll love this one.

Put your weighed salt, the thyme, cloves, juniper berries, 4 bay leaves and 4 cloves of peeled garlic into a food processor. Finely grate in the orange zest and the nutmeg and add a good pinch of black pepper. Blitz to make a flavoured salt, then rub really well over the duck legs, lamb breast and pork belly in a large tray. Cover with clingfilm and place in the fridge overnight to marinate.

The next day, preheat the oven to 180°C/350°F/gas 4. Brush the salt off the meat and pat the meat dry with kitchen paper. Cut the duck legs into thighs and drumsticks, and divide both the lamb and pork into 8 equal pieces. Put the duck, lamb and pork into a snug-fitting tray and roast for 1 hour 30 minutes. When the time's up, remove most of the rendered fat from the tray to a bowl, toss the sausages in the tray with the other meat and return to the oven for 20 minutes while you make the sauce.

Peel the onion and finely chop with the celery, leek and rosemary leaves, then add to a large ovenproof casserole pan with 2 tablespoons of reserved fat and fry for 15 minutes on a medium heat. Tip in the tomatoes and 2 tins' worth of water, breaking the tomatoes up with a spoon. Bring to the boil, then simmer for 5 minutes. Remove the tray from the oven and add the meat to the sauce. Stir the wine around the tray to pick up any sticky goodness from the bottom, then add to the sauce and stir together.

For an amazing topping, drain the beans into a large bowl and add the breadcrumbs. Remove and discard the stalks from the remaining bay leaves, then smash them up in a pestle and mortar with the remaining peeled clove of garlic and a pinch of salt until completely pulped. Muddle in a good lug of oil and grate in the lemon zest, then mix with the beans and breadcrumbs and scatter over the cassoulet. Bake for 1 hour, or until thick, golden and bubbling. Serve with loads of steamed seasonal greens.

ROYAL PASTA DOUGH

This is definitely a royal pasta dough – silky, velvety pasta, made with a simple blend of Tipo 00 flour (00 means it's super-fine) and fine semolina, which has wonderful flavour and golden colour. This blend of flours along with free-range egg yolks gives you the ultimate in pasta dough. And the best bit is, it's still super-cheap for the volume of pasta that it gives you. Enjoy this rolled or cut into a hundred different shapes, and feel the pride in making pasta yourself from scratch.

× ROYAL PASTA DOUGH ×

SERVES 8

30 MINUTES

PLUS RESTING

327 CALORIES

400g good-quality Tipo 00 flour,
  plus extra for dusting

75g fine semolina

12 large eggs

2 tablespoons extra virgin olive oil

×

Of course the world of pasta is full of rules and old wives' tales about what you can and can't do, but throughout Italy, in every village, town and region, they all regularly contradict each other. This method will get you into a good place, but of course you can roll it out thicker for a thicker noodle, which will simply have to be cooked for longer. The most important question to consider is, does it eat well with the sauce you're going to pair it up with? Only you can answer that. The sauce and the pasta shape should be in harmony – the pasta is equal to the sauce.

THE DOUGH

Pile the flour and semolina into a large bowl and make a well in the middle. Separate the eggs and add the yolks to the well, putting the egg whites into a sandwich bag and popping into the freezer for making meringues another day (page 320). Add the oil and 4 tablespoons of cold water to the well, then use a fork to whip up with the eggs until smooth, then gradually bring the flour in from the outside. When it becomes too hard to mix, get your clean floured hands in there and bring it together into a ball of dough. Knead on a flour-dusted surface for around 4 minutes, or until smooth and elastic (eggs can vary in size and flour can vary in humidity; this dough shouldn't be too wet or dry, but tweak with a touch more water or flour if you need to – use your common sense). Wrap in clingfilm and leave to relax for 30 minutes.

ROLLING OUT

Traditionally, Italians would have used a very large rolling pin, and you can do it that way if you like, it just requires a large flat surface and a bit of elbow grease. In this day and age, I think it's fun and advisable to use a pasta machine. Attach it firmly to a nice clean table and divide your pasta dough into four pieces, covering everything with a damp clean tea towel to stop it drying out as you go.

STAGE 1

One at a time, flatten each piece of dough by hand and run it through the thickest setting, then take the rollers down two settings and run the dough through again to make it thinner. Importantly, fold it in half and run it back through the thickest setting again – I like to repeat this a few times because it makes the dough super-smooth and turns it from a tatty sheet into one that fills out the pasta machine properly.

STAGE 2

Start rolling the sheet down through each setting, dusting with flour as you go. Turn the crank with one hand while the other maintains just a little tension to avoid any kinks, folds or ripples. Take it right down to the desired thickness, which is about 2mm for shapes like linguine, tagliatelle and lasagne. For anything turned into a filled pasta such as ravioli and tortellini, go as thin as 1mm, because when it's folded around a filling it will double up to 2mm. Turn the page for some ideas to have fun with shapes.

PLAY TIME

As a chef, pasta changed my life with the vast amount of different shapes and sizes, and the ownership and pride it gave me when making it – it really took my cooking to the next level. Now you've made your dough (page 214), to turn it into any of the shapes on this page go to youtube.com/jamieoliver and Gennaro will show you how, step by step, as well as much, much more.

× PRAWN LINGUINE ×

SERMES 4

<u>1 HOUR</u>
<u>500 CALORIES</u>

12 large raw shell-on king prawns

1 good pinch of saffron

olive oil

1 onion

4 anchovy fillets

1 splash of crisp, dry Riesling

1 x 400g tin of plum tomatoes

2 cloves of garlic

200g ripe cherry tomatoes

1 fresh long red chilli

½ a bulb of fennel

½ x royal pasta dough (page 214)
   or 320g dried linguine

1 large handful of rocket

1 lemon

extra virgin olive oil

Prawn linguine is definitely close to people's hearts – it's one of the bestselling dishes on the Jamie's Italian menu. Sweet prawns, freshly made pasta, rich tomatoes, lemony rocket and a kick of chilli – it's definitely comfort food. In the restaurants, our sauce base takes hours to make, so I've adjusted that complex recipe to make it more home friendly and help you achieve maximum flavour from all those lovely ingredients.

Peel the prawns, reserving all the heads and shells. Run a knife down the back and pull out the veins. Keep 4 prawns whole, running your knife down those ones again to butterfly them. Chop the rest of the prawns into small chunks to help distribute that sweet taste throughout the dish. Put the saffron into a little bowl with a thimble of boiling water. Place the prawn heads and shells in a large pan on a medium heat with a lug of olive oil and fry while you peel and finely chop the onion, then add it to the pan. Cook until the onion starts to soften, stirring occasionally. Add the saffron with its soaking water and the anchovies. Turn the heat up, add the wine and cook it away, then add the tinned tomatoes, 1 tin's worth of water and a pinch of salt and pepper. Bring to the boil, then simmer for 12 minutes. Cool a little, and in small batches, blitz in a blender until smooth, then pass through a coarse sieve and season to taste.

Put a large pan of salted water onto boil for the pasta. Peel and finely slice the garlic, quarter the cherry tomatoes and finely slice the chilli. Trim and finely slice the fennel, preferably on a mandolin (use the guard!). You can make this with fresh or dried pasta, so if using fresh (page 214), cut the sheets into linguine.

Now it's time to focus. Great pasta is all about timing and confidence – the sauce takes 4 minutes, so if using dried pasta, get that on first and start the sauce after 8 minutes; if using fresh, cook it halfway through the sauce process – I don't want you to overcook the prawns or pasta. Place a large pan on a high heat and, once hot, add a good lug of olive oil, quickly followed by the garlic and chilli. After 30 seconds, toss in the whole prawns, then after another 60 seconds add the chopped prawns, cherry tomatoes and fennel and toss again. Pour over the sauce and bring to a simmer. At this point, drain your cooked pasta and place it on top of the sauce. Toss again, quickly check the seasoning and divide between four bowls, followed by any leftover prawns and sauce. Top each portion with a clump of rocket, add a squeeze of lemon juice and drizzle with extra virgin olive oil. Eat it, and be proud of yourself.

× CRAB LINGUINE ×

SERVES 4
35 MINUTES
614 CALORIES

½ x royal pasta dough (page 214)
  or 320g dried linguine

300g white crabmeat

1 bulb of fennel

2 lemons

1–2 fresh red chillies

1 heaped tablespoon brown
  crabmeat

8 tablespoons extra virgin olive oil

1 handful of herby fennel tops or
  fresh baby basil leaves

Really good beautiful crabmeat isn't cheap these days – but this is super-quick to put together, and the results are exciting, delicious, comforting and a bit posh all at the same time. And actually, I quite like having a posh meal but sitting on the sofa in my jogging bottoms to eat it. When buying shellfish like crab or lobster, it's important to have a conversation with your fishmonger in advance to determine the best day to buy it, so you're getting it in mint condition and know that you'll get maximum flavour.

You can make this with fresh or dried pasta, so if using fresh (page 214), cut the sheets into linguine, then dry for an hour before cooking so it's more al dente.

Place the white crabmeat in a large bowl, then tear over any fennel tops from the bulb (often when you buy fennel from supermarkets the herby fronds will have already been removed, but if you've got any – great). Trim the base of the bulb and remove the outside layer if it's got any blemishes, then, using the coarse side of a box grater, grate the bulb into the bowl with the crab. Using the fine side of the grater, add just the yellow zest from ½ a lemon to the bowl. Deseed and very finely chop the chillies, then add half to the crab, reserving the rest for sprinkling later. To make the dressing, mix the brown crabmeat, the juice of both lemons and the oil together with a little splash of water. Mix with the white crabmeat and season to taste, if needed.

Put a large pan of salted water onto boil for the pasta. Transfer the dressed crabmeat to a large pan on a low heat to gently warm through, while you cook the pasta. If you've made fresh, the pasta will only take 2 minutes to cook – if you're using dried, simply cook according to packet instructions, but obviously don't put the crab on the heat until halfway through. Meanwhile, pick your fennel herbs or basil leaves.

Drain the pasta, reserving a cupful of cooking water, then toss the pasta through the sauce, adding half the picked herbs and loosening with a splash of reserved water, if needed. Divide between four warm bowls, sprinkle over the remaining chilli and fennel or basil leaves, and serve. I love it with a nice, cold glass of Soave or Riesling.

× BOLOGNESE RAVIOLI ×

SERVES 8–10
2 HOURS 30 MINUTES
PLUS COOLING
650 CALORIES

FILLING

400g minced pork

400g minced veal or beef

olive oil

2 cloves of garlic

2 onions

2 carrots

2 sticks of celery

200ml Chianti Classico

2 x 400g tins of plum tomatoes

100g Parmesan cheese,
  plus extra to serve

PASTA

1 x royal pasta dough (page 214)

fine semolina, for dusting

SAUCE

4 cloves of garlic

1–2 fresh red chillies

3 x 400g tins of plum tomatoes

a few sprigs of fresh basil

This beautiful Bolognese-filled ravioli is absolutely incredible, and is a homage to the tinned stuff I used to enjoy as a kid. That's the funny thing about memories and food – sometimes the memory is better than the reality. So without question, travelling and being enlightened to food made with passion, without compromise, gives you the tools to reinvent old classics, to be even better than your memories, just like I've done here.

Put all the minced meat into your largest pan on a high heat with a good lug of oil and a pinch of sea salt and pepper. Cook for 20 minutes, or until golden, stirring regularly. Meanwhile, peel and finely chop the garlic, onions, carrots and celery. When the mince has got a good colour, add all the chopped veg and cook for a further 10 minutes, then add the Chianti and cook it away. Pour in the tomatoes, breaking them up with a spoon, and add half a tin's worth of water. Bring to the boil, then simmer gently for 1 hour, or until the meat is tender and the sauce is super-thick. Remove from the heat to cool, then finely grate and stir in the Parmesan.

Now it's time to assemble your pasta. Following the instructions for making the pasta dough on page 214, roll out your dough to 1mm thick, then make your ravioli about 7cm square, using the pictures on page 226 as a guide. I work with a quarter of the pasta at a time to give more control. Use a heaped teaspoon of filling in the centre of each one, sealing the edges with a light brushing of water and pushing out the air – you should get about 50 to 60 ravioli from this amount of pasta. Place them on a semolina-dusted tray as you go. Freeze the remaining Bolognese (you'll have roughly half left) for a rainy day, or make a double batch of pasta and freeze as ravioli – you can cook them from frozen in the sauce. Put a pan of salted water onto boil for the pasta.

For the sauce, peel and roughly chop the garlic and deseed and finely chop the chillies. Place a pan on a medium heat, add a lug of oil and the garlic and chilli, and fry for a few minutes, or until very lightly golden. Add the tomatoes and simmer for 10 minutes, or until thickened and reduced, then remove from the heat and blitz until smooth with a stick blender. Taste and season to perfection, then place back on a very low heat. Cook the ravioli in the boiling salted water for 3 minutes, or until tender, then use a slotted spoon to transfer them to the sauce. Gently toss together and simmer for another couple of minutes, then divide between warm bowls, scatter with baby basil leaves and serve with a few extra gratings of Parmesan, if you like.

✕ TORTELLINI PRIMAVERA ✕

SERVES 6

3–4 HOURS
436 CALORIES

1.5kg chicken bones
(ask your butcher to cleaver
into 8cm chunks)

olive oil

2 large chicken legs

1 bulb of garlic

2 sticks of celery

2 carrots

60g Taleggio cheese

20g Parmesan cheese

1 lemon

½ x royal pasta dough (page 214)

fine semolina, for dusting

500g fresh peas in their pods
(150g podded weight)

a few fresh herby fennel tops

3 sprigs of fresh basil

extra virgin olive oil

Around northern Italy, especially Milan and Bologna, they make beautiful, clean, tasty broths with small delicate seasonal tortellini. So here's my favourite comforting version, celebrating sweet spring peas, delicate chicken and tiny amounts of pungent Taleggio. As Gennaro says, these really are little parcels of spring–summer love.

Preheat the oven to 200°C/400°F/gas 6. Place the bones in a roasting tray, season with sea salt and black pepper, drizzle with olive oil, toss, and roast for 1 hour. At this point, transfer the bones to a large casserole pan. Pour a little water into the roasting tray and use a wooden spoon to scrape up all the sticky goodness from the bottom of the tray, then add to the pan with 4 litres of cold water. Add the chicken legs and the whole bulb of garlic, halve and add the celery and carrots, then bring to the boil and simmer over a very low heat for 1 hour 30 minutes, or until intense and delicious – you need enough broth for 6 portions, so top up slightly, if needed.

Remove the chicken legs to a board and strip all the meat and skin off the bone, returning the bones to the simmering broth. Scoop out the garlic and squeeze half the flesh from the skins. Very finely chop the chicken skin, roughly chop the meat, a little boiled carrot and the Taleggio, finely grate the Parmesan and lemon zest, then chop and mix it all together with the sweet garlic to make a delicious filling.

Now it's time to assemble your pasta. Following the instructions for making the pasta dough on page 214, roll out your dough to 1mm thick, then make your tortellini using a 7cm round cutter, using the pictures on page 230 as a guide. I work with a quarter of the pasta at a time to give more control. Use marble-sized balls of filling for each one, sealing the edges with a light brushing of water and pushing out the air – you should get around 60 tortellini. Place them on a semolina-dusted tray as you go. Pod all your peas and put to one side, adding the empty pods to the broth for 5 minutes for amazing added flavour. Pass the whole lot through a sieve – it will leave you with a deep, tasty, clear chicken broth. Have a slurp, and season to perfection.

Carefully cook the tortellini in a large pan of boiling salted water for 3 minutes, adding the peas for the last minute, then drain and place in the broth. Take to the table, divide between warmed bowls, scatter over a few fennel tops and baby basil leaves and drizzle with a little good-quality extra virgin olive oil.

✕ CRISPY DUCK LASAGNE ✕

SERVES 8–10
4 HOURS
PLUS COOLING & RESTING
835 CALORIES

1 whole duck (roughly 2kg)

olive oil

4 cloves of garlic

1 bunch of fresh marjoram (30g)

800g fresh or frozen spinach

1 whole nutmeg, for grating

1 onion

2 carrots

2 sticks of celery

200ml Chianti Classico

4 x 400g tins of plum tomatoes

2 fresh bay leaves

2 cloves

½ x royal pasta dough (page 214)

40g Parmesan cheese

WHITE SAUCE

100g unsalted butter

100g plain flour

1 litre semi-skimmed milk

75g Cheddar cheese

75g Fontina or Taleggio cheese

PANGRATTATO

200g stale bread

4 sprigs of fresh rosemary

Everyone loves a good lasagne, but I have to say this one really is very special. The stages of making the pasta and roasting the duck, then pulling all the meat off for the wonderful ragù sauce, are fun, simple and a real labour of love. This dish is going to create memories.

Preheat the oven to 180°C/350°F/gas 4. In a tray, rub the duck all over with oil, sea salt and black pepper, then roast for 2 hours, or until golden and crisp, draining off the fat into a jar. Leave to cool, remove all the skin and fat from the duck and place in a food processor, then strip all the meat off the bone into a bowl.

Peel and finely slice 2 cloves of garlic, then put into a large non-stick pan on a high heat with a little duck fat and the marjoram leaves. Cook until the garlic is lightly golden, then stir in the spinach and a good grating of nutmeg and cook for 15 minutes, or until the spinach has cooked right down and all the excess water has evaporated. Leave to cool while you make your ragù. Peel the onion and carrots, trim the celery, then roughly chop it all. Place all in a large pan on a medium heat with a little duck fat (keep any leftover fat in the fridge for making great roast potatoes) and crush in the remaining garlic. Fry for around 20 minutes, or until the veg are starting to caramelize, stirring regularly. Pour in the Chianti, turn up the heat and cook it away. Add the shredded duck meat and tinned tomatoes, along with 1 tin's worth of water, the bay leaves and cloves. Give it a good stir, simmer for around 1 hour, then season to perfection. Meanwhile, make your pasta dough (page 214).

Next make your white sauce. Melt the butter in a large pan over a medium heat, then stir in the flour to form a paste. Whisk in the milk, a little at a time, and continue to heat until you have a thick white sauce. Remove from the heat, grate and stir in the cheeses, season to taste and add a grating of nutmeg. To build your lasagne, start by rolling out the pasta dough into sheets. Cover the base of a baking dish (25cm x 30cm and 8cm deep) with a good layer of spinach, then cover with a single layer of pasta sheets. Stir a good grating of Parmesan into the ragù, then cover the pasta sheets with a layer of ragù, a thin layer of spinach, a layer of white sauce and another layer of pasta. Repeat twice more, finishing with a layer of white sauce. Top with a good grating of Parmesan, then bake at 180°C/350°F/gas 4 for 40 minutes, or until golden and bubbling. Leave to rest for around 20 minutes before serving.

Meanwhile, add the bread and rosemary leaves to the food processor with the duck skin and fat and pulse into fine crumbs. Fry in a large non-stick frying pan until golden and crisp, then serve on the side and let everyone sprinkle over their own portion.

× PROPER VEG LASAGNE ×

SERVES 10

4 HOURS
PLUS RESTING
716 CALORIES

1 x royal pasta dough (page 214)

1 x white sauce (page 236)

400g ricotta cheese

50g Parmesan cheese

SQUASH

1 large butternut squash (1.8kg)

1 teaspoon ground coriander

1 level teaspoon chilli powder

olive oil

VEG SAUCE

3 medium aubergines

20g dried porcini mushrooms

1 large red onion

2 carrots

2 sticks of celery

2 sprigs of fresh rosemary

150ml Chardonnay or Viognier

2 x 400g tins of plum tomatoes

4 cloves of garlic

4 tablespoons balsamic vinegar

SPINACH

8 sprigs of fresh marjoram
  or oregano

800g fresh or frozen spinach

I love this lasagne – you can taste all the different incredible veg elements and it's a fun assembly job. It will totally smash other veggie lasagne to pieces, as I've layered long lasagne sheets at the base so you can fold them in on top to create almost a lasagne pie with a wonderfully crisp pasta crust all the way round. Yum – enjoy!

Preheat the oven to 190°C/375°F/gas 5. Carefully halve the squash lengthways and deseed, then slice 2cm-thick, leaving the skin on. Toss in a large tray with the ground coriander, chilli powder, a pinch of sea salt and pepper and a lug of oil. Slice the aubergines into 2cm-thick rounds, lightly brush each side with oil and sprinkle with salt and pepper, then lay flat on a separate large tray. Roast both the squash and aubergine for 50 minutes, then remove, mashing up the squash really well.

For the veg sauce, just cover the porcini with boiling water and leave to rehydrate. Peel the onion and carrots, trim the celery, then finely chop it all with the rosemary leaves. Put a good lug of oil into a large casserole pan on a medium heat and add the rosemary and finely chopped veg. Cook for 15 minutes, until softened, then pour in the wine and completely cook it away. Chop and add the soaked porcini, followed by half the soaking water. Add the tinned tomatoes, then half fill each empty tin with water, swirl and add to the pan. Simmer for 5 minutes, then turn the heat off. When the aubergines are done, crush the garlic straight over them, drizzle with the balsamic and toss to coat, then scrape it all into the sauce. Simmer gently for 10 minutes on a medium heat, stirring occasionally, then season to perfection.

Put a large non-stick pan on a high heat with a splash of oil and the marjoram or oregano leaves. Cook for 1 minute, then stir in the spinach and cook for 15 minutes, or until it has cooked right down and all the excess water has evaporated. Make your white sauce (page 236) and pasta dough (page 214), leaving the pasta in long sheets.

Now it's assembly time – rub a deep 30cm circular ovenproof dish (or go traditional with 25cm x 35cm) with oil. Cover the base and sides of the dish with long sheets of pasta, allowing a nice amount to hang over each side. Spread one quarter of the veg sauce over the lasagne base, top with bombs of spinach, smashed squash and ricotta, then spoon over a fifth of the white sauce and finely grate over some Parmesan. Repeat three more times, then fold the overhanging pasta over the top and patch up any gaps with a little extra pasta. Cover with the remaining white sauce and a good grating of Parmesan, then bake on the very bottom of the oven for 45 minutes, or until golden and bubbling. Leave to rest for 20 minutes, then serve with a big salad.

× OSSOBUCO ALLA MILANESE ×

SERVES 6

2 HOURS 30 MINUTES

411 CALORIES

6 ossobuco (cross-cut veal
shanks, bone in, roughly 1.5kg in
total – order in advance from
your butcher)

1 whole nutmeg, for grating

plain flour, for dusting

2 knobs of unsalted butter

olive oil

2 onions

2 small carrots

2 cloves of garlic

2 sticks of celery

2 sprigs of fresh rosemary

200ml Pinot Bianco or Verdicchio

1 tablespoon tomato purée

1 litre fresh chicken stock

GREMOLATA

2 small cloves of garlic

1 bunch of fresh flat-leaf
parsley (30g)

1 lemon

*The marriage between the great ossobuco and risotto alla Milanese, commonly known
in Italy as risotto allo zafferano, that brilliant yellow saffron risotto, is fantastic, joyful
and comforting. This will serve 6 as a generous main, but if you shred the meat, removing
the bones, you can happily stretch it to serve 12 as a starter. Outside of the marriage,
ossobuco is great served simply with mashed potato, oozy polenta or good crusty bread,
but you'll find the recipe for risotto allo zafferano, the perfect partner, on page 246.*

Preheat the oven to 180°C/350°F/gas 4. Season the ossobuco lightly with sea salt,
pepper and a grating of nutmeg, then dust them in flour, shaking off any excess. Put
your widest ovenproof pan on a medium heat with the butter and a really good lug
of oil, then add the ossobuco, making sure they're not touching each other. Fry for
10 to 15 minutes, or until nicely golden, turning halfway – the more care you put
into building up good colour now, the better the depth of flavour will be later. While
they're cooking, peel the onions, carrots and garlic, trim the celery, then finely chop it
all with the rosemary leaves. When the veal has browned nicely, remove it to a plate.
Drain away most of the fat from the pan, then add all the chopped veg and rosemary
and cook for 15 minutes, stirring regularly. Pour in the wine and cook it away, then
stir in the tomato purée and stock. Bring to the boil, using a wooden spoon to pick
up all the sticky goodness from the bottom of the pan, then turn the heat off. Return
the meat to the pan, cover with a damp sheet of greaseproof paper and tin foil, then
carefully transfer to the middle of the oven. Cook for 2 hours, or until the meat
is tender and falling apart – check on it halfway, adding a splash of water, if needed.

With about 30 minutes to go on the ossobuco, start your risotto allo zafferano (page
246). When that's done, to make a quick gremolata, peel and roughly chop the garlic
with the parsley leaves, finely grate over the lemon zest, then chop and mix together
until fine. Divide the risotto between warm bowls, then place the ossobuco on top.
Season the cooking liquor to perfection (loosening with a few splashes of boiling
water if needed) and spoon over the top, then scatter over the gremolata – as soon
as it hits the heat of the meat it will explode with wonderful fragrant flavour.

× RISOTTO ALLO ZAFFERANO ×

SERVES 6
40 MINUTES
436 CALORIES

1.2 litres fresh chicken stock

1 onion

1 celery heart

2 knobs of unsalted butter

1 good pinch of saffron threads

450g Arborio risotto rice

200ml Pinot Bianco or Verdicchio

80g Parmesan cheese

extra virgin olive oil

This classic risotto is wonderful with ossobuco (page 244), but can absolutely be enjoyed in its own right as a starter or as an alternative to a pasta course. It's very simple and humble in its core ingredients, apart from one, which just happens to be the most expensive ingredient on the planet by weight – saffron! Thankfully, you don't need much of it to achieve that brilliant bright yellow vivacity you see here.

Firstly, the better your stock, the better your risotto. Of course you can make it with organic stock cubes, or you can make your own. Whichever way, pour your stock into a pan on a low heat and leave it simmering away, so it's hot when you need it.

Peel the onion. Click off 6 sticks of celery and return them to the fridge for another day, leaving you with the central yellow heart (the best and often neglected bit). Finely chop with the onion and put into a large high-sided pan (if your pan is too shallow the stock will evaporate too quickly later) on a medium-low heat with 1 knob of butter. Cook for 15 minutes, or until soft but not coloured, stirring occasionally. Meanwhile, put the saffron threads in a bowl and cover with a small ladleful of hot stock.

Stir the rice into the pan for a couple of minutes, then turn the heat up to medium-high, add the wine and cook it away completely, then add the saffron stock and stir for a few minutes until absorbed. Add the remaining stock a ladleful at a time, only adding more once each ladleful has been nearly absorbed, and stirring regularly for 16 minutes in total, or until the rice is cooked and a pleasure to eat, but still holds its shape. Add a final splash of stock to give you a loose, oozy consistency.

Remove from the heat, beat in the remaining knob of butter and finely grate in most of the Parmesan, then season the risotto to perfection, if needed. Cover with a lid and leave to sit for 2 minutes (a nonna in Italy taught me how important this stage is – it allows the rice to relax and become really creamy), then stir well. Finish with a drizzle of extra virgin olive oil, grate over the remaining Parmesan and serve right away.

× MAKING KIEŁBASA ×

MAKES 14

4 HOURS

PLUS CHILLING

295 CALORIES

1.5kg pork shoulder butt or collar, trimmed of any sinue

500g pork belly, skin removed

1 level teaspoon ground allspice

40g butcher's curing salt

2 cloves of garlic

8 sprigs of fresh marjoram

1 whole nutmeg, for grating

3 metres of sausage casings (ask your butcher or buy online)

×

To make and smoke your own sausages, you need to invest in a decent hand-crank mincer, or an electric one, which is even better and not much more expensive (about £20–£50). It must have a sausage funnel attachment and a coarse die plate. A dustbin incinerator makes a brilliant makeshift smoker – again about £20. I got all this online from Amazon along with my butcher's curing salt, sausage casings and a thermometer. You also need oak logs and some wood chips.

Kiełbasa are legendary smoked sausages synonymous with Poland. I've developed this recipe specifically for the home with my old butchers, Matthew and Adam, who now run the wonderful artisan Cobble Lane Cured. We've given you every possibility of mastering sausages from scratch, but you can buy them if you prefer and skip straight to page 252.

Dice all the meat into 2½cm cubes. In a pestle and mortar, pound up the allspice, salt, peeled garlic and marjoram leaves, grate in quarter of the nutmeg and add 1 heaped teaspoon of black pepper, then massage into the pork and refrigerate overnight.

The next day, soak the sausage casings in cold water until pliable, changing the water regularly. Follow the instructions to set up your mincer with a coarse plate and the sausage funnel attachment. Feed the end of the casing onto the funnel, leaving a 5cm overhang. Get a mate to push the pork mixture into the machine, mincing it directly into the casing – as soon as a little mince comes out of the funnel, stop the machine and tie a knot in the casing. Start the machine again holding the casing fairly firmly so the meat fills it tightly and evenly, letting it slide through your hands to make one massive sausage. Every 20cm, pinch and twist twice to make links, then cut into pairs.

To build your smoker, dig a 15cm-deep hole, 30cm wide. At opposite sides of the circle dig out 6cm-wide gaps to create airflow channels, then make a small fire in the hole using oak logs. Let it burn down to glowing cinders while you get a 2cm-thick cane and saw it about 2cm longer than the diameter of your dustbin. Squeeze the cane into the bin so it holds in place firmly near the top, then hang the sausage pairs from it and leave it beside the fire, with the lid off, so the sausages start to dry.

When the fire's cindered down, add soaked wood chips to generate smoke, then place the bin directly on top of the fire. Fill the gap between the base of the bin and the ground with stones or mud, leaving only the airflow channels free. Look into the bin; you don't want any flames coming through the base holes – if it's too lively, just block off a channel to calm the fire. You just want smoke and ambient heat like an outdoor oven. Block up 80% of the holes around the sides of the dustbin with foil, corks or stones. Hang a thermometer in the middle and check the temperature regularly until it reaches 40°C, then maintain that steady temperature, opening or closing the channels, and feeding the fire with logs or wood chips, as needed, for 1 hour 30 minutes. At this point, stoke the fire up to 80°C, and once there, smoke for 15 minutes, then cool (this is important) and place the sausages in the fridge for up to 1 week until needed for cooking. Turn the page for how to cook and serve.

× COOKING & SERVING KIEŁBASA ×

SERVES 14

1 HOUR

223 CALORIES

14 kiełbasa (page 250)

POTATOES

2.5kg small red potatoes

2 sprigs of fresh rosemary

1 bulb of garlic

olive oil

2 knobs of unsalted butter

PICKLED CABBAGE

1 red cabbage

1 pinch of ground cloves

1 tablespoon yellow mustard seeds

4 tablespoons red wine vinegar

HORSERADISH CREAM

3 heaped tablespoons fresh
   or jarred horseradish

300ml soured cream

½ a lemon

GARNISHES

2 handfuls of cornichons

a nice selection of mustards

Once you've made or bought your incredible kiełbasa, it's time to cook and serve them in style. I love them with crispy skinned squashed potatoes roasted with rosemary and garlic, a quick pickled red cabbage spiked with cloves and mustard seeds, some lovely little cornichons and horseradish cream, and, of course, a nice cold beer on the side.

When you're ready to start cooking, preheat the oven to 200°C/400°F/gas 6. Scrub the potatoes clean, then parboil in a large pan of boiling salted water for around 12 minutes, or until tender but holding their shape. Drain and leave to steam dry. Strip off the rosemary leaves and squash the garlic cloves (leaving the skins on). Put a good splash of olive oil and the butter into two large roasting trays with the rosemary leaves, garlic and potatoes. Season with sea salt and pepper, toss well to coat, then roast for 40 minutes. Remove from the oven and gently squash all the potatoes to increase that crispy surface area and expose some of the fluffy insides. Return to the oven until perfectly golden and crisp.

Meanwhile, make your pickled cabbage. Finely slice the cabbage, ideally with a mandolin (use the guard!), or with a fine slicer in a food processor, and put into a large bowl. Add the ground cloves, mustard seeds, vinegar and 1 level teaspoon each of salt and pepper, then toss to coat. Leave to infuse in the fridge until needed. Next, make your horseradish cream. Put the horseradish into a bowl, finely grating it if using fresh. Add the soured cream, squeeze in the lemon juice, then season to perfection.

To cook the kiełbasa you can barbecue or pan-fry them. Score a criss-cross on the end of each sausage, then, all the way along the length on both sides of the sausages, thinly score at a slight angle at ½cm intervals – this is a cool, authentic Polish technique. Toss the sausages in a little oil, then barbecue or pan-fry with a little extra oil, turning regularly and cooking for around 8 minutes, or until hot in the middle and crispy and golden on the outside. Serve with your potatoes, cabbage, horseradish cream, cornichons and mustards. What an absolute feast.

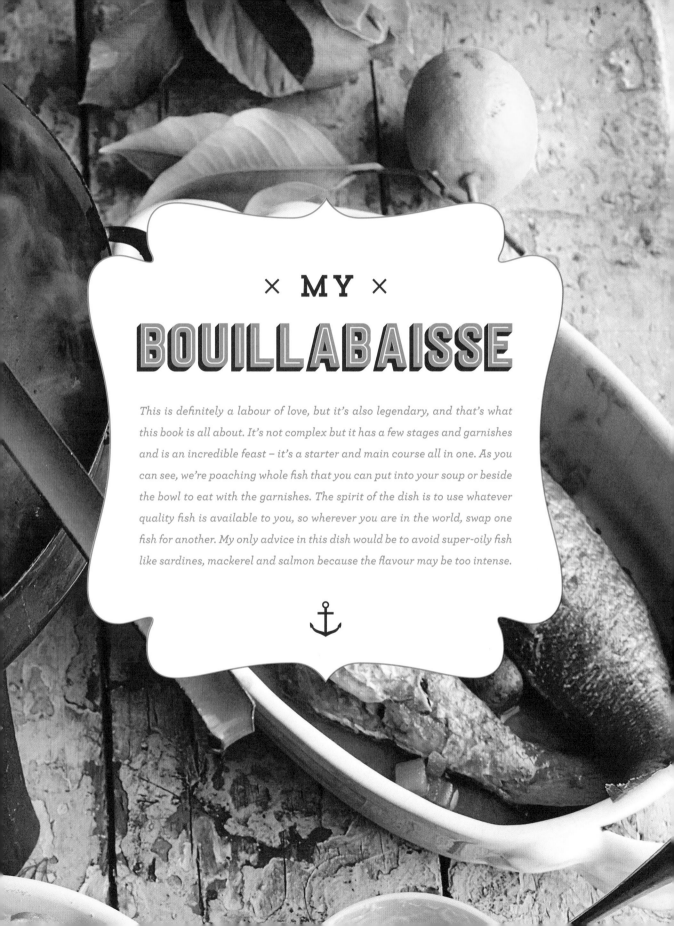

× MY ×
BOUILLABAISSE

This is definitely a labour of love, but it's also legendary, and that's what this book is all about. It's not complex but it has a few stages and garnishes and is an incredible feast – it's a starter and main course all in one. As you can see, we're poaching whole fish that you can put into your soup or beside the bowl to eat with the garnishes. The spirit of the dish is to use whatever quality fish is available to you, so wherever you are in the world, swap one fish for another. My only advice in this dish would be to avoid super-oily fish like sardines, mackerel and salmon because the flavour may be too intense.

⚓

× MY BOUILLABAISSE ×

SERVES 10
4 HOURS (OVER 2 DAYS)
695 CALORIES

DAY 1

1 x 1.5kg whole live lobster
  (or 2 small ones)

10 large raw shell-on king prawns

1 large dressed crab

5 fresh bay leaves

1 heaped teaspoon cayenne
  pepper

olive oil

1.5kg large ripe tomatoes,
  on the vine

DAY 2

2 onions

2 carrots

5 cloves of garlic

2 bulbs of fennel

1kg baby new potatoes

1 French baguette

1 x mayonnaise four ways
  (page 258)

1 fresh red chilli

6 sprigs of fresh dill

3 lemons

150ml good French rosé

4 whole fish, such as red mullet,
  bream, sea bass, gurnard, gills
  removed, scaled and gutted

500g cockles or clams

DAY 1 – THE FISH BASE

Place the live lobster in the freezer for 30 minutes so it's docile. Preheat the oven to 200°C/400°F/gas 6. Remove the heads and shells from the prawns, run your knife down their backs and remove the veins, then pop in the fridge. Put the shells into a large roasting tray. Fill your largest deep pan with water, season with sea salt and bring to a rolling boil. Swiftly plunge the lobster head first into the water, place the lid on and cook for 8 minutes (or slightly less if you're using 2 small ones). Remove and leave to cool. Rip the lobster tail off the body, squeeze the tail shell in until you hear it crack, then rip it open the other way to expose the meat, pull it out and roughly chop it. Rip the claws off the body, then use a rolling pin on a board to crack them open. Remove all the lobster meat to another bowl, removing any shell or bones (check out jamieoliver.com/how-to), add the white crab meat, cover and refrigerate. To the tray, add the brown crab meat (discard the shell), lobster shells, bay leaves and cayenne. Drizzle with oil, toss, roast for 30 minutes to release all the flavours, then add the tomatoes on the vine and roast for a further 30 minutes. In small batches, place the shells in a food processor, scraping up all the good bits from the bottom of the tray. Put the lid on, cover with a tea towel, then hold and process (noisy, but necessary!). Pour into your largest pan, cover with 4 litres of water, and simmer for 1 hour with the lid ajar. Pass through a coarse sieve into a large bowl and pop into the fridge.

DAY 2 – THE SOUP

Peel the onions, carrots and garlic, then finely chop with the fennel (reserving any tops) and put into your largest pan over a medium heat with a good lug of oil. Cook slowly for 30 minutes, stirring occasionally, while you boil the new potatoes, then drain. Preheat the oven to 180°C/350°F/gas 4. Finely slice the baguette, drizzle with a little oil and toast on trays in the oven until crisp. Warm up your serving bowls as the oven cools and make your mayos (page 258). Finely chop the chilli and dill and mix with the crab and lobster meat, along with the zest and juice of 1 lemon. Pour the wine into the veg pan and cook away, then add the fish base, bring to a simmer and add the whole fish, making sure they're fully submerged (top up with water, if needed). Simmer for 15 minutes, skimming if required. Taste and season to perfection, then add the cockles or clams and the prawns for 4 minutes, or until the shellfish pops open (discard any that remain closed). Spoon the soup into bowls, add the potatoes, croutons, reserved fennel tops and dollops of the mayos, as well as lemon juice to taste, then divide up the dressed lobster and crab. As the soup goes down, pull out the whole fish and pull off chunks of flaky meat to have in your soup or on the side with the garnishes.

× MAYONNAISE FOUR WAYS ×

MAKES 1 MEDIUM JAR
25 MINUTES
133 CALORIES
(PER TABLESPOON)

BASIC MAYO

2 large egg yolks

1 heaped teaspoon Dijon mustard

300ml mild olive oil

2–3 tablespoons white
   wine vinegar

optional: groundnut oil

optional: extra virgin olive oil

So why make mayonnaise from scratch when you can buy it in a jar? Because instead of being made with low-quality oils and vinegars you can use great oil and great vinegar, as well as super-fresh free-range yolks, to achieve big flavour, as pungent and as attitude-filled as you like. These four punchy-flavoured mayos will make magic happen.

For your basic mayo, place a large bowl on a damp cloth to keep it steady, then roll up one side of the cloth so your bowl sits tilted at a slight angle. Put the egg yolks into the bowl with the mustard and whisk together with a clean balloon whisk, then, whisking constantly, gradually add drips of the olive oil. As you add more, the drips can get bigger and move to a light drizzle. I recommend doing this with a friend so you can swap whisking and drizzling; it's very easy, it just takes a little time – if you add the oil too fast you'll split the mayonnaise. If this does happen, clean your whisk, get an extra egg yolk and slowly whisk drips of your split mixture into the new yolk (hopefully you won't need to do this!). When it gets really thick, loosen with a little of the vinegar. Once you've added all the olive oil, have a taste – it will still be strange-tasting and won't quite reference mayonnaise as you know it, but this is your basic mayo. Season it well with salt and just slightly overtang it with vinegar – this will improve it massively. If you're finding the taste of the olive oil too overpowering, you can whisk in some groundnut oil until it calms down, or, if you have the opposite feeling, finish it with a few splashes of extra virgin olive oil to up the pungency. It all depends on the kind of oil you use – trust your instincts and get tasting and tweaking, tasting and tweaking, until it's just right. Use the mayo as it is (it'll keep happily in the fridge for a week), choose a way to flavour it, or divide it up and make all four!

SAFFRON Soak a few saffron threads in a little boiling water before stirring in.

HARISSA Stir in harissa paste to taste, adding a splash of rosewater too, if you like.

LEMON AIOLI Peel garlic cloves and bash into a paste with a pinch of sea salt in a pestle and mortar, then stir in with some lemon zest and juice, to taste.

BASIL Pound fresh basil leaves to a paste with a pinch of sea salt in a pestle and mortar and stir in – either leave rustic or pass through a sieve until super-smooth.

✕ OVERNIGHT ROASTED PORK SHOULDER ✕

SERVES 12

WITH LOTS OF LEFTOVER MEAT
12–14 HOURS
902 CALORIES

PORK

1 x 5kg shoulder of pork, bone in,
   skin removed and reserved

olive oil

4 onions

2–3 eating apples

3 sticks of celery

1 bulb of garlic

1 bunch of fresh sage (30g)

4 fresh bay leaves

1 x 500ml bottle of cider

2 tablespoons fennel seeds

2 whole cloves

2 dried chillies

FENNEL & POTATO GRATIN

1.5kg Maris Piper potatoes

5 bulbs of fennel

4 cloves of garlic

4 anchovy fillets

4 sprigs of fresh rosemary

1 whole nutmeg, for grating

100g Parmesan cheese

400ml double cream

200ml single cream

This is one of those mega meals that's just perfect for a lazy Sunday. The beginning of the story is the night before if you want it for lunch, or early in the morning if you want it for dinner. It's a real joy, and with the right portion control, in my eyes, is not a bad thing. My nutrition ninjas aren't very happy about it, because it's a day and a half's worth of your recommended allowance of saturated fat, but for me it's simple – just make sure you lighten up your breakfast and lunch, then you can go to heaven for dinner.

Preheat the oven to full whack (240°C/475°F/gas 9). Toss the reserved pork skin in a little oil and sea salt (you can either slice it into long, thin strips or leave as one piece), lay it flat on a tray and roast until perfectly golden and crisp, keeping a close eye on it, then remove. Peel the onions, then cut into wedges with the apples. Trim and roughly chop the celery and break the garlic bulb into cloves. Scatter it all in your largest roasting tray with the sage and bay leaves, pour in the cider and add a good splash of water. Bash the fennel seeds, cloves, dried chillies and 1 heaped teaspoon of salt to a fine dust in a pestle and mortar, then massage all over the pork with a drizzle of oil. Sit the pork in the tray, cover tightly with a double layer of tin foil, place in the oven and turn the temperature down to 130°C/250°F/gas ½. Roast for 10 to 12 hours, or until the meat pulls easily away from the bone, then remove from the oven and cover with a couple of clean tea towels to keep warm.

Turn the oven up to 200°C/400°F/gas 6. Peel the potatoes, then cut lengthways into wedges along with the fennel. Parboil in a couple of pans of boiling salted water – the potatoes for 7 minutes and the fennel for 6 – then drain, leave to steam dry completely, and place in a large, high-sided roasting tray (25cm x 35cm). Peel the garlic and blitz until fine with the anchovies, rosemary leaves and a good splash of boiling water in a blender. Finely grate in half the nutmeg and most of the Parmesan and pour in the cream. Add a pinch of salt and pepper, blitz again, then pour over the veg. Grate over the remaining Parmesan and bake at the bottom of the oven for 45 to 50 minutes, or until golden and bubbling. Serve everything in the middle of the table with a whole load of simply steamed seasonal greens. You'll get a natural brothy gravy underneath the pork – reduce it on the hob before serving, if desired.

✕

*Freshen this up with a zingy salsa. Chop **2 eating apples** into fine matchsticks and toss in a bowl with **2 tablespoons of cider vinegar** and **4 tablespoons of extra virgin olive oil**. Pick, roll up and finely slice the leaves from **½ a bunch of fresh mint** and toss into the bowl with a pinch of salt and pepper. Simple.*

✕ MIGHTY GREEK MOUSSAKA ✕

SERVES 8

2 HOURS 45 MINUTES
PLUS RESTING
435 CALORIES

600g minced meat (I like a mixture of lamb and lean beef)

olive oil

2 onions

2 cloves of garlic

a few sprigs of fresh rosemary

a few sprigs of fresh sage

½ teaspoon dried oregano

2 fresh bay leaves

150ml red wine (look out for Agiorghitiko, or use an unoaked Merlot or Cabernet Sauvignon)

2 x 400g tins of plum tomatoes

4 aubergines

4 medium potatoes

50g unsalted butter

50g plain flour

750ml semi-skimmed milk

1 whole nutmeg, for grating

2 large eggs

½ a lemon

50g feta cheese

25g kefalotyri or pecorino cheese

A proper homemade moussaka makes me very, very happy. It's easy to make, but has a few stages – trust me, though, whatever effort you put in, you get twice as much back in pleasure when you're eating it. Make it in advance for a casual dinner party, and just reheat it when you're ready. If anyone cooked this for me, I'd be incredibly grateful.

Start by making a ragù. Fry the minced meat in a very large pan on a high heat with a little oil for 15 minutes, or until golden, stirring regularly. Meanwhile, peel and finely chop the onions and garlic, then pick and finely chop the herb leaves. Add it all to the pan with the dried oregano and 1 bay leaf, reduce to a medium heat and fry for a further 10 minutes. Stir in the wine and cook it away, then add the tinned tomatoes and a splash of water. Bring to the boil, then reduce to a simmer for 1 hour with the lid ajar, or until super-thick and delicious. Season lightly.

Meanwhile, preheat the oven to 180°C/350°F/gas 4. Slice the aubergines lengthways 1cm thick, then season generously with sea salt and leave to drain in a colander for 20 minutes. Peel the potatoes and slice 1cm thick, then parboil in a large pan of boiling salted water for 5 minutes. Drain, toss with a little oil and seasoning, then use them to cover the base of a deep roasting tray (25cm x 30cm), slightly overlapping the slices. Roast the potatoes for 40 minutes, or until lightly golden. Meanwhile, wipe the aubergine slices with kitchen paper and fry them in a little oil in batches in a large frying pan on a high heat for a few minutes on each side, or until golden.

While the aubergines are cooking, in a medium pan on a medium heat, melt the butter, then stir in the flour to form a paste. Whisk in the milk a little at a time until you have a smooth white sauce. Season with salt and pepper, add a good grating of nutmeg and the remaining bay leaf, simmer for 15 minutes, then importantly, remove from the heat. Discard the bay leaf, beat the eggs with the lemon zest and juice, then, whisking as you go, slowly add to the white sauce.

To layer up, spread half the ragù over the roasted potatoes, crumble over half the feta, then cover with half the aubergines in a single layer. Repeat with the remaining ragù, feta and aubergines, gently pour over the white sauce, then finely grate over the kefalotyri or pecorino cheese. Dust with black pepper and drizzle with oil. Cook for 40 minutes, or until golden, then remove and (this is important) leave to rest for 30 minutes. Serve with a delicious Greek salad. While portioning the moussaka you'll notice that a rich oil comes out – this is normal and delicious.

SIMPLE, DELIGHTFUL &
JUST A LITTLE BIT WRONG

GUILTY

· PLEASURES ·

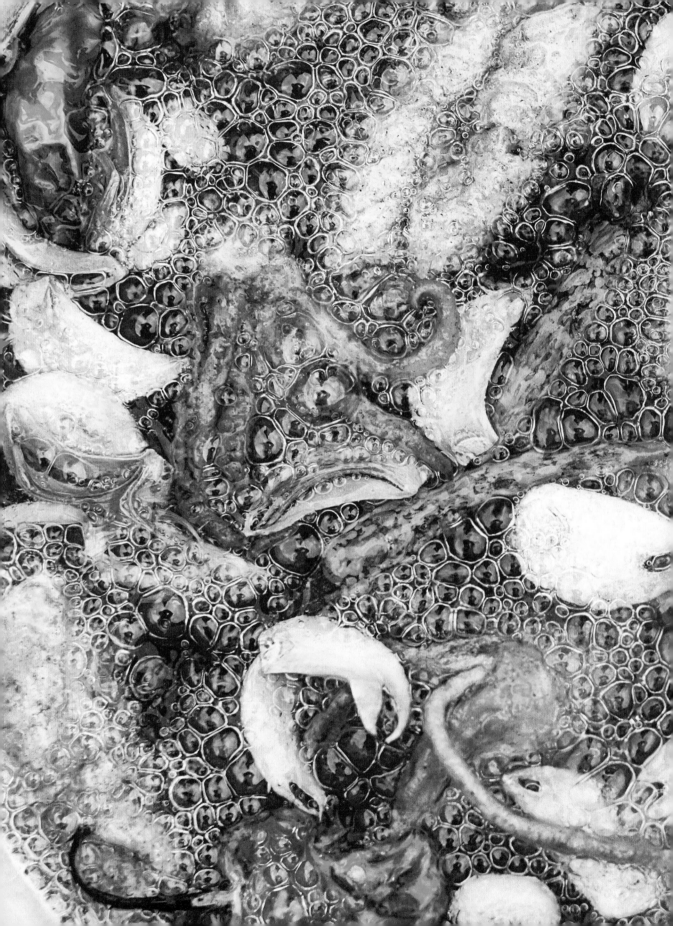

SALT & PEPPER SQUID

× SALT & PEPPER SQUID ×

SERVES 4

45 MINUTES

343 CALORIES

½ a bunch of fresh mint (15g)

4 spring onions

8 medium whole squid (500g)

vegetable oil

1 heaped tablespoon white pepper

100g plain flour

1 small handful of mixed
   fresh chillies

4 cloves of garlic

1 tablespoon white or red
   wine vinegar

Crispy but tender squid with a hum of pepper heat, complemented by fragrant herbs, crispy garlic and a hit of vinegar – this is my evolution of the classic dish, which I know you guys all love. Traditionally it comes from Cantonese cuisine, originating in the Guangdong province, and it was one of the very few spicy dishes this cuisine embraced. They achieved heat by using finely ground peppercorns instead of chillies, which they didn't have, but I couldn't resist adding a few here for double pleasure.

Pick the mint leaves into a small bowl of cold water to ensure they stay super-fresh. Trim and halve the spring onions across the middle, then finely slice lengthways into shreds and add to the water bowl. Get your fishmonger to prepare the squid for you, or, if you'd rather do it yourself, simply go to jamieoliver.com/how-to and you'll find a video to guide you. Pat the squid dry with kitchen paper, then use a regular eating knife to lightly score the inside of the squid at ½cm intervals at an angle. Turn the squid through 180° and do the same again to create a criss-cross pattern.

When you're ready to cook, just under half fill a large sturdy pan with oil – the oil should be 8cm deep, but never fill your pan more than half full – and place on a medium to high heat. Use a thermometer to tell when it's ready (180°C), or add a piece of potato and wait until it turns golden – that's the sign that it's ready to go. While it heats, tip the white pepper and flour into a large bowl with a pinch of sea salt. Add the squid, toss and mix to coat, then leave in the flour for a few minutes while you prick the chillies – if some are bigger, halve and deseed them first, then peel and finely slice the garlic 1mm thick, ideally on a mandolin (use the guard!).

When you're ready to fry, add half the squid and chillies – it's important to cook in two batches so you don't overcrowd the pan. When it's all looking golden and lovely (after about 1½ minutes), add half the garlic for a final minute. Use a slotted spoon to scoop everything into a bowl or pan lined with kitchen paper to drain while you cook the second batch. Whip out the paper, then cut the squid into bite-sized pieces and return to the bowl. Drizzle with the vinegar, add a good pinch of seasoning, the drained mint leaves and spring onion curls, toss it all together and serve right away.

№.1

TOASTED CHEESE SANDWICH

⟫⟫⟫——→

⨯ NO.1 TOASTED CHEESE SANDWICH ⨯

SERVES 1   15 MINUTES

A toasted cheese sandwich is a beautiful thing, but I'm not messing about here – this is the ultimate one and it's going to blow your mind. But there is a particular sequence of events that needs to happen in order to achieve the most ridiculously tasty, chomp-worthy sandwich. Follow this recipe, and it will always make you feel good. It is also especially useful when you're suffering from a light hangover. This is when the condiments – dolloped onto a side plate like a painter's palette – really come into their own.

With the No. 1 toasted cheese sarnie we don't score any points for buying expensive, artisan bread. It's important to go for something neutral, and in my eyes, only a white bloomer will do. Lightly butter the bread on both sides (oh, and if you've got any leftover mashed potato, spread that across one piece of the bread – it's insanely good). To one piece of bread, add a nice grating of good-quality cheese that melts well, like Cheddar, Red Leicester or a mixture of the two. Place your second piece of bread on top, then cook in a sturdy non-stick frying pan on a medium heat for about 3 minutes on each side. This is important, because if it gets too coloured too quickly, you won't get the gorgeous ooze and melt in the middle, and this is about encouraging that internal cheese lava flow. As it cooks, I like to rest something flat with a little weight on top to ensure maximum surface area and crunch.

When lightly golden on both sides, lift the toastie out of the pan and grate a little layer of cheese into the pan where it was sitting. Place the toastie back on top and grate some more cheese on the top side. Leave it for just over 1 minute – wait for the cheese to bubble and the fat to spill out of it, then add a little pinch of cayenne pepper. Give the toastie a poke with a fish slice, and once it has a cheesy, doily-like crust on the bottom that moves as one, lift the toastie out of the pan and hold it on the fish slice for 30 seconds so the melted cheese hangs down, sets hard and forms an impressive cheese crown. Flip it onto the other side and once golden, serve, remembering to let it cool for a couple of minutes before attempting to tuck in.

The final debate is what do you want on the side? Tomato ketchup, brown sauce, a shake of Tabasco or hot sauce, mango chutney or a mixture – all are fine choices.

× BUTTER & SAGE ×

GNUDI

× BUTTER & SAGE GNUDI ×

SERVES 6–8

45 MINUTES
PLUS CHILLING
455 CALORIES

GNUDI

1kg best-quality ricotta

100g Parmesan cheese

1 whole nutmeg, for grating

fine semolina, for dusting

TO SERVE

good-quality unsalted butter

1 bunch of fresh sage (30g)

Parmesan cheese, for grating

1 lemon

Gnudi is a fantastic dish – you must make it. It's elegant, light in texture, easy to make and for most people, very unusual. My dear friend April Bloomfield, from the very cool Spotted Pig in New York, has recently made this dish most famous, but it certainly dates back at least a good thirty or forty years, and is made all over Tuscany. Gnudi means naked, and quite simply this is a ricotta ravioli without the pasta (aka naked). The proviso for this dish being genius to the point where your guests won't stop talking about it is to use top-quality ricotta, butter and Parmesan, as well as beautiful freshly picked sage.

Put the ricotta into a bowl with a pinch of sea salt and black pepper, then finely grate in the Parmesan and a few scrapings of nutmeg. Beat it together, then have a taste to check the balance of seasoning is right – you want the nutmeg to be very subtle. Generously cover a large tray with semolina, then roll the ricotta mixture into 3cm balls, rolling them in the tray of semolina as you go until really well coated. You should get around 40 gnudi from this amount of mixture. Shake and cover really well with the semolina and leave for 8 hours or preferably overnight in the fridge (don't cover the tray) – the semolina will dehydrate the ricotta, giving the gnudi a lovely fine coating.

The gnudi will only take 3 minutes to cook and I like to cook them in 2-portion batches to take care of them. So, shake the excess semolina off 2 portions-worth of gnudi and cook them in boiling salted water while you melt a large knob of butter in a frying pan on a medium heat and pick in about 20 sage leaves to crisp up. Remove the crispy leaves to a plate and scoop the gnudi directly from the water into the frying pan, adding a spoonful of the cooking water. When the butter and water have emulsified, take off the heat and grate over a layer of Parmesan, add just a few drops of lemon juice, then toss together. Serve in warm bowls straight away with an extra grating of nutmeg and Parmesan and the crispy sage leaves, while you get on with the next batch, wiping the frying pan clean between batches. Welcome to the naked club.

×

Gnudi can be easily transformed with the addition of one seasonal ingredient. Asparagus tips, podded peas, wild mushrooms or a few fresh tomatoes – any of the above with that sage butter will rock the party. In summer, some smashed fresh basil leaves in the ricotta mixture are lovely; or in winter, a splash of quality red wine use to deglaze the frying pan adds much deliciousness.

× PIZZA PERFECTION ×

SERVES 8

1–2 HOURS
PLUS PROVING
700 CALORIES

DOUGH

1kg strong bread flour,
  plus extra for dusting

1 x 7g sachet of dried yeast

SAUCE

2 cloves of garlic

3 tablespoons olive oil

2 x 400g tins of plum tomatoes

1 bunch of fresh basil (30g)

TOPPING

4 x 125g balls of buffalo mozzarella

Parmesan cheese

extra virgin olive oil

·················· × ··················

To get the ultimate in crispy bases, you need to invest in a pizza stone, or you can get a 2cm-thick piece of granite cut to the size of your oven – when this heats up it will give your dough a wonderful rise, getting close to what you'd achieve in a wood oven.

Being a pizza lover, and loving using wood-fired ovens, I'm not bad at making pizzas. But being able to spend time with my dear friend Chris Bianco from Arizona – who's one of the world's very best pizza makers and has taken my perception of pizza to another level – I've written this dough recipe, inspired by him. It's designed to give you a super-reliable, high-quality dough to work with at home, and hopefully will give you a better understanding of how to achieve a great crust with a soft fluffy interior and a very light, crisp base, as well as show you how to be restrained with the toppings. You're gonna love it.

Pile the flour, yeast and 1 level teaspoon of sea salt into a large bowl. Make a well in the middle and pour in 675ml of tepid water. Gradually mix it into the flour, bringing it in from the outside as you go. Once combined, knead on a flour-dusted surface for 15 minutes, or until super-smooth and elastic, then place in a lightly oiled bowl. Cover with a damp tea towel and prove in a warm place for 1 hour, or until doubled in size.

Meanwhile, to make the sauce, peel and finely slice the garlic and put into a large frying pan on a medium heat with the olive oil. Cook for a few minutes, or until soft, stirring regularly, then add the tomatoes, pick in half the basil leaves and leave to tick away for 5 minutes. Taste and season to perfection, then let it cool a little and blitz in a blender until super smooth (any leftover sauce will keep happily in the fridge for a couple of days to be used for pasta). Once the dough has doubled in size, knock it back, then divide and knead it into 8 equal-sized pizza balls. Leave on a flour-dusted tray, covered, to prove for a further 30 minutes (you can freeze the dough at this stage).

When you're ready to cook, place your pizza stone in the oven and preheat to full whack (240°C/475°F/gas 9). One-by-one, use your hands to gently pull and stretch out the dough, passing it between them and letting gravity stretch it out to about 23cm. Pinch the edges up to create a natural crust, then spread over a light layer of tomato sauce. Tear over half a ball of mozzarella, finely grate over some Parmesan, drizzle with a little extra virgin olive oil and whack in the oven for 10 minutes, or until golden and puffed up at the edges. Pick over a few fresh basil leaves and serve while you cook another. Like anything, the quality of your pizza, perfecting it in your oven with the flour that's available to you and mastering your technique just comes down to practice, which is why it's nice to cook them one at a time and let everyone share slices while the next one cooks. Master this, and you'll never look back.

✕ LOBSTER MAC 'N' CHEESE ✕

SERVES 6

2 HOURS
849 CALORIES

1 x 1.5kg whole live lobster
   (or 2 small ones)

2 onions

4 cloves of garlic

50g unsalted butter

1 small pinch of saffron

½ teaspoon cayenne pepper

2 anchovy fillets

200ml white Burgundy,
   such as Pouilly-Fussé

50g plain flour

1.1 litres semi-skimmed milk

2 teaspoons English mustard

400g dried amori pasta
   or macaroni

70g mature Cheddar cheese

70g Gruyère cheese

70g Parmesan cheese

✕

A few freshly picked rosemary leaves tossed in a drizzle of olive oil and sprinkled over the top for the last 10 minutes of cooking will be delicious.

Mac 'n' cheese is one of the most famous comfort foods in the world, and I wanted to take it from the everyday to the absolute next level by making it with lobster, which is incredibly delicious, super-special and turns it into a total showstopper. If you ask a fishmonger, pretty much all of them can order in a large lobster and it'll probably work out cheaper than serving your guests fillet steak, so it's great for a special occasion – I'm into that, and I'm sure at the right time and in the right place, with the right people, you will be too.

To start, place the live lobster in the freezer for 30 minutes so it's docile. Meanwhile, fill your largest deep pan with water, season with sea salt and bring to a rolling boil. Swiftly plunge the lobster head first into the water, place the lid on and cook for 8 minutes (or slightly less if you're using 2 small ones). Remove and leave to cool.

Peel and finely chop the onions and garlic. Get yourself a large ovenproof casserole pan (ideally 30cm wide and 10cm deep) that you want to serve up in. Put the butter into the pan on a medium heat, add the onions, garlic, saffron, cayenne and anchovies and cook for 10 minutes. Turn the heat up to high, add the wine and cook it away, then reduce the heat back to medium and stir in the flour, followed by the milk and mustard. Mix well and simmer for 10 minutes while you prepare the lobster.

Twist the lobster head and body apart – importantly, shake out all the tasty juice and bits from the head into the sauce. Squeeze the tail shell in until you hear it crack, then rip it open the other way to expose all that lovely tail meat. Rip the claws off the body, then use a rolling pin on a board to crack them open and poke out any meat you can find. Roughly chop all the meat, reserving the tail shell and head (go to jamieoliver.com/how-to for help on how to do this).

Preheat the oven to 180°C/350°F/gas 4. Cook the pasta in a pan of boiling salted water according to packet instructions, then drain, reserving a little cooking water. Remove the sauce from the heat, stir in the pasta and lobster meat and grate in the Cheddar and Gruyère. Mix well, taste and correct the seasoning – you don't want the sauce to be super-thick now, so loosen it with a little cooking water if needed, remembering that it will thicken as it bakes. Finely grate over the Parmesan (I didn't do it in the picture, but you can add a sprinkling of breadcrumbs before the cheese too, if you like). For a bit of fun, pop the lobster head and tail into the pan at either end. Cook in the oven for about 35 minutes, or until golden, bubbling and delicious. Serve with a smile, a big seasonal salad, and a glass of cold Soave.

✕ TEAR 'N' SHARE GARLIC BREAD ✕

MAKES 35 PIECES
1–2 HOURS
PLUS PROVING
121 CALORIES (PER PIECE)

800g strong bread flour,
  plus extra for dusting

1 x 7g sachet of dried yeast

100g stale breadcrumbs

BUTTER

1 bulb of garlic

500g unsalted butter
  (at room temperature)

1 lemon

1 bunch of fresh flat-leaf
  parsley (30g)

1 level teaspoon cayenne pepper

✕

*Any leftover butter would be
delicious used as a stuffing for
my chicken Kievs (page 52).*

Everyone loves garlic bread, and as you'd expect, this version totally over delivers. Soft, spongy and with the crunchiest backsides you've ever seen, as well as being bombed with pungent garlic butter – what's not to love? One of my favourite ways to eat this is simply with a massive green salad for lunch, but of course the great thing about garlic bread is that it can be a side for many things – chilli, pasta, soup, part of a picnic – you name it.

Put the flour, yeast and 1 teaspoon of sea salt into a large bowl and make a well in the middle. Gradually pour in 550ml of tepid water, continuously stirring and bringing in the flour from the outside as you go to form a rough dough. Transfer to a flour-dusted surface and knead for 10 minutes, or until smooth and springy. Place in a bowl, cover with a damp tea towel and prove in a warm place for 1 hour, or until doubled in size.

Meanwhile, make the butter – this is a big batch, to make good use of your time, and you can freeze the extra for rainy days. Use a garlic crusher to crush the garlic into the softened butter, finely grate over the zest of ½ a lemon, finely chop and add the parsley (stalks and all), the cayenne and a pinch of salt, then mix it all together. Remove one quarter to use in this recipe, then place the rest on a sheet of greaseproof paper, roll it up into a log and twist the ends like a Christmas cracker, then pop into the freezer. After 30 minutes, get the butter out and slice it up to pre-portion, then re-roll and return to the freezer, where it will keep very happily for up to 6 months.

Spread one third of your soft butter portion all around the base and sides of a large metal tray (25cm x 35cm), then scatter in the breadcrumbs and shake around into an even layer so they stick to the butter. Divide up the dough into 35 pieces, then, one-by-one, roll each one into a ball and place in the tray in rows – 5 balls across and 7 balls long is perfect. Bomb over another third of the soft butter, in and around the balls. Leave to prove for another 1 hour 30 minutes, or until doubled in size again.

Preheat the oven to 190°C/375°F/gas 5. Sprinkle the balls with a little salt, then bake on the bottom shelf of the oven for 30 minutes, or until lovely and golden. Bomb over that final third of your soft butter and spread it around to give the bread a beautiful shine. Whack the tray in the middle of the table or at the centre of your picnic for sharing, and let everyone tear off their own pieces.

✕ SOUTHERN FRIED CHICKEN ✕

SERVES 4
2 HOURS 15 MINUTES
PLUS BRINING & TENDERIZING
523 CALORIES

4 chicken thighs, skin on, bone in

4 chicken drumsticks

200ml buttermilk

4 sweet potatoes

200g plain flour

1 level teaspoon each baking
    powder, cayenne pepper, hot
    smoked paprika, onion powder,
    garlic powder

2 litres groundnut oil

BRINE

1 tablespoon black peppercorns

100g sea salt

100g brown sugar

4 sprigs of fresh thyme

4 fresh bay leaves

4 cloves of garlic

PICKLE

1 teaspoon fennel seeds

100ml red wine vinegar

1 heaped tablespoon golden
    caster sugar

½ a red cabbage (500g)

This is an incredible fried chicken recipe, one which I've subtly evolved from that of my dear friend Art Smith, one of the kings of southern American comfort food. I've finished the chicken in the oven, purely because you really do need a big fryer to do it properly as well as good temperature control, and this method is much friendlier for home cooking.

To make the brine, toast the peppercorns in a large pan on a high heat for 1 minute, then add the rest of the brine ingredients and 400ml of cold water. Bring to the boil, then leave to cool, topping up with another 400ml of cold water. Meanwhile, slash the chicken thighs a few times as deep as the bone, keeping the skin on for maximum flavour. Once the brine is cool, add all the chicken pieces, cover with clingfilm and leave in the fridge for at least 12 hours – I do this overnight. After brining, remove the chicken to a bowl, discarding the brine, then pour over the buttermilk, cover with clingfilm and place in the fridge for a further 8 hours, so the chicken is super-tender.

When you're ready to cook, preheat the oven to 190°C/375°F/gas 5. Wash the sweet potatoes well, roll them in a little sea salt, place on a tray and bake for 30 minutes. Meanwhile, make the pickle – toast the fennel seeds in a large pan for 1 minute, then remove from the heat. Pour in the vinegar, add the sugar and a good pinch of sea salt, then finely slice and add the cabbage. Place in the fridge, remembering to stir every now and then while you cook your chicken.

In a large bowl, mix the flour with the baking powder, cayenne, paprika and the onion and garlic powders. Just under half fill a large sturdy pan with oil – the oil should be 8cm deep, but never fill your pan more than half full – and place on a medium to high heat. Use a thermometer to tell when it's ready (180°C), or add a piece of potato and wait until it turns golden – that's a sign it's ready to go. Take the chicken out of the fridge, then, one or two pieces at a time, remove from the buttermilk and dunk into the bowl of flour until well coated. Give them a shake, then place on a large board and repeat with the remaining chicken pieces.

Turn the oven down to 170°C/325°F/gas 3 and move the sweet potatoes to the bottom shelf. Once the oil is hot enough, start with 2 thighs – quickly dunk them back into the flour, then carefully lower into the hot oil using a slotted spoon. Fry for 5 minutes, turning halfway, then remove to a wire rack over a baking tray. Bring the temperature of the oil back up, repeat the process with the remaining 2 thighs, then pop the tray into the oven. Fry the 4 drumsticks in one batch, then add them to the rack of thighs in the oven for 30 minutes, or until all the chicken is cooked through. Serve with your baked sweet potatoes, cabbage pickle and some salad leaves.

× AUBERGINE PARMIGIANA SANDWICH ×

SERVES 16

2 HOURS 40 MINUTES
PLUS PROVING
476 CALORIES

FOCACCIA

1 x 7g sachet of dried yeast

1kg strong bread flour,
  plus extra for dusting

quality extra virgin olive oil

PARMIGIANA

8 medium aubergines

200g stale bread

200g Parmesan cheese

8 cloves of garlic

1 bunch of fresh basil (30g)

olive oil

1 teaspoon dried oregano

300ml red wine (Barbera d'Alba
  or d'Asti from Piedmont is
  perfection, or use a Valpolicella
  or Chianti)

4 x 400g tins of plum tomatoes

3 x 125g balls of mozzarella cheese

250g rocket

1 lemon

Having a mouthful of this sandwich should be a human right. Aubergine parmigiana, which is a beautiful veg side dish or main in its own right, is at the heart of this story, but rammed into a soft light focaccia as a sarnie it's a total game changer. It's great party food, especially at lunchtime with a delicious green salad and a few nice cold beers.

Whisk the yeast into 600ml of tepid water and leave for 5 minutes. Put the flour and 1 teaspoon of sea salt into a large bowl and create a well in the middle. Pour in the yeasty water and use a spoon to bring in the flour until it becomes too hard to mix, then bring it together with clean floured hands and knead for 5 minutes, or until elastic. Cover and leave in a warm place for 1 hour, or until doubled in size. Knock back the dough, then push it into a large roasting tray (30cm x 40cm). Drizzle with 4 tablespoons of extra virgin olive oil and poke it all over with your fingertips, right to the bottom. Sprinkle with salt and pepper, then leave until doubled in size again.

While the bread is proving, preheat the oven to 180°C/350°F/gas 4. Slice the aubergines lengthways 1½cm-thick. Season generously with salt and leave to drain in a colander for 20 minutes. Tear the bread into a food processor and whiz to fine crumbs, sprinkle over a large tray and bake for 10 minutes. Switch to the fine grater blade and whiz up the Parmesan. Peel the garlic and finely slice with the basil stalks, then fry in a large pan on a medium heat with a splash of olive oil and the oregano until lightly golden. Pour in the wine, bring to the boil and cook away, then squash in the tomatoes and add 1 tin's worth of water. Bring back to the boil, then simmer for 20 minutes. Wipe the aubergine slices with kitchen paper and fry them in a little olive oil in batches in a large frying pan on a high heat for a few minutes on each side, or until golden.

Cover the base of a roasting tray (25cm x 35cm) with one-third of the aubergines, top with one-third each of the tomato sauce, basil leaves, breadcrumbs and Parmesan, then tear over a ball of mozzarella. Repeat twice, then drizzle with a little olive oil. Once the focaccia has doubled in size, very gently place it in the middle of the oven. Place the parmigiana at the bottom of the oven and cook both for 40 minutes, or until the focaccia is lightly golden and cooked through, and the parmigiana is bubbling. When you remove the focaccia and parmigiana from the oven, drizzle the focaccia all over with at least another 4 tablespoons of extra virgin olive oil, and, (this is important) leave the parmigiana to rest for 30 minutes. Divide them both up into portions and stuff the sandwiches, adding some lemon-dressed rocket. It's messy, but awesome.

STICKY CHINESE
RIBS

× STICKY CHINESE RIBS ×

SERVES 6–8

3 HOURS 20 MINUTES

451 CALORIES

1 rack of pork belly ribs, trimmed
of excess fat (1.5–2kg)

olive oil

3 tablespoons Chinese five-spice

2 spring onions

2 fresh chillies

1 bunch of radishes

GLAZE

3 red onions

3 star anise

1 level teaspoon Chinese five-spice

4 tablespoons fresh apple juice

3 tablespoons hoisin sauce

2 tablespoons runny honey

1 tablespoon tomato ketchup

1 tablespoon rice wine vinegar

Having super-tender fall-off-the-bone pork ribs, shining with a sticky Chinese glaze, always excites me. I remember when I first tried ribs like these – I was about 7 or 8 years old, having a family meal at our local Chinese restaurant, and I remember thinking wow – I'd never tried anything like that before. Bundled with other great dishes like noodles and stir-fried rice, it was beyond exciting. My face and hands were absolutely covered in sauce and that's how you should be after tucking into these little beauties. Get stuck in.

Preheat the oven to 160°C/325°F/gas 3. Get yourself three layers of tin foil, 1-metre long. Place the ribs in the centre, drizzle them with oil and rub all over with the five-spice and a good pinch of sea salt and pepper. Seal into a tight parcel and pop on a tray in the middle of the oven for 3 hours, or until just tender and cooked through.

Meanwhile, for the glaze, peel and slice the onions and put them into a frying pan on a medium heat with a lug of oil and the star anise. Cook for 15 minutes, or until soft and starting to caramelize, stirring occasionally. Stir in the five-spice for 2 minutes, stir in the rest of the glaze ingredients and leave to bubble away for another 2 minutes, then turn the heat off and leave to cool a little. Fish out the star anise, transfer the mixture to a blender and blitz until smooth, loosening with a splash of water, if needed, then pass through a fine sieve so it's super-super smooth. Have a taste and season if required. Trim the spring onions and deseed the chillies, then finely slice both lengthways and put them into a bowl of ice-cold water so they curl up. For a laugh you can randomly score the radishes and pop them into the water for a bit of a naff 80s feel; otherwise, leave them whole or cut them into quarters.

When the time's up, transfer the ribs to the tray, discarding the foil, and turn the oven up to 200°C/400°F/gas 6. Brush a good layer of glaze over the ribs and return them to the oven for 8 to 10 minutes, then I like to keep brushing on glaze and popping them back into the oven every minute after that for a few more minutes, to build up a really good layer of dark, sticky glaze. Serve the ribs with a bowl of any leftover glaze for dunking, and with the radishes, chillies and spring onions on the side.

×

This is definitely an opportunity to have a finger bowl on the side and a tea towel at the ready.

× SUPER EGGS BENEDICT ×

SERVES 4
40 MINUTES
418 CALORIES

4 spring onions

olive oil

400g baby spinach

1 whole nutmeg, for grating

1 lemon

4 English muffins

8 small eggs

100g wafer-thin smoked ham

HOLLANDAISE

100g unsalted butter

2 large egg yolks

1 teaspoon Dijon mustard

white wine vinegar

×

My top chef's tip here is that the best way to keep hollandaise in a stable, warm condition is to put it into a preheated Thermos flask. Then, if you've got mates coming round, you can just knock out Benedicts in batches, pouring the sauce straight from the flask – it makes life a lot easier and prevents it from splitting.

I do love eggs Benedict. Hot fluffy muffins are important, but really good wafer-thin smoked ham is essential. For fun, I've given you a simple method for creating a double-yolker egg, which also helps you achieve the perfect shape. There's more hollandaise here than you need, but the reality is it's really hard to make a smaller batch because you're emulsifying the butter. However, you can refrigerate what you don't need and use it almost like a mayonnaise over the next few days. Feel free to swap out the ham for beautiful smoked salmon, or even a slow-roasted portobello mushroom, if you prefer.

Preheat the oven to 180°C/350°F/gas 4. Trim and finely chop the spring onions and put them into a large frying pan on a medium-low heat with a little drizzle of oil. Add the spinach with a grating of nutmeg and a good pinch of sea salt and pepper. Cook down until dark and delicious, and any excess water has cooked away, then add a squeeze of lemon juice to taste, and keep warm.

To make the hollandaise, melt the butter in a small pan. Put the egg yolks into a heatproof bowl over a pan of gently simmering water and whisk with 1 tablespoon of lemon juice and the mustard. Whisking constantly, very slowly (otherwise it will split) pour the melted butter into the egg mixture, until well combined, adding a splash of water to loosen, if needed. Whisk in a splash of vinegar and season to perfection. Turn the heat off and keep warm over the pan of water, stirring occasionally, and loosening with an extra splash of water, if needed (or see tip, left).

Warm the muffins in the oven. Meanwhile, simply press an oiled sheet of good-quality clingfilm into an oiled teacup, then crack 2 eggs into it to cheat a double-yolker. Bring the sides up, ease out any air, twist together and tie a tight knot to pouch the egg into a parcel – it's very easy. Repeat with the remaining eggs (a drizzle of truffle oil, a shake of Tabasco or a few fresh soft herbs can be added to your parcels for extra flavour). Poach the parcels in a pan of gently simmering water for 8½ minutes. To check they're done, lift one out with a slotted spoon and gently squeeze – use your instincts.

Halve the warm muffins, then divide over the spinach and waves of delicate ham. Unwrap the poached double-yolker eggs and balance on top, spoon a tablespoon of hollandaise over each one, then bust the eggs open and enjoy.

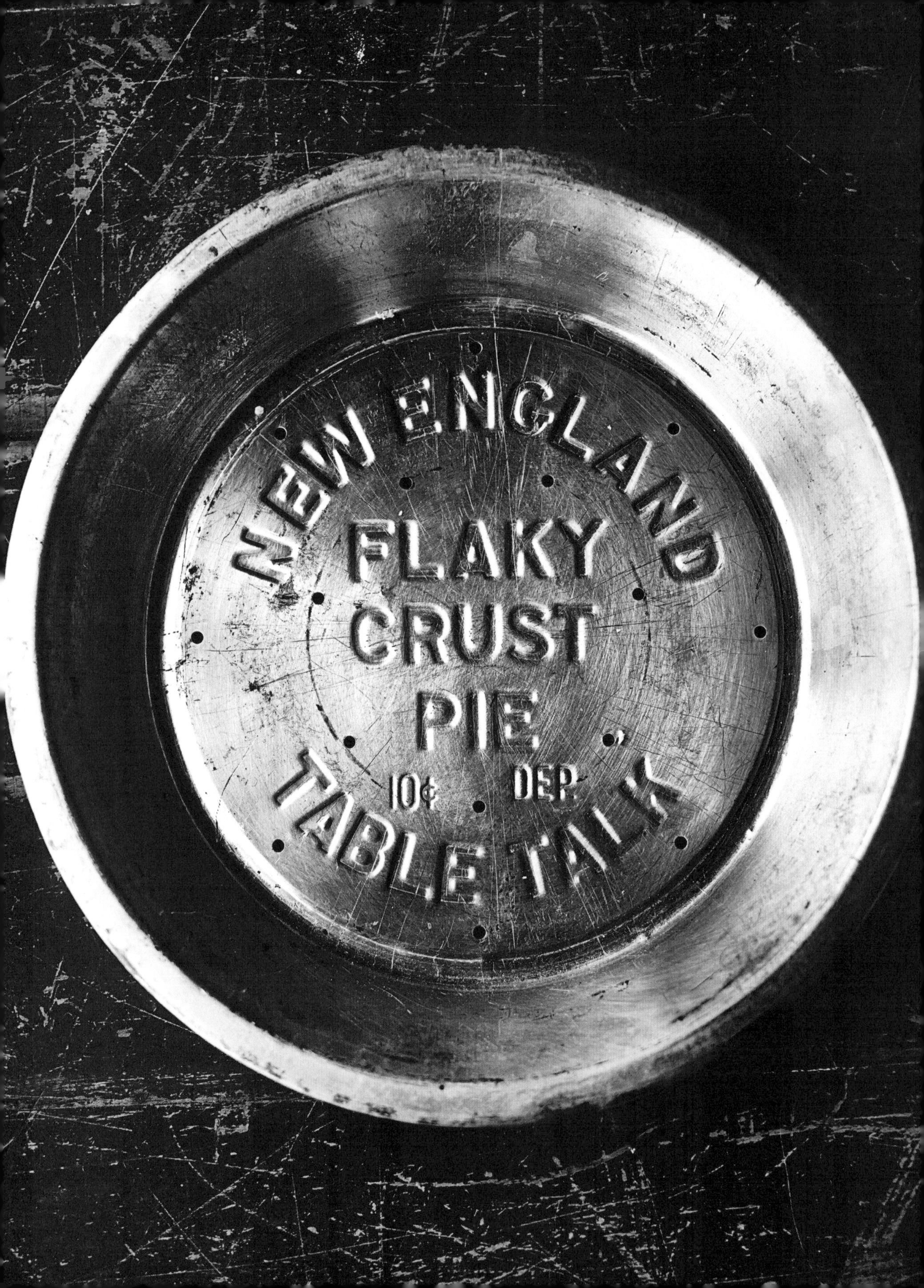
NEW ENGLAND
FLAKY
CRUST
PIE
10¢ DEP
TABLE TALK

× CHICKEN & MUSHROOM PIE ×

SERVES 8

3 HOURS 45 MINUTES

PLUS COOLING

673 CALORIES

PASTRY

250g unsalted butter (cold)

400g plain flour, plus extra
  for dusting

FILLING

2 onions

2 medium carrots

2 sticks of celery

2 large leeks

250g button mushrooms

1 x 1.6kg whole chicken

olive oil

½ a bunch of fresh thyme (15g)

375ml New World Chardonnay

2 heaped tablespoons plain flour

300g mixed wild mushrooms

2 teaspoons English mustard

1 large egg

To come home to this pie is a gift. In my office, we say that if you cook it for your loved one, it's the dish that gets you married. Master it and good things will happen – say no more.

Cube up the butter and put it into a large bowl along with the flour and a pinch of sea salt. Rub the butter into the flour until it resembles cornflakes, add just enough cold water so it comes together – don't overwork it – then wrap in clingfilm and chill in the fridge. Prep all the veg for the filling: peel and roughly chop the onions and carrots. Clean and roughly chop the celery, leeks and button mushrooms. Next, simply hack up the chicken into thighs, drumsticks, wings and manageable chunks of breast, all kept on the bone with the skin on for maximum flavour.

Place a large casserole pan on a medium heat, add a lug of oil, then working in batches fry the chicken pieces for 20 minutes, or until nice and golden all over. Remove the chicken to a plate, then add the prepped veg to the pan, strip in the thyme leaves and fry for 15 minutes, stirring regularly. Stir in the wine, scraping all the sticky goodness from the bottom of the pan, and cook it away, then stir in the flour. Return the chicken to the pan, tear in the wild mushrooms, add the mustard and pour in 1.2 litres of water. Bring to the boil, then simmer gently for 1 hour. Have a taste and correct the seasoning – make sure you get this right now to ensure your pie is super-delicious. Remove the chicken from the pan with tongs, leaving the sauce to gently tick away. Once the chicken is cool enough to handle (or wear gloves), carefully pick through it, discarding the skin and bones. Stir the meat back into the pan and reduce to a nice thick consistency (no one likes a watery pie!), then leave to cool completely.

When you're ready to put your pie together, preheat the oven to 180°C/350°F/gas 4. Roll out two-thirds of your pastry to about 3mm thick on a flour-dusted surface. Eggwash the edges of a 25cm pie tin, then loosely roll the pastry around the rolling pin and unroll it over the dish, easing it into the sides and leaving a generous overhang. Spoon in half the cooled filling (freeze the rest for another lucky day), then eggwash the pastry rim. Roll out the remaining pastry and top your pie. Take a bit of pride in pinching the edges together, flouring your fingers as you go – I've got big hands and I can do it neatly, so anyone can. Trim away any excess, cut a cross in the centre, then brush all over with more eggwash. Bake on the bottom of the oven for 45 to 50 minutes, or until golden and cooked through. Serve with simply cooked seasonal veg, such as peas, spring greens or kale, cooking them once the pie comes out of the oven – you don't want the pie to be screaming hot. Enjoy – this pie won't fail you.

⨯ BEEF & BARLEY BUNS ⨯

SERVES 10

5 HOURS
PLUS INFUSING
405 CALORIES

FILLING

2 onions

2 carrots

500g minced beef

olive oil

2 fresh bay leaves

1 star anise

30g pearl barley

10 sprigs of fresh thyme

200ml Shiraz

1 litre fresh chicken stock

5 jarred pickled walnuts

DOUGH

1 x 7g sachet of dried yeast

1 tablespoon golden caster sugar

100g unsalted butter

550g strong bread flour,
  plus extra for dusting

175ml semi-skimmed milk

HORSERADISH SAUCE

3 heaped tablespoons jarred
  grated horseradish

4 heaped tablespoons crème fraîche

1 tablespoon white wine vinegar

These mouthfuls of heavenly pleasure are a signature dish at Fifteen London – people love them. It's like the best mince your nan would make, wrapped up in a delicate soft bun. I've slightly adapted the recipe here, but it was originally created by my dear friend and wonderful head chef at Fifteen, Jon Rotheram. He used to be at the famous St John Hotel, cooking great British food in the heart of Chinatown, so being surrounded by dim sum every day he developed these lovely morsels to embrace the best of both worlds.

For the filling, peel and very finely chop the onions and carrots. Fry the minced beef in a large non-stick frying pan on a high heat with a splash of oil until browned, stirring regularly. Stir in the onions, carrots, bay, star anise and pearl barley. Strip in the thyme leaves and fry for another 5 minutes, then stir in the wine to pick up all the sticky goodness from the bottom of the pan. When the wine has cooked away, pour in the stock. Finely chop the pickled walnuts and add to the pan with a good splash of pickled juice from the jar. Cover with a lid or tin foil and simmer gently for 2 hours, then remove the lid and give it a final 40 minutes, or until well thickened, but not completely dry, stirring regularly. Season to perfection, then cool and chill overnight to infuse.

The next day, to make the dough, add the yeast and sugar to 150ml of tepid water, give it a stir, then leave for 10 minutes. Meanwhile, rub the butter and flour together until you have a crumble consistency, then pour in the yeast mixture and the milk, along with 1 level teaspoon of sea salt. Mix it all together with a spoon until it becomes too hard to mix, at which point use your hands to knead the dough until smooth, silky and elastic. Divide into 20 even-sized balls (roughly 45g each), then leave to prove on a flour-dusted surface covered with a damp tea towel, until doubled in size.

Preheat the oven to 170°C/325°F/gas 3. One-by-one, flatten each dough ball in the palm of your hand. Add a heaped dessertspoon of filling to the centre, discarding the bay and star anise (you only need half the filling, so freeze the rest for your next batch of buns). Pull the sides of the dough up around the filling and pinch together, patting into an even round. Place on 2 greased and lined baking trays, crease-side down, and bake at the bottom of the oven for 20 minutes, or until lightly golden. If you want, you can bake a batch an hour or two in advance, then just pop them back into the oven for a few minutes before serving to warm through. Mix the sauce ingredients together, season to perfection, and serve on the side. If you can get fresh horseradish, use a grating of that instead of the jarred stuff. These buns are best eaten warm, not hot.

✕ UNBELIEVABLE PROVENÇAL BAKE ✕

SERVES 8

SERVES 8

2 HOURS

380 CALORIES

FILLINGS

600g ripe plum tomatoes

½ a bunch of fresh basil (15g)

½ a lemon

red wine vinegar

125g Comté cheese

125g Gruyère cheese

½ a bunch of fresh flat-leaf
    parsley (15g)

200g handcut wafer-thin ham (I like
    a mixture of smoked and cured)

WHITE ONION SAUCE

2 onions

1 large knob of unsalted butter

4 tablespoons plain flour

700ml semi-skimmed milk

1 teaspoon English mustard

1 whole nutmeg, for grating

CRÊPES

30g unsalted butter,
    plus extra for cooking

120g plain flour

2 large eggs

70ml semi-skimmed milk

The combo of sweet tomatoes, smoked ham and gooey, melty cheese is obviously bound to give you a home run of a dish, so this crispy stodgy crêpe delight is a real classic. Crêpes are so easy to make, and using them in savoury bakes in both France and Italy is fairly common, and gives truly wonderful results. Like lasagne, don't serve this straight from the oven – let it rest, so it's easier to cut and portion up. This will make you happy.

Score a cross on each tomato, then carefully plunge them into a large pan of boiling water for 45 seconds, then drain in a colander and place in cold water. Peel away and discard the skins, then deseed the tomatoes and chop the flesh into 1cm chunks. Pick and finely chop the basil leaves, finely grate the lemon zest, then toss both with the tomatoes, a good splash of vinegar and a good pinch of sea salt.

To start the sauce, peel and finely chop the onions. Melt the butter in a pan on a medium heat, add the onions and cook for 15 minutes, or until soft, stirring regularly. Meanwhile, for the crêpes, melt the butter and let it cool a little while you pile the flour into a bowl with a pinch of salt. Make a well in the middle, whisk in the eggs, then gradually whisk in the milk and 70ml of water until smooth. Stir in the melted butter, then leave to sit while you finish the sauce. Stir the flour into the onions to make a kind of roux, then gradually whisk in the milk until smooth. Stir in the mustard and a few scrapings of nutmeg, season, simmer for 15 minutes, then remove from the heat.

Put a 26cm frying pan on a medium heat with a tiny knob of butter. Once melted, add just enough batter to coat the base of the pan, gently swirling to cover. Cook until lightly golden, then flip and cook on the other side. Repeat with the remaining batter, wiping out the pan with a ball of kitchen paper and adding a tiny knob of butter each time – you should end up with 6 crêpes. Grate and mix the cheeses, pick and roughly chop the parsley leaves, and tear up the slices of ham.

Preheat the oven to 180°C/350°F/gas 4. Get yourself a deep ovenproof pan 26cm in diameter. Repeat layers of crêpe, sauce, tomato (leaving any juices behind in the bowl), ham, cheese and parsley until you've used up all the ingredients, finishing with a layer of just sauce and cheese. Bake on the bottom shelf of the oven for 40 minutes, or until golden and bubbling, resting for 10 minutes before serving. I like it with a mixed garden salad with a French dressing made with walnut oil, and I also like to shave some walnuts on a box grater over the top of the salad for added crunch – delicious.

✕ NEXT-LEVEL STEAK & ONION SANDWICH ✕

SERVES 4

<u>50 MINUTES</u>

<u>553 CALORIES</u>

400g flank skirt steak or bavette

2 sprigs of fresh rosemary

2 large onions

5 fresh bay leaves

20g unsalted butter

olive oil

70g dark brown sugar

125ml red wine vinegar

1 ciabatta loaf

extra virgin olive oil

optional: English mustard

½ a lemon

1 handful of watercress

I've got really early memories of my dad making steak sandwiches, which were absolutely gorgeous and always such a treat. In this recipe I want to take the joy of a steak sandwich to the next level by kind of taking the mighty steak off its pedestal a bit and putting most of the focus on awesome onions, to create the best steak sandwich ever.

Remove the steak from the fridge and let it come to room temperature, pick over the rosemary leaves, then cover it with greaseproof paper and bash it with the base of a pan to tenderize and make it all roughly the same thickness. Meanwhile, peel the onions, also removing the first layer of flesh (reserve this for a soup or stew), then slice into 2cm-thick rounds. Put the bay, butter, a lug of oil and the sugar into a large non-stick frying pan on a medium heat. Once the butter has melted, place the onions into the pan in a single layer, season with sea salt and black pepper and cook for 5 minutes. Pour in the vinegar, pop the lid on, reduce the heat to low and cook for around 35 minutes, or until beautifully golden and caramelized on the bottom only, adding splashes of water to loosen, if needed.

Meanwhile, pop the ciabatta into the oven, turn onto 110°C/225°F/gas ¼ and leave to warm through. Season the steak all over with salt and pepper. Place a large non-stick heavy-bottomed pan on a high heat. Once screaming hot, drizzle the steak with olive oil, then put it into the pan and cook for 3 minutes on each side for medium, or to your liking. Remove to a plate, rest for 1 minute, then slice 1cm thick and toss through its own resting juices with a drizzle of extra virgin olive oil.

Cut the warm ciabatta in half and rub the inside of each piece in the steak resting juices. Spread on some mustard, if you like, then layer over the caramelized onions, the steak and pinches of lemon-dressed watercress. Pop the other piece of bread on top, press down lightly, carve up into decent chunks and get involved.

DESSERTS, PUDS & BEAUTIFUL SWEET TREATS

SWEET

× INDULGENCE ×

✕ DREAMY MARSHMALLOW PAVLOVA ✕

SERVES 16

2 HOURS
PLUS COOLING
331 CALORIES

MERINGUES

8 large egg whites

400g caster sugar

MARSHMALLOW

½ x magnificent marshmallows
(minus the cornflour and icing
sugar – don't make until
assembly – page 372)

BERRIES

600g seasonal berries (my ultimate
is wild strawberries when they're
in season, or even mulberries, but
any berries will be delicious)

1 tablespoon lemon juice

1 heaped tablespoon caster sugar

1 tablespoon balsamic vinegar

2 sprigs of fresh mint

CHANTILLY CREAM

1 vanilla pod

2 tablespoons caster sugar

400ml double cream

200ml Greek yoghurt

This is the pavlova my dreams are made of. Thin crispy meringue exterior with a soft chewy centre, seasonal berries – in this case bubble-gummy wild strawberries – Chantilly cream, and from my dreamland, the surprising guest appearance of cloud-spongy homemade marshmallow. I want you to share this dream – it's a good one.

Preheat the oven to 130°C/250°F/gas ½. Whisk the egg whites and a pinch of sea salt in a free-standing electric mixer until they form stiff peaks, then with the mixer still running, very gradually and carefully add the sugar, turn to the highest setting and leave to mix for 8 minutes, or until fully dissolved (rub a pinch of the mixture between your thumb and forefinger – if it feels smooth you're good to go). Line two large baking trays with greaseproof paper, then draw a 24cm circle on each sheet of paper. Divide the mixture between the two sheets and spread it out to just inside your circles, then use the back of the spoon to flick up peaks and make troughs in the mixture to give you free-form, rustic meringues that are also elegant and delicate. Bake for 1 hour 20 minutes, then turn the oven off, leaving the meringues in there until the oven is cool.

When you're ready to assemble the pavlova, make your magnificent marshmallow (page 372). As soon as it's made, divide in big beautiful spoonfuls between the two meringues before it sets, being mindful to spoon in between the lovely peaks and wisps of meringue, so it's as pretty as possible. At this point, identify the dreamiest meringue and put the scruffier one onto a cake stand to form the base of your pavlova.

Put the most perfect-looking half of your berries to one side, then place the other half in a bowl (removing any stalks). Add the lemon juice, sugar and balsamic, toss together and leave to macerate for 10 minutes while you make the Chantilly cream. Halve the vanilla pod lengthways and scrape all the seeds into a large bowl with the sugar. Pour in the cream and whisk by hand until it forms soft peaks (all elegance will be lost if you overwhip the cream – if anything, underwhip it), then fold in the yoghurt.

Spoon three-quarters of the cream into the centre of the base meringue and carefully smooth it out to the edge, trying not to completely cover the marshmallow. Spoon over the macerated berries and juices, then place the second meringue on top. Dot over the remaining cream in between the marshmallow and meringue wisps, then sprinkle with the reserved berries. Pick a few baby mint leaves over the top, and serve.

× SCRUMPTIOUS ×
STICKY TOFFEE PUDDING

✕ SCRUMPTIOUS STICKY TOFFEE PUDDING ✕

SERVES 16

1 HOUR 15 MINUTES
567 CALORIES

4 Earl Grey tea bags

450g fresh Medjool dates

1 level teaspoon ground cinnamon

1 whole nutmeg, for grating

170g unsalted butter, plus extra for
   greasing (at room temperature)

340g self-raising flour, plus
   extra for dusting

170g golden caster sugar

170g dark muscovado sugar

4 large eggs

Maldon sea salt

CARAMEL SAUCE

250g unsalted butter

125g dark muscovado sugar

125g golden caster sugar

50ml dark rum

300ml double cream

I grew up with sticky toffee pudding and it's only ever made me happy in life. As a child I remember asking Mum, Nan or Grandad, 'What's for dessert, what's for dessert?' and if it was sticky toffee pudding, that was just the best news – no matter what else was for dinner! And being honest, not much has changed. The reason that this recipe is the best I've ever had is because it relies on the fantastic Medjool dates, though you can use any other really high-quality dates; with muscovado sugar, subtle spices and Earl Grey tea, it makes for a winning combo. It's great served in a Bundt tin like this and looks pretty spectacular, but feel free to go old school and traybake it, if you prefer. Enjoy.

Preheat the oven to 180°C/350°F/gas 4. Put the tea bags into a jug, cover with 300ml of boiling water and leave to steep for 3½ minutes. Meanwhile, destone the dates and put into a food processor with the cinnamon, then finely grate in half the nutmeg. Scoop out the tea bags and pour the tea over the dates, pushing them down so they're submerged. Leave them to soak with the lid on for 10 minutes, then blitz to a purée, stopping occasionally to scrape down the sides, which will help it along.

Butter and lightly flour a 26cm Bundt tin or a 20cm x 30cm baking dish. In a large mixing bowl, cream the butter and sugars together using a wooden spoon. Beat in the eggs, one-by-one, then, using a large metal spoon, stir in the flour and fold in the puréed dates. Pour the pudding mixture into your chosen receptacle, then bake for 45 to 50 minutes, or until an inserted skewer comes out clean.

When your pudding is almost ready, make the sauce. Cube the butter and melt in a small pan on a medium heat. Add both the sugars, then, once nicely mixed, carefully add the rum (it may splatter) and double cream. Bring to the boil, then simmer for around 5 minutes, or until a lovely deep golden colour.

As soon as the pudding is ready, if using a Bundt tin, flip out onto a platter and brush all over with enough sauce to form a delicate, crispy surface but also keep your sponge nice and bouncy, or, if you're traybaking it in a dish, poke small holes in the top and pour over one-third of the sauce. Sprinkle with a little sea salt for contrast, and serve with a jug of sauce and a little double cream, ice cream or custard, if you like.

PINEAPPLE

UPSIDE-DOWN CAKE

✕ PINEAPPLE UPSIDE-DOWN CAKE ✕

SERVES 12
1 HOUR 20 MINUTES
503 CALORIES

225g unsalted butter, plus
extra for dusting

150g coconut milk

75g desiccated coconut

1 ripe pineapple

400g caster sugar

4 large eggs

200g self-raising flour

1 jar of stem ginger in syrup

1 lime

15 glacé cherries

I really like pineapple – I like it fresh, I like it in cocktails, I like it with mint sugar and yoghurt for breakfast, and I grew up loving upside-down cakes. My primary school actually used to make a brilliant version, often using tinned pineapple, and served with hot custard, so this brings back many fond memories for me. I recommend buying your pineapple a week ahead – it should smell sweet and the central leaves should be easily removable – this will give you the most intense flavour. Also, this delicious cake can be made in advance and reheated later with great results, which is always very useful.

Preheat the oven to 180°C/350°F/gas 4 and grease a deep 23cm loose-bottomed cake tin, then place on a baking tray (to catch any caramel if it sneaks out during cooking). In a small pan, bring the coconut milk to the boil, then stir in the desiccated coconut and put aside to cool. Meanwhile, cut the pineapple in half lengthways, putting one half in the fridge for another day. Remove the skin from the remaining half, then remove the core by doing a v-cut and slice into 2cm-thick half-moons (like you see in the picture). Melt 25g of butter and 200g of sugar in a non-stick frying pan on a medium heat – don't stir it. As the sugar starts to dissolve, add the pineapple slices in one layer. Turn the heat up a little so the pineapple releases all its lovely juices, and let it bubble away until dark golden and caramelized on one side only. Using spoons, arrange the pineapple slices in a lovely fan shape across the base of the prepared cake tin, golden side down, then drizzle the caramel over the pineapple.

In a large bowl, cream together the remaining 200g of butter and sugar until pale and fluffy. Beat in the cool coconut mixture, then one-by-one beat in the eggs and finally, fold in the flour. Pour the cake mixture over the pineapple and bake for 45 minutes, or until golden and an inserted skewer comes out clean. Leave the cake to cool in the tin for 5 minutes, then carefully turn out onto a wire rack.

Meanwhile, put 4 tablespoons of stem ginger syrup into a small pan. Gently heat up, squeeze in the lime juice, finely chop and add a piece of stem ginger, then add the cherries and a splash of water. Simmer and reduce until you have a lovely thick syrup, then simply pour over the sponge, piling those shiny cherries in the centre. Serve with cream or double vanilla ice cream (page 342). Retro and so worth it.

CHOCOLATE
CELEBRATION
CAKE

× CHOCOLATE CELEBRATION CAKE ×

SERVES 16

2 HOURS
542 CALORIES

SPONGE

250g unsalted butter, plus extra
for greasing

150g quality dark chocolate (70%)

2 tablespoons olive oil

300g caster sugar

6 large eggs

150g self-raising flour

4 tablespoons quality cocoa
powder

CHOCOLATE RICE LAYER

300g quality dark chocolate (70%)

or quality milk chocolate,
plus extra to serve

75g unsalted butter

1 tablespoon runny honey

100ml double cream

100g puffed rice cereal

NOUGAT FROSTING

2 large egg whites

3 tablespoons runny honey

200g caster sugar

1 level teaspoon cream of tartar

½ teaspoon vanilla extract

optional: ½ teaspoon orange
blossom or rose water

Every household needs a blooming good chocolate cake in their repertoire, whether it's just for the hell of maintaining your chocolate quota, or of course for those special occasions where you need a freshly baked cake, or need to arrive somewhere with a showstopper in hand. Regardless, this chocolate celebration cake will reset everyone's expectations of what a chocolate cake should be – it's delicious, it has incredible texture, it looks absolutely amazing, and it's a pleasure to make and watch people enjoying.

Preheat the oven to 180°C/350°F/gas 4. Grease and line a deep 23cm loose-bottomed cake tin, lining the sides with a double layer of greaseproof paper. For the sponge, smash up the chocolate and melt in a large heatproof bowl with the butter, oil and sugar over a pan of gently simmering water until smooth and glossy. Remove the bowl from the heat and leave to cool for 10 minutes, then, using an electric hand whisk at high speed, one-by-one beat in the eggs until combined. Sift in the flour and cocoa with a good pinch of sea salt and beat for a short while until just combined. Pour into the prepared tin and bake for around 50 minutes, or until an inserted skewer comes out ever so slightly gooey (the top of the cake will rise up and crack slightly, but don't worry, it'll end up covered by all your lovely toppings). Leave to cool in the tin for 15 minutes, then transfer to a wire rack to cool completely. Place on a cake stand, use a long knife to carefully slice the sponge into 3 equal rounds and remove the top two sponges to separate plates (go to jamieoliver.com/how-to to see how to do this).

For your chocolate rice layer, smash up the chocolate and melt with the butter, honey, cream and a pinch of salt in a large heatproof bowl over a pan of gently simmering water until smooth and glossy. Leave to cool for 5 minutes (to avoid soggy cereal!), then stir in the puffed rice until evenly coated. Divide the mixture onto the 3 cooled sponge layers and spread out evenly across the tops, going right to the edges.

To make the nougat frosting, place the egg whites in a heatproof bowl with the honey, sugar, cream of tartar, a good pinch of salt and a splash of water. Place over a pan of gently simmering water, turn up the heat, and with an electric hand whisk beat for 6 to 7 minutes, or until it starts to form peaks. Remove the bowl from the heat, add the vanilla extract and orange blossom or rose water (if using), then carry on beating the mixture until thick. Leave to cool for 5 to 10 minutes, then evenly top each sponge layer and stack them up neatly. To finish the cake off nicely, use a large knife to shave some extra chocolate, then sprinkle it over the top (there's a video on jamieoliver.com/how-to to show you how to do this). Add your candles or sparklers, get them lit and indulge in chocolate celebration cake heaven. Enjoy!

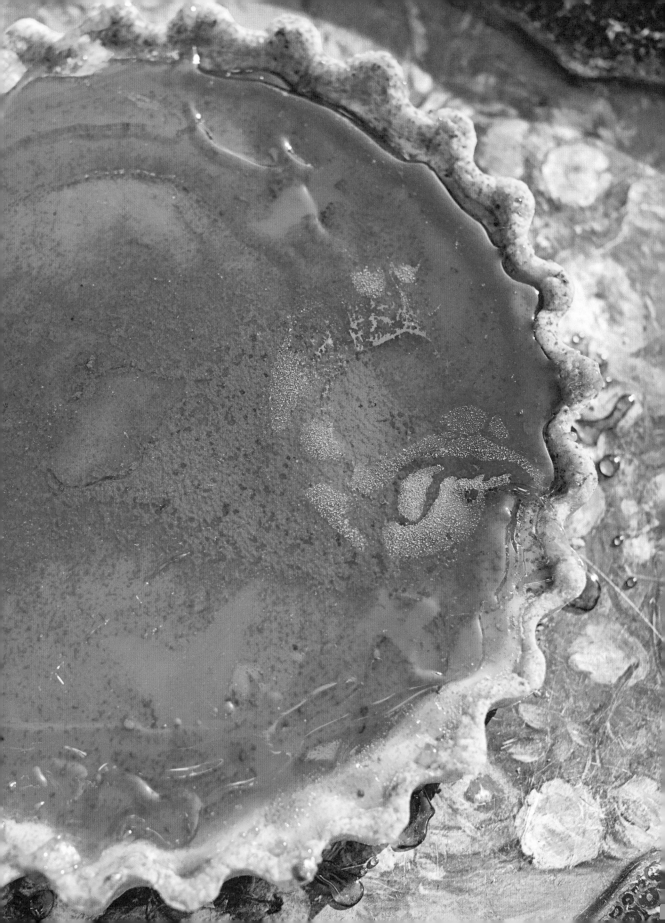

× MILK TART ×

SERVES 10

1 HOUR 20 MINUTES
PLUS CHILLING & COOLING
317 CALORIES

PASTRY

250g plain flour, plus extra
   for dusting

50g icing sugar

125g unsalted butter (cold)

1 large egg

1 splash of semi-skimmed milk

FILLING

600ml semi-skimmed milk

1 vanilla pod (look for a really
   nice, fat juicy one)

1 knob of unsalted butter

2 large eggs

2 tablespoons cornflour

1½ tablespoons plain flour

75g golden caster sugar

1 teaspoon ground cinnamon

OPTIONAL: CARAMEL

130g caster sugar

Great as a dessert or for afternoon tea, the much-loved South African milk tart or 'melktert' was introduced by Cape Malays, who used spices to add flavour to the food of Dutch spice traders back in the seventeenth century. It's a simple, light, milkier custard tart with a dusting of cinnamon, and I couldn't help but evolve it by pouring a golden caramel over the top, giving it a naughty, shardy, delicate brûlée-like crunch. Double yum.

For the pastry, sieve the flour and icing sugar into a bowl. Cut the butter into cubes, then gently rub it into the flour and sugar until the mixture resembles breadcrumbs. Add the egg and a pinch of sea salt, gently work it together using your hands, then add the milk to bring it into a scruffy ball. Don't overwork it or it will become elastic and chewy, rather than crumbly and short. Wrap in clingfilm, then chill for 30 minutes.

Lightly oil the inside of a deep 24cm non-stick loose-bottomed tart tin. Dust a clean surface and a rolling pin with flour, then roll out the pastry to ½cm thick, dusting with flour if required. Loosely roll the pastry around the rolling pin, then unroll over the tart tin, pushing it into the sides. Trim off any excess and use that to patch any holes, prick the base all over with a fork, then pop into the freezer for 20 minutes.

Preheat the oven to 180°C/350°F/gas 4. Loosely criss-cross 2 large pieces of quality clingfilm over the pastry case. Fill up with uncooked rice or ceramic baking beans, loosely fold in the clingfilm, then bake blind for 10 minutes. Remove from the oven, lift out the clingfilm-wrapped rice or beans, saving them for next time. Return the pastry case to the oven for 10 minutes, or until almost biscuit-like, then remove.

Meanwhile, for the filling, pour the milk into a small pan, halve the vanilla pod lengthways and scrape out the seeds, then add both seeds and pod to the milk. Gently simmer for 15 minutes, then remove from the heat, and stir in the butter to melt. In a bowl, beat the eggs with the cornflour, plain flour and sugar, then, when the milk has cooled a little, gradually whisk it into the egg mixture. Tip back into the pan and place over a low heat for 5 to 10 minutes, or until thickened, whisking constantly, then discard the vanilla pod. Pour into the pastry case and dust with the ground cinnamon through a sieve from a height. Bake for 20 minutes, then transfer to a wire rack to cool.

For an optional extra, just before serving make a caramel topping. Melt the sugar in a non-stick frying pan with a splash of water over a medium heat until lightly golden – do not stir – then pour over the tart (you can see how to do this on jamieoliver.com/how-to). Cool fully at room temperature, then tap and crack the caramel and serve.

× CHOCOLATE PROFITEROLES ×

SERVES 8–10
1 HOUR
PLUS COOLING
554 CALORIES

CHOUX PASTRY

150g plain flour

125ml semi-skimmed milk

100g unsalted butter

1 heaped teaspoon caster sugar

4 large eggs

CRÈME PÂTISSIÈRE

250ml semi-skimmed milk

200ml double cream

1 vanilla pod

2 large eggs

75g golden caster sugar

30g cornflour

SAUCE

200g dark chocolate (70%)

150ml semi-skimmed milk

I started making profiteroles at my mum and dad's pub as a very young boy – my dad was famous for having one of the best dessert trolleys in Essex, and I reckon in the whole country too. Sadly, gone are the days of lovely old Mary, Linda, Joan and Jenny, pushing the sweet trolley around the restaurant, serving up everyone's favourite dessert, but that doesn't mean we can't still enjoy these little beauties. Profiteroles are a great old classic that people just love, especially if you serve each portion with its own little jug of silky chocolate sauce so that everyone can pour it over the top themselves.

Preheat the oven to 200°C/400°F/gas 6. To make the choux pastry, sieve the flour into a bowl and add a pinch of sea salt. Pour the milk into a small pan, place over a high heat and bring to the boil. Chop the butter into small chunks and add to the milk with the sugar. When the milk starts to boil again, tip in the flour and remove from the heat. Beat well with a wooden spoon until the mixture comes together into a thick dough. Place the pan back on the heat for 30 seconds and stir the dough around in the pan, then turn the heat off and allow to cool for a minute or so. Whisk the eggs in a bowl, then beat about a quarter of the egg into the dough. Add the rest of the egg in 3 batches, beating each one in well before adding the next, until you have a lovely glossy dough. Spoon the mixture into a piping bag with a nozzle roughly 2cm wide. Pipe around 30 profiteroles onto a couple of lined baking trays and, with a wet finger, lightly push the pointed tops down – this will prevent them from burning in the oven. Bake for around 20 minutes, or until perfectly golden, then transfer to a wire rack to cool.

Meanwhile, make the crème pâtissière. Pour the milk and cream into a pan. Halve the vanilla pod lengthways, scrape out the seeds, add both pod and seeds to the pan and simmer for 5 minutes. In a separate bowl, whisk the eggs, sugar and cornflour together. Gradually add the hot creamy liquid to the egg mixture, mixing constantly. Return to a low heat for 2 minutes, or until thickened, mixing constantly, then cool.

For the sauce, snap the chocolate into a heatproof bowl, add the milk, then melt over a pan of gently simmering water while you use the handle end of a wooden spoon to make a hole in the side of each profiterole. Spoon the crème pâtissière into a piping or sandwich bag, then fill each profiterole and serve with hot or cold chocolate sauce.

× DOUBLE VANILLA ICE CREAM ×

MAKES 1 LITRE

1 HOUR
PLUS CHURNING
127 CALORIES (PER SCOOP)

2 vanilla pods

500ml whole milk

250ml double cream

7 large eggs

150g golden caster sugar

Vanilla is the mother flavour of all ice creams – done well, it's so simple and delicious. At its heart is the wonderful vanilla pod, one of the most extraordinary ingredients on the planet. It tastes incredible and is able to take the front seat in delicious flavour as it does here, yet it's also always happy to work with just about any complementary flavour. So here is my ultimate basic ice cream recipe, and on the pages that follow are four tasty derivatives and twists on it that work right into this staged recipe – have fun with it!

STAGE 1

Halve the vanilla pods lengthways and scrape out the seeds. Place the pods and seeds into a medium pan and pour in the milk and cream. Put the pan on a low heat and warm very gently for 15 minutes, then remove and put aside to cool slightly.

STAGE 2

Separate the eggs and, in a large bowl, whisk the yolks with the sugar until pale (freeze the egg whites in a sandwich bag for making meringues another day, page 320).

STAGE 3

Whisking constantly, gradually pour the warm milk mixture through a sieve into the egg mixture until smooth and combined, pushing through all the vanilla seeds.

STAGE 4

Pour the custard into a pan on a very low heat. Stirring constantly, cook for 10 to 15 minutes, or until thickened and coating the back of a spoon (like you see in the picture). Transfer to a clean bowl and leave to cool completely.

STAGE 5

If using an ice cream machine, pour in the recommended volume of cooled custard and churn until you have smooth and light ice cream. If working by hand, pour the custard into a container and freeze, whisking it well every 30 minutes with a fork to break up any ice crystals, for around 3 to 4 hours in total, or until nicely set.

MINT CHOC CHIP
ICE CREAM

MAKES 1 LITRE
1 HOUR 10 MINUTES
PLUS CHURNING
140 CALORIES (PER SCOOP)

Start the double vanilla ice cream recipe (page 342), adding
1 teaspoon of natural peppermint extract and the leaves
from 1 bunch of fresh mint to the milk and cream at
stage 1. Before starting stage 2, strain the milk mixture to
remove the mint leaves. Continue through the rest of the
double vanilla ice cream stages. At stage 5, once you've
churned your ice cream, finely chop or grate 100g of quality
dark chocolate (70%). Sprinkle and stir the chocolate chips
into the ice cream, then freeze until required.

SALTED CARAMEL
ICE CREAM

MAKES 1 LITRE
1 HOUR 15 MINUTES
PLUS CHURNING
144 CALORIES (PER SCOOP)

Make your double vanilla custard as per stages 1 to 4 (page
342) and leave to cool. Line a tray with greaseproof paper.
Pour 250g of caster sugar and a good pinch of sea salt into
a large non-stick frying pan with 4 tablespoons of water
and allow to caramelize on a medium heat (but don't stir).
When deep golden, carefully pour half onto the tray and tilt
to spread out thinly. Return the rest to the heat until dark
golden, then carefully whisk into the custard. Churn the
ice cream as instructed in stage 5. Once the caramel sheet
is set, smash into shards and either fold through the ice
cream and freeze until required, or sprinkle it over to serve.

RUM & RAISIN
ICE CREAM

MAKES 1 LITRE
1 HOUR 10 MINUTES
PLUS SOAKING & CHURNING
106 CALORIES (PER SCOOP)

Place 100g of raisins (or currants if you want a smaller, finer fruit), in a bowl and cover with 150ml of quality dark spiced rum, such as Bacardi Oakheart. Leave to soak for at least 2 hours, or until plump. Lift out half the raisins, then blitz the other half with the rum in a food processor until smooth. Make your double vanilla custard as per stages 1 to 4 (page 342) and leave to cool, then, before churning at stage 5, stir through the whole and blitzed rummy raisins. Churn the ice cream as instructed and freeze until required.

RASPBERRY RIPPLE
ICE CREAM

MAKES 1 LITRE
1 HOUR 20 MINUTES
PLUS CHURNING
106 CALORIES (PER SCOOP)

Make your double vanilla custard as per stages 1 to 4 (page 342) and leave to cool. Put 250g of raspberries into a pan with 50g of golden caster sugar and 60ml of Valpolicella (this is an Italian light, red wine that can be served chilled, but feel free to use a sweet red wine instead). Place on a medium heat for 10 minutes, squashing the berries with a spoon as you go. Push through a coarse sieve, scraping all the good bits from the bottom but discarding any seeds, and leave to cool. At stage 5, pour your churned ice cream into a freezer dish, then ripple and fold through the raspberries in a figure of eight and freeze until required.

× THE JAFFA CAKE ×

SERVES 16

1 HOUR 30 MINUTES
PLUS CHILLING
482 CALORIES

225g unsalted butter, plus extra for
    greasing (at room temperature)

300g golden marzipan

100ml single cream

225g golden caster sugar

10 large eggs

½ tablespoon vanilla extract

1 orange

150g self-raising flour

100g cornflour

150g rindless bitter orange
    marmalade

25ml whisky

300g dark chocolate (70%),
    plus extra to serve

40g candied orange peel

The inspiration for this cake comes from a fantastic German Christmas cake where you make a kind of batter sponge that you cook layer by layer, under the grill. It's a really fun and satisfying process – the comfort is definitely in the making. I've evolved the recipe to include flavours in between the layers, reminiscent of the old-school classic Jaffa cake that we enjoyed as kids (and adults!) – chocolate, orange and sponge. What a combo.

Preheat the grill to medium-high. Grease and line the base of a deep 23cm loose-bottomed cake tin. Roughly chop the marzipan and blitz with a splash of cream, 175g of butter and the sugar in a food processor until pale and creamy. Separate the eggs, then beat in the yolks one-by-one, followed by the vanilla extract, the rest of the cream and the orange zest. Sift the self-raising flour and cornflour, then use a large metal spoon to fold into the cake batter. Whisk the egg whites with a pinch of sea salt till they form firm peaks, then gently fold them into the batter with the spoon.

Melt the marmalade in a small pan over a low heat, loosening with the whisky, and keep warm. Smash up 100g of the chocolate and melt with 25g of butter in a heatproof bowl over a pan of gently simmering water. Keep both to one side ready for layering.

To assemble the cake, use a ladle to spoon just enough batter into the prepared cake tin to cover the base in a thin layer. Spread it out evenly, then cook on the top shelf under the grill for 3 to 4 minutes, or until set and golden all over – this is really important, otherwise your layers won't show. Ladle another thin layer of batter on top, and return to the grill. Continue layering and grilling, mixing up the layers with thin layers of marmalade and melted chocolate as you go. Repeat until the batter is used up, brush the top of the cake with a good layer of marmalade, then run a knife around the outside. Leave to cool, then cover with clingfilm and chill for a few hours.

A couple of hours before you're ready to serve, melt the remaining 200g of chocolate and 25g of butter in a heatproof bowl set over a small pan of gently simmering water. Once glossy, leave to cool for 5 minutes. Remove the cake from the tin and set it on a serving plate. Pour over the chocolate sauce and use a spatula to spread it evenly over the top, letting it drizzle down the sides, smoothing out if you like. Leave it to set, avoiding the fridge, which can make the chocolate go dull, then top with strips of candied orange peel. Really nice with shavings of chocolate on top (there's a video on jamieoliver.com/how-to to show you how to do this).

AMAZING

APPLE

PIE

✕ AMAZING APPLE PIE ✕

SERVES 8

2 HOURS 30 MINUTES
PLUS COOLING
590 CALORIES

FLAKY PIE PASTRY

250g unsalted butter (cold)

350g plain flour, plus extra
for dusting

1 tablespoon golden caster sugar

FILLING

2kg apples (I like a mixture
of Bramley, Russet, Braeburn,
Cox and good old Granny Smith)

1 lemon

50g unsalted butter

100g light brown muscovado sugar

1 good pinch of ground cinnamon

TOPPING

1 large egg

20g demerara sugar

✕

*Whenever I'm making a pie
I generally make one, two or
three extras, so feel free to up
this recipe, and pop them into
the freezer for another day.*

This is the very best apple pie I've ever tasted, but that's not by luck. It might just be pastry and apples, but how you make that pastry and which apples and sugar you choose are what make all the difference. And as you can see from the pictures (page 351), I like to have some fun with how an apple pie looks, so as I'm rolling out pastry for multiple pies (see tip) and I start to run out, I love that it challenges me to do lots of different and exciting patterns. Remember, it's those little details that really count.

To make the pastry, chop the butter into 1cm chunks and pop into the freezer until super-cold. Put the flour, a good pinch of sea salt, the golden caster sugar and cold butter into a food processor and pulse until just combined but still a little chunky. Pour in 150ml of ice-cold water and pulse again until it just forms a very rough dough. At this point, use your hands to bring the dough together into two equal flat rounds, wrap them in clingfilm and pop into the fridge to rest for at least 1 hour.

Meanwhile, for the filling, peel and core the apples. Cut half into rough chunks and quarters, and the other half into 1cm chunks, then squeeze over the lemon juice to prevent them from turning brown. Melt the butter and muscovado sugar in a large saucepan on a medium heat, then add the cinnamon. When the mixture starts to bubble, add the chunkier half-batch of apples and cook for around 10 minutes, or until they start to soften but are still holding their shape. Stir in the rest of the apples and cook for a further 4 minutes, then take off the heat and leave to cool completely.

Preheat the oven to 190°C/375°F/gas 5. On a flour-dusted surface, roll out one piece of pastry, turning and dusting with flour as you go, until it's 3mm thick. Loosely roll the pastry around your rolling pin, then unroll it over a 26cm pie dish, making sure you have a decent overhang. Pile the filling into the pie dish and gently pat it down. Whisk the egg and brush around the edges of the pastry. Roll out the remaining piece of pastry and use your rolling pin again to unroll it on top of the pie – let it sink naturally onto the apples, then gently press down at the edges. Trim off any excess (feel free to decorate the top), then crimp the edges together with a fork or by pinching with your fingers. Eggwash the top of the pie, then scatter over the demerara sugar from a height. Cut a cross in the middle, then bake at the bottom of the oven for 50 minutes to 1 hour, or until golden. Serve with lashings of custard or cream.

✕ JAMAICAN GINGER CAKE ✕

SERVES 10

1 HOUR 20 MINUTES
PLUS COOLING
359 CALORIES

125g dark soft brown sugar

100g golden syrup

115g black treacle

75ml spiced dark rum

150ml semi-skimmed milk

1 thumb-sized piece of ginger

4 balls of stem ginger in syrup

115g unsalted butter, plus extra for
    greasing (at room temperature)

225g self-raising flour

1 teaspoon bicarbonate of soda

1 teaspoon ground cinnamon

1 teaspoon ground ginger

1 large egg

ICING

100g icing sugar

1 clementine

Many of us grew up enjoying some kind of ginger cake – my mum had a good recipe, so did my nan, and there'd always be a load on sale down at my local village hall, but the quality of ingredients you can get these days is off the hook. It's not just dried ginger any more, this cake embraces fresh ginger and stem ginger in syrup too. Not only that, some good Jamaican spiced rum makes this just the best ginger cake ever, and it lasts really well. Dark, spicy and delicious, this is definitely one for your comfort repetoire.

Place a medium pan on a low heat and add the sugar, golden syrup, treacle, rum and milk. Cook for a few minutes to dissolve the sugar, then increase to a medium heat and bring to the boil, then remove. Peel the fresh ginger, then finely grate into the mixture along with half of the stem ginger. Stir, then leave to cool completely.

Meanwhile, preheat the oven to 170°C/325°F/gas 3. Grease a 1.5-litre loaf tin and line with greaseproof paper. Put the flour, bicarbonate of soda, cinnamon and ground ginger into a food processor, cube and add the butter, then pulse to fine crumbs.

Once the syrupy pan mixture has cooled, beat in the flour mixture. Crack in the egg and beat until you have a smooth, runny batter, then pour into the prepared tin and bake for around 50 minutes, or until evenly coloured and just cooked through – you want it to still be a bit sticky in the middle. Leave to cool in the tin for 10 minutes, then turn out onto a wire rack to cool completely. Sift the icing sugar into a bowl, then finely grate in the clementine zest and squeeze in just enough juice to give you a thick but spoonable icing. Once the cake is cool, drizzle the icing over the top (as you can see from the picture, if you're not patient enough like me, half of your icing will run straight off, which is not what you want!). Matchstick the remaining 2 balls of stem ginger, sprinkle down the centre of the cake, then let the icing set before serving.

× HUMMINGBIRD CAKE ×

SERVES 14

1 HOUR
PLUS COOLING
684 CALORIES

250ml olive oil, plus extra
  for greasing

350g self-raising flour

1 level teaspoon ground cinnamon

350g golden caster sugar

4 medium very ripe bananas

1 x 425g tin of pineapple chunks

2 large eggs

1 teaspoon vanilla extract

50g pecans

ICING

400g icing sugar

150g unsalted butter
  (at room temperature)

200g cream cheese

2 limes

BRITTLE

100g caster sugar

50g pecans

Quite simply, this beautiful cake is bloody delicious – bake it, and get it in your gob. Light fluffy sponge with banana and pineapple galore, a crunchy dusting of pecan brittle, and a little reminder that zesty cream cheese icings rock – it's near perfection. For special occasions, to treat your loved ones, or purely for those moments when you just need a good slice of cake, this hummingbird beauty is guaranteed to hit the spot.

Preheat the oven to 180°C/350°F/gas 4. Grease and line two 23cm loose-bottomed cake tins. Sift the flour and cinnamon into a mixing bowl, then add the sugar and a large pinch of sea salt. Peel the bananas and mash them up with a fork in another bowl. Drain and finely chop the pineapple and add to the bananas with the oil, eggs and vanilla extract. Mix until combined, then fold into the dry mixture until smooth. Finely chop the pecans and gently fold in, then divide the batter evenly between your prepared tins. Bake for 35 to 40 minutes, or until risen, golden and the sponges spring back when touched lightly in the centre. Run a knife around the edge of the tins, then leave to cool for 10 minutes before transferring to wire racks to cool completely.

Meanwhile, to make the icing, sift the icing sugar into a free-standing electric mixer, add the butter and beat until pale and creamy. Add the cream cheese, finely grate in the zest of 1 lime and a little squeeze of juice, then beat until just smooth – it's really important not to over-mix it. Keep in the fridge until needed. To make a brittle topping, place the caster sugar and a splash of water in a non-stick frying pan on a medium heat. Shake flat and don't stir it, just swirl the pan occasionally until dissolved and lightly golden. Add the pecans and a pinch of salt, spoon around to coat, and when nicely golden, pour onto a sheet of oiled greaseproof paper to set (check out the video on jamieoliver.com/how-to). Once cool, smash up to a dust (you'll need about half to top the cake – save the rest for sprinkling over ice cream, see pages 342–5).

To assemble the cake, place one sponge on a cake stand and spread with half the icing. Top with the other sponge, spread over the rest of the icing, then grate over the zest of the remaining lime. Scatter over the brittle dust and decorate with a few edible flowers, such as violas, borage or herb flowers, if you feel that way inclined. With a cup of tea on the side, this will make everyone who eats it extremely happy. Serve in a bluebell wood on a fallen tree, as you do.

✕ DEVIL'S DOUBLE CHOC MALT COOKIES ✕

MAKES 24
40 MINUTES
PLUS CHILLING
181 CALORIES

50g unsalted butter

200g quality dark chocolate (70%)

1 x 397g tin of condensed milk

25g ground almonds

2 heaped teaspoons Horlicks

200g self-raising flour

100g Maltesers

50g quality white chocolate

I was very young when the realization of the joy of the cookie hit me. I've never really met anyone that doesn't like a freshly baked cookie, and if anything, since I was a kid it's just become easier to get pre-made commercial, average, frankly boring cookies. So for me, baking your own is the only way to pass that perfection down the family to the next generation. The problem is, what flavour to choose – there's so many. Well, I've made it easy for you – this in my view is the best flavour combo. Bake these, and your face will hurt because you'll be smiling, chewing and gurning for another one.

Melt the butter and chocolate in a pan on a low heat until smooth and combined, stirring occasionally. Remove from the heat and stir in the condensed milk, followed by the almonds and Horlicks. Sift in the flour and a pinch of sea salt, mix together, then chill in the fridge for 20 to 30 minutes (no longer). Once cool, but still pliable, smash up the Maltesers and roughly chop the white chocolate, then mix it all together.

Preheat the oven to 170°C/325°F/gas 3. Divide the mixture into 24 equal-sized balls and place on a couple of large baking trays lined with greaseproof paper. Flatten each a little – like squashed golf balls (you can freeze them at this stage to bake another day if you like) – then bake for around 12 minutes, or until chewy in the middle and firm at the edges. Leave to sit in the tray for 5 minutes, then transfer to a wire rack to cool.

If you want to take these devilish cookies to another level, either sandwich 2 cookies with a good spoonful of your favourite ice cream (pages 342–5), or even some homemade marshmallow (page 372), and squeeze . . . heaven, or simply drizzle all the cookies with melted chocolate while they cool . . . amazing!

♔

BONKERS

BREAD & BUTTER

PANETTONE PUDDING TART

BONKERS BREAD & BUTTER PANETTONE PUDDING TART

SERVES 12–14

1 HOUR
PLUS RESTING
548 CALORIES

125g unsalted butter, plus extra
for greasing

4 tablespoons demerara sugar

750g plain panettone

1 vanilla pod

300ml double cream

300ml whole milk

5 large eggs

100g golden caster sugar

60g quality dark chocolate (70%)

60g bitter orange marmalade

OK guys, we all know we love bread and butter pudding, but it's time for a change. This version is super-fun – ripping up a panettone, layering it with chocolate, marmalade and custard, then baking it until golden and gorgeous in a tart tin. It's a total showstopper, unexpected, and from a flavour and comfort perspective I'm sure there won't be much conversation happening round the table when you bring this bad boy out.

Preheat the oven to 180°C/350°F/gas 4. Lightly grease a 28cm loose-bottomed tart tin. Bash 2 tablespoons of demerara sugar in a pestle and mortar until fine, then mix with the remaining demerara so you have a range of textures. Tip into the tart tin and shake around to coat. Tap gently, then tip any excess back into the mortar for later. Slice the edges off the panettone in strips and use them to line the base and sides of the tart tin, pressing down hard to compact and create a pastry-like shell.

Halve the vanilla pod lengthways and scrape out the seeds, then put both seeds and pod into a pan on a medium heat, along with the cream, milk and butter, and simmer for 5 minutes, or until the butter has melted. Meanwhile, in a large bowl, whisk the eggs and golden caster sugar for 2 minutes, or until smooth. Whisking constantly, add the hot cream mixture to the bowl until combined, then discard the vanilla pod.

Now it's time to build this crazy comfort pudding. Pour one-third of the custard into the base of the tart and leave to soak in for a couple of minutes. Meanwhile, tear up all the remaining panettone into rough chunks, soak them in the bowl of creamy custard for a minute or two (the more it sucks in, the better!), then layer up in the shell you've created, snapping up and adding little chunks of chocolate and dollops of marmalade between the layers – there's no need to be neat about it, you want a range of heights, saturation and textures. Pour over any leftover custard, leaving it to soak in if necessary, then sprinkle with the remaining demerara sugar. Bake for around 25 minutes, or until set. Allow the pudding to rest for 10 minutes, then serve with cream, custard or ice cream, if you like – it's delicious cold too, if you've got any leftovers!

× RHUBARB & POTTED CUSTARD ×

SERVES 8

1 HOUR 20 MINUTES
PLUS CHILLING
445 CALORIES

CUSTARD

3 sheets of gelatine (5g)

500ml semi-skimmed milk

300ml double cream

1 vanilla pod

75g golden caster sugar

20g custard powder

RHUBARB

600g forced rhubarb

100g golden caster sugar

optional: 1 tablespoon
    balsamic vinegar

1 tablespoon rose water

2 oranges

CRUMBLE

25g crystallized ginger

50g unsalted butter (cold)

50g light brown muscovado sugar

100g plain flour

TO SERVE

extra virgin olive oil

Rhubarb and custard is a totally classic combination in any form, whether it's just as your nan used to make it, a boiled sweet in a bag or this little beauty. The potted custard just subtly nods towards an Italian panna cotta, but I'm mixing up the texture with the crumbly bits on top – yum. These are brilliant when you want to get ahead for a dinner party, or just to have ready-made in the fridge for an ad hoc delicious dessert.

To make the custard, soak the gelatine in ice-cold water to soften. Pour 400ml of milk and the cream into a pan. Halve the vanilla pod lengthways and scrape out the seeds, add both pod and seeds to the pan, then simmer gently for 10 minutes. In a bowl, dissolve the sugar and custard powder in the remaining 100ml of milk. Pour half the infused milk into the bowl and whisk together, then pour that back into the pan and simmer for 5 more minutes, whisking regularly. Drain the gelatine sheets and whisk them into the custard, still on the heat, until dissolved, then pass through a sieve. Divide between 8 small ramekins or pots, leave to cool, then cover with clingfilm (make sure it's not touching the custard) and pop into the fridge overnight to set.

Trim and cut the rhubarb into 5cm batons, then lay in a single layer in a snug-fitting baking dish. Sprinkle over the sugar, balsamic (if using) and rose water, then squeeze over the orange juice. Cook at the bottom of the oven for 25 minutes, or until the rhubarb has softened, but still holds its shape. Leave to cool.

Meanwhile, to make the crumble, preheat the oven to 180°C/350°F/gas 4. Finely chop the crystallized ginger, then put into a food processor and pulse with all the remaining crumble ingredients until a chunky crumble forms. Scatter over a baking tray, gently pinching the crumble together to create some bigger pieces so you have a range of textures, and bake for 20 to 25 minutes, or until dark golden, turning halfway.

To serve, pour some boiling water into a bowl, submerge three-quarters of each custard pot for about 15 seconds, or until you can see the edge coming away from the pot, then turn out onto a plate. Repeat, then divide the rhubarb and its beautiful juice between the plates and break and scatter over the crumble (serving any extra in a little bowl so everyone can help themselves to more as they tuck in). Add a few drops of quality extra virgin olive oil, which will be bizarrely good, and if you've got any edible flowers like violas or pansies, a few of their petals camps it up even more.

✕ BRAZILIAN TEARDROP DOUGHNUTS ✕

MAKES 50

1 HOUR 15 MINUTES
92 CALORIES
(PER DOUGHNUT)

BOOZY CHOCOLATE SAUCE

1 lime

1 orange

100g golden caster sugar

50ml cachaça or light rum

200g dark chocolate (70%)

100ml single cream

SPICED SUGAR

120g golden caster sugar

1 tablespoon ground cinnamon

DOUGHNUTS

vegetable oil

270g plain flour

50g golden caster sugar

2 large eggs

400ml buttermilk

1 heaped tablespoon
   baking powder

I've evolved these amazing doughnuts from the brilliant Portuguese 'bolinhos de chuva', which roughly translates as 'little cakes of rain', and that's reflected in their delightful shape. Mums, nans and aunties are said to make these when it's cold and rainy, to put a little smile on the kids' faces. I couldn't resist doing an adults' version by adding Brazilian cachaça to some oozy chocolate sauce to serve with them. They were so good, they sent people into a state of emotional bliss, thus me renaming them 'teardrop' doughnuts – a little homage to the energy and fun Brazilians seem to apply to most things in life.

To make the sauce, finely zest and juice the lime and orange into a small pan, add the sugar and cachaça or rum and place over a high heat. Reduce by one-third, then remove from the heat. Bash up and add the chocolate and stir with a spatula until melted, then whisk in the cream and either leave to cool, or keep in a warm place until needed. To make the spiced sugar, simply mix the sugar and cinnamon on a tray.

For the doughnuts, just under half fill a large sturdy pan with oil – it should be 8cm deep, but never fill your pan more than half full – and place on a medium to high heat. Use a thermometer to get it to 180°C, or add a small drop of the batter as it's heating up and when it's dark golden and floating you'll be about right. Meanwhile, to make the doughnut batter, mix the flour, ½ a teaspoon of sea salt and the sugar together in a bowl. In a second bowl, whisk the eggs into the buttermilk one-by-one, then slowly pour into the dry ingredients, beating constantly with a whisk until perfectly smooth. Just before you start cooking, stir through the baking powder, then add heaped teaspoons of batter to the hot oil. The technique is to use one spoon for the batter, hold it over the oil and use another spoon to ease it off, but let gravity actually take it off the spoon just like a teardrop (beware of splashes). Cook 6 to 8 at a time, frying them for about 3 minutes, and turning with a slotted spoon until golden all over. Scoop out, drain quickly on kitchen paper, then toss in the spiced sugar.

I like to pour the chocolate sauce over a board or serving platter, then dot over the hot doughnuts and let everyone tuck in, so that the sauce gets nice and evenly distributed – a few gratings of lime zest over the top is delicious too.

× MOLTEN CHEESECAKE ×

SERVES 12

1 HOUR
PLUS CHILLING
709 CALORIES

½ x magnificent marshmallows (page 372) or 300g quality shop-bought marshmallows

175g unsalted butter, plus extra for greasing

250g dark chocolate digestives

100g Hobnobs

2 vanilla pods

100g caster sugar

3 tablespoons cornflour

900g full-fat cream cheese (at room temperature)

125g soured cream

2 large eggs

BERRY DRIZZLE

250g raspberries, plus extra to serve

50g caster sugar

1 lemon

1 teaspoon good balsamic vinegar

I'm not really sure what to say about this dessert. It's horribly beautiful, deliciously filthy and very naughty on the nutrition front, but it's a wicked one-off treat. Creamy vanilla cheesecake with the ultimate biscuit base, covered in molten marshmallow with a tart berry drizzle – wow. It's going to put humongous smiles on all your lucky friends' faces.

Make the magnificent marshmallows (page 372). Preheat the oven to 170°C/325°F/gas 3, and grease the bottom and sides of a 23cm loose-bottomed cake tin. Melt the butter in a pan over a medium heat. Finely crush all the biscuits, then mix them with the melted butter. Lightly and evenly press them into the base of the prepared tin and bake in the oven for 10 minutes, then remove and leave to cool.

Halve the vanilla pods lengthways, scrape out the seeds and place in a bowl along with the sugar, cornflour, cream cheese and soured cream. Beat well with an electric hand whisk on a high speed until creamy, adding the eggs one at a time. Once smooth and fluffy, pour the mixture onto the biscuit base, smooth out the top, then bake in the centre of the oven for 40 minutes, or until lightly golden. Leaving it in the tin, allow to cool, then place in the fridge for at least 4 hours, or until needed.

To make the berry drizzle, blitz the raspberries in a blender with the sugar, a squeeze of lemon juice and the balsamic. Have a taste and tweak with more lemon juice or sugar if needed. You can serve it like this, or push it through a coarse sieve to make it super-smooth, if you're like me and hate raspberry seeds!

When you're ready to serve, tear up the marshmallows, dot over the top of the cheesecake and whack under the grill on a medium heat for 3 to 5 minutes, or until golden and melted. Keep an eye on it, as it can burn easily (if you do catch a few bits because you weren't concentrating – it does happen – you can often just remove the burnt bits with a spoon and pop back under the grill; don't stress about it). Leave to sit for a few minutes, then run a palette knife carefully around the diameter of the tin to loosen. Release the clasp and carefully remove the tin, allowing the marshmallow to ooze down the sides, then you're ready to plate up. As well as the all-important tart berry drizzle, it's good served with more fresh raspberries on the side too.

× MAGNIFICENT MARSHMALLOWS ×

MAKES 32 PIECES

50 MINUTES
PLUS COOLING
75 CALORIES (PER PIECE)

50g cornflour

50g icing sugar

50g liquid glucose syrup (get it from
  the supermarket or a chemist)

450g caster sugar

10 sheets of gelatine

2 large egg whites

2 vanilla pods

optional: 1½ teaspoons natural
  food colouring

CHOOSE YOUR FLAVOUR

rose water

orange blossom water

natural lemon extract

natural orange extract

natural peppermint extract

Making and serving marshmallows is just one of those magnificently therapeutic, fun things to do. It's kind of weird, but feels like magic – and as much as I love a homemade marshmallow (which does taste better than a bought one), it's the outrageous pleasure that they give my kids when they taste that freshly made gooey delicious treat that's important for me. And they make really good presents and gifts. You can cut and shape them however you please, and flavour them in really fun ways, toast them over fires, melt them over cheesecake (page 370), have them sandwiched between chocolate-drizzled cookies (page 360) or even melted over ice cream (pages 342–5). Heaven!

This is a precise recipe, so make sure you read through the method carefully before you start, get all your ingredients weighed out and get your equipment ready to go. You'll be working with hot sugar and syrups, so it's best to keep your kids out of the kitchen until those marshmallows are cooling, ready to eat.

Sift the cornflour and icing sugar into a bowl. Finely sift half the mixture over a deep baking tray (20cm x 30cm) and set the other half aside in the sieve until later. Mix the liquid glucose syrup and caster sugar together in a pan over a low heat with 250ml of cold water. Heat gently, stirring until all the sugar has dissolved and you have a clear syrup. Meanwhile, soak the gelatine leaves in a small pan with 125ml of water.

Once the sugar syrup is clear, turn up the heat, pop in a sugar thermometer and allow the syrup to boil vigorously (please don't stir it). When it reaches 110°C, place the gelatine pan over a medium heat and stir until dissolved. Whisk the egg whites in a free-standing electric mixer until you have stiff peaks. Once your syrup has reached 122°C, very carefully and slowly pour it down the sides of the bowl of the moving mixer, then pour in the dissolved gelatine. Halve the vanilla pods lengthways and scrape out the seeds, add the seeds to the mixer bowl, then continue to whisk for 6 to 8 minutes, or until the mixture has significantly increased in volume, but is thick and still pourable. You can have a plain white vanilla marshmallow, or you can add any of the flavours listed, to taste (remembering to start small as you can always add more, but you can't take it away!). Add any natural food colouring at the same time (if using) – I like to try to match the colour of the marshmallow to the flavour I'm using, whisking for a further 2 to 3 minutes to give you a nice even colour and flavour. Either way, pour the marshmallow mixture into your prepared tray, use a palette knife to smooth it out, then sift over the remaining mixed cornflour and icing sugar and leave somewhere cool for 2 to 3 hours, or until set and soft.

✕ BEAUTIFUL BLACK FOREST GATEAU ✕

SERVES 12

2 HOURS
PLUS COOLING
836 CALORIES

SPONGE

185g unsalted butter, plus extra
  for greasing

150g quality dark chocolate (70%)

125ml semi-skimmed milk

175g self-raising flour

225g golden caster sugar

150g soft light brown sugar

1 tablespoon cocoa powder

3 large eggs

75ml buttermilk

FILLINGS & TOPPINGS

700ml double cream

25ml Kirsch

1 tablespoon runny honey

100g quality dark chocolate (70%),
  plus extra to serve

1 vanilla pod

50g icing sugar

75g shelled hazelnuts

1 x 370g pack of quality all-natural
  cherry pie filling

1 packet of popping candy

Without doubt this is one of the most indulgent and famous desserts of the 70s and 80s. So this is our opportunity to take this wonderful Germanic dessert from the Black Forest region and let it relive its original glory with gorgeous fluffy sponge, Chantilly cream, chocolate ganache and smacks of cherry, all of which will seduce you into a chocolate gateau coma. This is a big, bold, fun, special occasion dessert.

Preheat the oven to 150°C/300°F/gas 2. Grease and line a deep 20cm loose-bottomed cake tin. Snap the chocolate into a medium pan, then add the butter, milk and a pinch of sea salt. Place over a low heat until melted together, then remove and leave to cool slightly while you mix the flour, sugars and cocoa powder together in a large bowl, then beat in the eggs, one-by-one. Beat the buttermilk into the melted chocolate mixture, then stir that into the egg mixture. Pour into your prepared cake tin, using a spatula to smooth out the top. Bake for 1 hour 10 minutes, or until cooked through. To check, poke a skewer into the middle – if it comes out clean it's cooked. Leave to cool in the tin for 5 minutes, then transfer to a wire rack to cool completely.

Meanwhile, make the ganache. Put 200ml of cream, the Kirsch and honey into a pan over a medium heat and bring to a simmer. Snap the chocolate into a heatproof bowl. Pour the creamy mixture over the chocolate, whisking until smooth and shiny. For the Chantilly cream, pour the remaining cream into a bowl. Halve the vanilla pod lengthways, scrape out the seeds and add them to the cream. Sift in the icing sugar, then whisk to soft peaks and leave in the fridge until needed. Toast the hazelnuts in a pan on a medium heat until golden, then lightly crush in a pestle and mortar.

Cut the sponge horizontally into 3 rounds (check out jamieoliver.com/how-to for guidance). Brush the base sponge with a few tablespoons of cherry pie filling, then spread over half the ganache and one third of the Chantilly cream. Drizzle over a few more tablespoons of cherry pie filling, then sprinkle with a little popping candy and one third of the crushed hazelnuts. Repeat these layers again, place the remaining sponge on top, then pipe or spoon on the rest of the cream. Scatter with the rest of the hazelnuts, drizzle with some of the cherry pie filling juice, if you like, then shave and scatter over some chocolate (there's a video on jamieoliver.com/how-to to show you how to do this). This is really nice served with fridge-cold, super-ripe fresh cherries, whenever they're in season.

☓ TUTTI FRUTTI PEAR TARTE TATIN ☓

SERVES 6–8
1 HOUR
499 CALORIES

3 firm pears, such as
  Conference, Williams

25ml amaretto

150g caster sugar

50g unsalted butter

1 vanilla pod

2 fresh bay leaves

1 orange

1 handful of flaked almonds

375g all-butter puff pastry

plain flour, for dusting

Having made tarte tatins for twenty-odd years, I've always found them exciting, and everyone seems to just love the caramelized, almost burnt edges that you get on the pastry. Here I've used vanilla, bay, and citrus to create the most unusually wonderful tutti frutti-style caramel that works a treat with the beautiful fresh pears.

Preheat the oven to 200°C/400°F/gas 6. Peel the pears, then cut some into halves and some into quarters, removing the stalks and any woody bits from the core. In a shallow bowl, drizzle them with the amaretto and leave aside.

Place a 26cm non-stick ovenproof frying pan on a medium-low heat, then sprinkle in the sugar in an even layer. Once lightly golden, chop and dot in the butter and carefully melt everything together, but don't stir it – just gently swirl the pan to combine. Give it a good 5 minutes, and when it's a deep dark golden colour, halve the vanilla pod lengthways and scrape out the seeds, then add both pod and seeds to the pan along with the bay leaves. Use a speed-peeler to strip in the zest from half the orange. Position the pears in the pan in a single layer, being careful not to touch the caramel, sprinkle over the flaked almonds, then turn up to medium-high and cook for 5 to 6 minutes to soften the pears – you want the juices to cook away so you're left with a thick caramel.

Meanwhile, roll out the pastry on a flour-dusted surface so it's about 3cm bigger than the pan all the way round and just under 1cm thick. Carefully place over the pears, tucking in all the excess around them and in under itself at the edges, creating little waves. Bake for 20 to 25 minutes, or until the pastry is puffed up and golden and the edges are dark and caramelized (don't worry if they get really dark – it's all good).

When the time's up, carefully remove from the oven – remember the handle will be hot too! Place a large board, platter or plate on top of the pan, then, using a couple of tea towels to protect your hands, confidently, carefully and swiftly flip it over – if you let it cool down too much in the pan, it's more likely to stick, so it's best to get it out while it's hot. Drizzle any juices that escape back over the fruit, and serve with a drizzle of single cream, a nice scoop of ice cream or lashings of custard.

× GERMAN COFFEE CAKE ×

SERVES 18

1 HOUR 25 MINUTES
PLUS COOLING
318 CALORIES

STREUSEL

150g unsalted butter, plus extra
    for greasing

150g plain flour

½ teaspoon baking powder

100g golden caster sugar

CARAMEL

100g caster sugar

½ teaspoon granulated instant
    coffee

SPONGE

225g unsalted butter
    (at room temperature)

225g golden caster sugar

4 large eggs

225g self-raising flour

½ teaspoon baking powder

50ml espresso (cold)

1 teaspoon granulated
    instant coffee

2 tablespoons Camp coffee

This is my homage to the brilliant German or Saxon Streuselkuchen, which translates as sprinkle or crumb cake, as it has a wonderful crumble-like topping over a gorgeous spongy cake. It's known to be a coffee cake, not because it has coffee in it (until now!), but because it was always eaten with whipped cream and a mug of coffee at teatime, to tide you over until supper. I've evolved this recipe by putting three types of coffee in it – it smells absolutely incredible as it bakes, and is great served still warm, with coffee or tea.

Preheat the oven to 180°C/350°F/gas 4. Grease and line a deep baking tray (30cm x 35cm), and line another baking tray with greaseproof paper. Make a caramel by sprinkling the sugar into a small non-stick pan with a splash of water over a high heat and leaving for a few minutes (swirl it gently, but don't stir). Once golden, sprinkle in the granulated coffee, then pour the caramel onto the greaseproof paper-lined tray and leave to cool and set. For the streusel, cube the butter and put into a bowl with the flour, baking powder and sugar, then rub together with your fingertips until you have fine crumbs. Place in the fridge to chill until needed.

Next make the sponge batter. Cream the butter and sugar together until pale and fluffy. Beat in the eggs one-by-one, then fold in the flour and baking powder with a metal spoon. Mix in the cold espresso, granulated and Camp coffees, then transfer to the deep lined tray and smooth out into an even layer. Smash up the caramel into small bits and mix with your chilled streusel mixture. Rustically sprinkle half of it over the sponge batter from a height, then get the other half of the mixture and squeeze and clump bits together with your fingers. Drop these in and around the sponge as well – it's a rustic finish, so being uneven is all good. Bake for around 35 minutes, or until golden and cooked through. Leave to cool for 10 minutes, then turn out onto a wire rack to cool completely. Pop the kettle on, then slice and serve.

PEANUT BUTTER & JELLY

BROWNIES

. . . .

× PEANUT BUTTER & JELLY BROWNIES ×

SERVES 15

1 HOUR
PLUS COOLING
411 CALORIES

CUSTARD

250ml semi-skimmed milk

1 vanilla pod

2 large egg yolks

50g golden caster sugar

1 heaped tablespoon cornflour

20g unsalted butter
  (at room temperature)

2 heaped tablespoons smooth
  peanut butter

BROWNIES

230g unsalted butter, plus extra
  for greasing

250g quality dark chocolate (70%)

230g golden caster sugar

4 large eggs

150g plain flour

2 tablespoons raspberry jam

75g fresh raspberries

Frankly, this is an outrageous little recipe. I don't know why, but the somewhat confused combo of peanut butter and jelly always succeeds in putting a very large smile on people's faces, so let's embrace it. And by the way, jelly means jam in this context (that's what it's called in the US where this unlikely combo is most famous). You can use any wonderful seasonal jam you can get your hands on – raspberries, strawberries, blackcurrants or cherries when paired with chocolate, all feel good.

To make the custard, put the milk into a pan, halve the vanilla pod lengthways and scrape out the seeds, then add both pod and seeds to the pan and lightly simmer on the hob, stirring occasionally. Meanwhile, in a bowl, use a balloon whisk to combine the egg yolks, sugar, cornflour and soft butter. Whisking constantly, gradually pour the hot milk into the bowl, until combined. Return the custard mixture to the pan, place over a low heat and stir gently for 2 to 3 minutes, or until thickened. Stir in the peanut butter, then leave the custard to cool completely.

Preheat the oven to 180°C/350°F/gas 4. For the brownies, grease and line a deep baking tray (20cm x 30cm). Melt the butter in a non-stick pan on a very low heat, then snap up and add the chocolate. Stir regularly with a spatula until melted and combined, then remove from the heat and stir in the sugar. Leave to cool slightly, then whisk in the eggs, one at a time, until silky. Sift in the flour and mix well.

Pour the chocolatey brownie mix into the prepared tray, then swirl through the chilled nutty custard (discarding the vanilla pod). Erratically distribute little spoonfuls of jam over the surface, then poke in the fresh raspberries (or any other fresh seasonal berries that correspond with the jam you're using). Bake for around 25 minutes, or until cooked on the outside but still a bit gooey in the middle. Leave to cool for 1 hour if you can bear it, then cut into portions and serve.

× ULTIMATE HOT CHOCOLATE ×

MAKES 1 JAR
(16 SERVINGS)
15 MINUTES
PLUS CHILLING
222 CALORIES

200g quality dark chocolate (70%),
  plus extra to serve

100g quality cocoa powder

100g icing sugar

50g cornflour

50g Horlicks

Hot chocolate is undoubtedly a beautiful thing. In recent years, wonderful artisan chocolate makers have started serving some incredible hot chocolates using just water, chocolate and spices, no dairy. These really reflect the fineness of chocolate, so I did consider this style when giving you the ultimate in hot chocolate recipes, but something didn't sit quite right with me. If I'm honest, I'm looking for something a little more trashy and naughty. What I've come up with here is the best of both worlds, using great chocolate and cocoa but thickening it up. These quantities make enough for 16 servings, so make a batch, pop it in a jar, and simply use it whenever you fancy – boom – to create the perfect mugful. You could even give a jar to your friends as a gift.

Place the chocolate in the fridge for 30 minutes, then unwrap and blitz until fine in a food processor. Add the rest of the ingredients with a good pinch of sea salt, and pulse until nicely mixed. Decant into an airtight jar, pop the lid on and give it a good shake up, then pop on your shelf until you're ready for the perfect mug of chocolatey heaven.

To make a hot chocolate, simply put 2 heaped tablespoons of mixture and 1 mug of milk per person into a pan. Bring to a simmer over a medium heat for 5 minutes, whisking regularly, then pour your thickened, silky, frothy hot chocolate into mugs and top with an extra grating of chocolate. Leave to cool just a little, then sit back, relax and indulge.

Feel free to embellish your mug of hot chocolate with a little extra deliciousness – a few marshmallows, a dollop of whipping cream, a pinch of cinnamon, a little grating of white chocolate or nutmeg, even a bit of orange zest – the choice is yours.

× NUTRITION ×

16 — Calories 415kcal · Fat 21.1g · Saturates 10.8g · Carbs 17.3g · Sugar 12.1g

19 — Calories 334kcal · Fat 9.6g · Saturates 3.7g · Carbs 55.5g · Sugar 3.7g

24 — Calories 508kcal · Fat 19.9g · Saturates 9.9g · Carbs 64.2g · Sugar 5.8g

28 — Calories 450kcal · Fat 15.1g · Saturates 3.9g · Carbs 51.7g · Sugar 10.3g

34 — Calories 690kcal · Fat 29.2g · Saturates 9.6g · Carbs 73.5g · Sugar 16.7g

36 — Calories 430kcal · Fat 17.2g · Saturates 7.0g · Carbs 44.4g · Sugar 7.8g

40 — Calories 388kcal · Fat 12.2g · Saturates 4.7g · Carbs 49.7g · Sugar 10.3g

42 — Calories 530kcal · Fat 33.0g · Saturates 13.0g · Carbs 41.8g · Sugar 9.0g

46 — Calories 817kcal · Fat 44.1g · Saturates 9.3g · Carbs 61.5g · Sugar 28.1g

50 — Calories 242kcal · Fat 17.1g · Saturates 8.2g · Carbs 14.6g · Sugar 2.8g

50 — Calories 388kcal · Fat 8.7g · Saturates 3.5g · Carbs 68.8g · Sugar 3.2g

52 — Calories 878kcal · Fat 40.7g · Saturates 16.4g · Carbs 77.6g · Sugar 4.5g

58 — Calories 363kcal · Fat 22.0g · Saturates 8.8g · Carbs 9.9g · Sugar 4.9g

61 — Calories 316kcal · Fat 5.7g · Saturates 1.7g · Carbs 45.9g · Sugar 6.2g

64 — Calories 828kcal · Fat 49.5g · Saturates 5.9g · Carbs 58.5g · Sugar 2.6g

66 — Calories 330kcal · Fat 20.3g · Saturates 2.4g · Carbs 34.8g · Sugar 1.2g

68 — Calories 605kcal · Fat 48.4g · Saturates 9.0g · Carbs 32.5g · Sugar 15.2g

72 — Calories 498kcal · Fat 31.4g · Saturates 8.6g · Carbs 17.9g · Sugar 13.0g

74 — Calories 204kcal · Fat 11.3g · Saturates 1.7g · Carbs 20.6g · Sugar 7.9g

78 — Calories 764kcal · Fat 34.1g · Saturates 10.2g · Carbs 86.4g · Sugar 10.3g

	80		90		94		98		100
Calories 317kcal		Calories 505kcal		Calories 694kcal		Calories 738kcal		Calories 981kcal	
Fat 15.2g		Fat 27g		Fat 38.1g		Fat 34.5g		Fat 35.0g	
Saturates 3.7g		Saturates 5.3g		Saturates 14.5g		Saturates 8.3g		Saturates 6.4g	
Carbs 10.2g		Carbs 40.1g		Carbs 37.3g		Carbs 61.8g		Carbs 119.2g	
Sugar 7.3g		Sugar 19.8g		Sugar 8.0g		Sugar 10.9g		Sugar 13.5g	

	104		108		112		118		120
Calories 526kcal		Calories 535kcal		Calories 475kcal		Calories 450kcal		Calories 254kcal	
Fat 21.9g		Fat 12.7g		Fat 25.5g		Fat 28.6g		Fat 4.9g	
Saturates 8.3g		Saturates 2.8g		Saturates 4.4g		Saturates 6.0g		Saturates 0.6g	
Carbs 54.2g		Carbs 86.2g		Carbs 36.4g		Carbs 14.7g		Carbs 23.4g	
Sugar 7.6g		Sugar 19.3g		Sugar 6.7g		Sugar 10.5g		Sugar 19.5g	

	124		128		134		136		140
Calories 382kcal		Calories 282kcal		Calories 835kcal		Calories 299kcal		Calories 732kcal	
Fat 17.3g		Fat 12.7g		Fat 46.0g		Fat 7.1g		Fat 47.0g	
Saturates 4.1g		Saturates 6.3g		Saturates 20.8g		Saturates 2.2g		Saturates 10.4g	
Carbs 19.4g		Carbs 31.2g		Carbs 66.2g		Carbs 52.1g		Carbs 46.4g	
Sugar 15.8g		Sugar 1.7g		Sugar 9.6g		Sugar 11.8g		Sugar 4.7g	

	144		146		148		150		152
Calories 312kcal		Calories 490kcal		Calories 479kcal		Calories 502kcal		Calories 567kcal	
Fat 4.7g		Fat 23.5g		Fat 29.2g		Fat 33.5g		Fat 28.3g	
Saturates 1.2g		Saturates 10.6g		Saturates 6.7g		Saturates 6.1g		Saturates 11.8g	
Carbs 60.0g		Carbs 50.6g		Carbs 41.9g		Carbs 24.7g		Carbs 46.6g	
Sugar 8.4g		Sugar 11.0g		Sugar 6.4g		Sugar 12.7g		Sugar 10.4g	

	158		160		162		166		168
Calories 539kcal		Calories 309kcal		Calories 476kcal		Calories 291kcal		Calories 914kcal	
Fat 21.4g		Fat 24.1g		Fat 28.7g		Fat 11.4g		Fat 52.4g	
Saturates 6.6g		Saturates 4.2g		Saturates 7.7g		Saturates 3.8g		Saturates 17.8g	
Carbs 59.8g		Carbs 16.5g		Carbs 33.9g		Carbs 35.4g		Carbs 50.8g	
Sugar 24.6g		Sugar 2.0g		Sugar 2.5g		Sugar 8.9g		Sugar 2.5g	

172	174	176	180	182
Calories 457kcal	Calories 520kcal	Calories 655kcal	Calories 584kcal	Calories 718kcal
Fat 23.1g	Fat 33.9g	Fat 33.8g	Fat 16.5g	Fat 24.5g
Saturates 12.7g	Saturates 7.0g	Saturates 12.6g	Saturates 2.2g	Saturates 9.3g
Carbs 52.2g	Carbs 41.3g	Carbs 65.7g	Carbs 67.3g	Carbs 93.9g
Sugar 7.2g	Sugar 14.1g	Sugar 10.7g	Sugar 5.7g	Sugar 6.8g

184	188	192	194	198
Calories 442kcal	Calories 414kcal	Calories 494kcal	Calories 644kcal	Calories 84kcal
Fat 24.1g	Fat 15.1g	Fat 29.1g	Fat 14.5g	Fat 0g
Saturates 8.9g	Saturates 2.1g	Saturates 6.7g	Saturates 4.9g	Saturates 0g
Carbs 44.0g	Carbs 63g	Carbs 16.3g	Carbs 106.3g	Carbs 3.3g
Sugar 16.5g	Sugar 5.7g	Sugar 14.8g	Sugar 12.0g	Sugar 3.3g

198	199	199	204	208
Calories 165kcal	Calories 157kcal	Calories 192kcal	Calories 553kcal	Calories 279kcal
Fat 0.1g	Fat 0g	Fat 2.2g	Fat 28.5g	Fat 5.7g
Saturates 0g	Saturates 0g	Saturates 0.7g	Saturates 9.5g	Saturates 1.6g
Carbs 15.5g	Carbs 14.2g	Carbs 11.1g	Carbs 35.8g	Carbs 41.8g
Sugar 14.9g	Sugar 14.2g	Sugar 10.9g	Sugar 19.9g	Sugar 3.2g

210	214	222	224	228
Calories 755kcal	Calories 327kcal	Calories 500kcal	Calories 614kcal	Calories 650kcal
Fat 43.6g	Fat 11.9g	Fat 22.1g	Fat 36.2g	Fat 27.0g
Saturates 16.6g	Saturates 2.8g	Saturates 4.3g	Saturates 6.3g	Saturates 8.9g
Carbs 27.6g	Carbs 42.4g	Carbs 51.9g	Carbs 45.2g	Carbs 57.9g
Sugar 5.6g	Sugar 0.7g	Sugar 8.7g	Sugar 2.9g	Sugar 12.0g

232	236	238	244	246
Calories 436kcal	Calories 835kcal	Calories 716kcal	Calories 411kcal	Calories 436kcal
Fat 22.1g	Fat 48.9g	Fat 34.4g	Fat 15.1g	Fat 11.7g
Saturates 6.8g	Saturates 20g	Saturates 15.4g	Saturates 5.4g	Saturates 6.3g
Carbs 34.8g	Carbs 61.3g	Carbs 73g	Carbs 13.9g	Carbs 61.9g
Sugar 3.2g	Sugar 17.1g	Sugar 23.2g	Sugar 6.6g	Sugar 2.6g

#	Calories	Fat	Saturates	Carbs	Sugar
250	295kcal	21.0g	7.0g	0.2g	0g
252	223kcal	7.8g	4.2g	35.0g	4.6g
256	695kcal	39.4g	5.6g	46.0g	6.9g
258	133kcal	14.6g	2.2g	0g	0g
262	902kcal	66.5g	30.5g	36.1g	12.1g
266	435kcal	22.0g	10.4g	31.8g	12.5g
272	343kcal	18.7g	2.4g	22.6g	1.0g
282	455kcal	35.0g	21.8g	9.7g	3.7g
284	700kcal	23.2g	11.6g	97.6g	4.7g
286	849kcal	25.7g	13.9g	112.5g	15.5g
290	121kcal	4.3g	2.4g	18.7g	0.4g
292	523kcal	13.9g	3.4g	76.1g	23.6g
296	476kcal	17.8g	7.0g	59.5g	6.3g
300	451kcal	28.1g	9.2g	13.4g	11.9g
302	418kcal	22.7g	8.2g	30.6g	3.9g
306	673kcal	35.6g	17.7g	52.9g	6.2g
308	405kcal	17.4g	9.3g	48.8g	6.0g
312	380kcal	20.2g	11.5g	30.3g	10.0g
314	553kcal	22.3g	7.5g	60g	24.9g
320	331kcal	14.7g	9.2g	49.4g	48.6g
324	567kcal	34.4g	20.1g	63.9g	48.1g
328	503kcal	23.6g	14.8g	72.3g	59.5g
334	542kcal	33.7g	18.8g	55.6g	42.8g
338	317kcal	15.3g	8.4g	40.4g	16.4g
340	554kcal	36.8g	20.7g	48.3g	30.3g

Page	Calories	Fat	Saturates	Carbs	Sugar
342	127kcal	8.2g	4.6g	10.2g	10.2g
344	140kcal	9.5g	5.4g	10.4g	10.1g
344	144kcal	6.6g	3.7g	19.5g	19.5g
345	106kcal	6.1g	3.4g	10.1g	10.1g
345	106kcal	6.1g	3.4g	10.1g	10.1g
348	482kcal	24.6g	12.1g	61.0g	47.6g
352	590kcal	32.8g	18.8g	72.8g	34.2g
354	359kcal	10.7g	6.1g	62.1g	44.9g
358	684kcal	36.4g	11.0g	89.7g	69.0g
360	181kcal	8.1g	4.6g	24.9g	18.1g
364	548kcal	34.9g	17.9g	50.9g	29.4g
366	445kcal	26.7g	16.3g	49.4g	37.4g
368	92kcal	4.3g	1.7g	11.7g	7.3g
370	709kcal	49.4g	29.0g	63.2g	47.3g
372	75kcal	0g	0g	19.2g	17.0g
376	836kcal	58.7g	33.4g	72.8g	59.0g
378	499kcal	26.8g	15.2g	59.3g	35.1g
380	318kcal	19.0g	10.7g	35.3g	19.5g
384	411kcal	26.9g	14.6g	37.4g	27.2g
386	222kcal	8.4g	5.1g	29.9g	25.4g

THE JOB OF THE NUTRITION TEAM IS TO MAKE SURE THAT EVERY RECIPE JAMIE WRITES IS THE BEST IT CAN BE, WITHOUT COMPROMISING ON THE POINT OF THE DISH IN THE FIRST PLACE.

Every book has a different brief, and the nature of comfort food means that often the recipes in this book are indulgent. However, so that you can make an informed choice we have published the nutritional content for each recipe here, including figures per serving for calories, fat, saturated fat, carbohydrates and sugar. Remember that a healthy, balanced diet and regular exercise are the keys to a healthy lifestyle. For more information about our nutritional guidelines and how we analyse our recipes, please visit: jamieoliver.com/nutrition

Laura Parr – Head of Nutrition

FOOD STANDARDS

When it comes to buying ingredients, if it's within your means, I strongly advocate supporting higher welfare and sustainable options for meat, fish and eggs, plus anything containing egg, such as mayonnaise, egg noodles and pasta, as well as always choosing organic stock cubes.

When buying chicken or pork, the minimum standard I would recommend is RSPCA Freedom Food – start here, and upgrade to free-range or organic whenever you can. It's always good to buy beef from the country you live in, and if possible, opt for grass-fed cattle, which are healthier animals. British lamb is of a very high quality and is largely free roaming. And, be aware of sustainability when it comes to buying fish – look out for MSC-approved fish, or speak to your fishmonger to find out what's sustainably sourced.

Remember, buying a smaller amount of great-quality ingredients is a much better investment, and embrace seasonal produce to get stuff at its cheapest and at its best.

INGREDIENTS

You'll notice throughout the book that sometimes I've given you very specific recommendations for ingredients. This doesn't mean that you can't substitute in your own personal favourites; they're just the things that I believe will elevate your dish to that extra-special place and that are worth hunting out. So, for example, when I've suggested a certain type of wine for the base of a sauce or stew, the idea is that you can enjoy a glass of that wine when you serve up, safe in the knowledge that it's going to be a brilliant companion to your dish too.

SAFETY

Several of the recipes in this book require you to cook with hot oil. Please be extra careful and ensure there are no children or pets running around when you're cooking. Never leave the oil unattended and be sensible about heat control. When you've finished cooking, leave the oil somewhere safe to cool, pour it back into the bottle and dispose of it safely.

× FIND OUT MORE ×

For videos, features, lots of handy hints, tips and tricks on all sorts of different subjects, more nutritional advice, loads of fantastic, tasty recipes, plus much more, make sure you check out jamieoliver.com and youtube.com/jamieoliver

JAMIEOLIVER.COM

THANKS

· TO EVERYONE ·

GINNY ROLFE
FOOD TEAM

DAVID LOFTUS
PICTURES

REBECCA WALKER
WORDS

PETE BEGG
FOOD TEAM

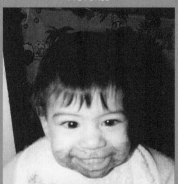

GEORGINA HAYDEN
FOOD TEAM

JAMES VERITY
DESIGN

BETHAN O'CONNOR
WORDS

SARAH TILDESLEY
FOOD TEAM

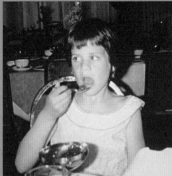

ABIGAIL FAWCETT
FOOD TEAM

CHRISTINA MACKENZIE
FOOD TEAM

PHILLIPPA SPENCE
FOOD TEAM

ROZZIE BATCHELAR
NUTRITION

JODENE JORDAN
FOOD TEAM

MADDIE RIX
FOOD TEAM

EMILY EZEKIEL
FOOD TEAM

LAURA JAMES
PROJECT MANAGER

SAM BALDWIN
FOOD TEAM RUNNER

CLAIRE SIMMONS
FOOD TEAM

× THANKS ×

To my lovely family – I couldn't do what I do without your love and support, so big hugs and kisses to Jools, Poppy, Daisy, Petal, Buddy and of course, Mum and Dad. Also to Gennaro for all of his services to both the porn and food industries over the last 25 years.

Big thanks to 'Lord' David Loftus for yet another book of beautiful photography – incredible work my friend. Thank you for your unfaltering dedication.

To my delightful food team, my second family, my buddies, many of who have worked alongside me over the last 15 years: helping me to build up our amazing team and embracing all the newbies who've joined us and are doing incredibly well. All of you do an amazing job to test, test, test and make sure every cookbook I do over delivers. I really appreciate it, and know the public do too. To the oldies but goodies, the one and only Ginny Rolfe, brilliant Pete Begg, and lovely ladies Bobby Sebire, Georgina Hayden, Sarah Tildesley, Abigail Fawcett, Christina Mackenzie, Phillippa Spence, Jodene Jordan, Joanne Lord and Helen Martin. And to the young guns, Charlie Clapp, Maddie Rix, Laura James, Sam Baldwin, Emily Ezekiel, Claire Simmons, Elspeth Meston and Amanda Luck. Thanks also to Joe Wright. And big thanks to my head pastry chef Ed Loftus for all the inspiration on the sweet indulgence chapter.

To my amazing nutrition team who always help me to be the best I can be without compromising the heart of a dish, as well as making things super-clear for you guys – to Laura Parr and her ninjas Rozzie Batchelar and Mary Lynch.

Thank you to my editorial team who do so much more than just make sense of my rants – they help me strike the balance between content, design, and all the little things that help you guys get a clear, beautiful well-expressed recipe – to my editor Rebecca Walker, and to Bethan O'Connor.

To my unbelievable publishers of 15 years, Penguin. They're an incredible, collaborative publisher to work with, and there are many unsung heroes behind the scenes making sure everything is spot on. What an amazing crew of super-professional people. Special thanks to Tom Weldon and Louise Moore, who've been with me since the very beginning, and have always allowed me to do what I've felt passionate about. To my Glaswegian brother, John Hamilton, who has art directed every single book I've done – thank you as ever. Big thanks to Juliette Butler in production, who we've challenged a lot on this book with our cover requests – I think you might deserve a holiday.

Thank you to the Ed2 team for double, triple and quadruple checking everything is well written. Not much gets past these guys, but putting up with the Oliver can be a little bit like having a grammatical enema, I'm sure. So to the unflappable Nick Lowndes, the legend that is Annie Lee, Caroline Pretty, Pat Rush and Caroline Wilding – thank you.

I'm going to bundle together rights, sales, publicity, marketing and brand, not because they're not all wonderful in their own right, but because it only works when they all work tightly together as an incredible team, which they do. Although I don't get to see you very often, you're the ones who have the task of inspiring the book buyers to consider us on their shelves every year, and I never take that for granted – thank you. To Chantal Noel and her team: Khan Lawrence, Lucy Beresford-Knox, Alison Faulkner, Celia Long and Alex Elam. To the sales gang: Anna Derkacz, Zoe Caulfield, Olivia Hough, Rebecca Cooney, Stuart Anderson, Roseanne Bantick, Isabel Coburn, Neil Green, Jonathan Parker and Samantha Fanaken. To Katya Shipster and Francesca Pearce in publicity and to new girl in the mix, Bek Sunley, on brand and marketing, with Merle Bennett.

× THANKS ×

I also want to give a shout out to all our international publishers and their teams. I'm really blessed, and still to this day can't believe we publish in 34 languages and 38 countries around the world. I've never managed to make it to some of them but, without doubt, I thank you for all of your support over the years and for taking my recipes to places I can only dream of.

Thank you to our compadres, James Verity, Mark Arn and the rest of the gang at creative agency Superfantastic, for the genius design, layouts and general over delivery. Creating a great cookbook is far from simple, and achieving a balance between clarity and beauty requires a lot of effort, so thank you guys – this book is amazing, as ever.

To the rest of the dear people around me at Jamie Oliver Ltd who help me do what I do in many different ways. Ultimately we're all passionate about getting everyone cooking fresh food from scratch and enjoying good times with their families. So I'm constantly thankful and appreciative of John Jackson and Paul Hunt, Tara Donovan, Louise Holland and Claire Postans. Thank you to Giovanna Milia in legal, Therese MacDermott for keeping us in check, my PR manager Peter Berry, Rosangela Amadei and Eloise Bedwell in marketing, and of course to my hardworking personal team, Holly Adams, Amelia Crook, Max Shadbolt, Paul Rutherford and the rest of the gang. There are so many more people from the office I could list here, but there simply isn't the space – you all know who you are – thank you for everything that you do. A special thanks as well to all the brilliant office testers we have on board – your role in creating this book is so important, and I really appreciate your feedback and enthusiasm. And a big shout out to my mate Paul Green from the restaurant gang, who's helped me out with all the beautiful wine recommendations throughout the book.

Last but not least, to all the guys at Fresh One Productions – my old family of TV makers. Again, many of the people who've worked on this production have been with me for years, led by my dear friend Zoe Collins, who I pinched from Radio One back in the day – she's such a talent and has worked across everything I've ever been proud of on TV. Thanks as well to the lovely Jo Ralling, who makes sure everything that needs to happen, does so in a charming way. They've put together an unbelievable team on *Comfort*, headed up by series producer Emily Kennedy and series director Mike Matthews. There'll be a few people from the crew that might not get a mention here, as we'll still be working on the show when this book prints, so if you're not listed, please know that doesn't mean I don't appreciate all your efforts. To brilliant Gudren Claire and her team – Sean Moxhay, Susan Cassidy and Leona Ekembe. To Mike Sarah, our lighting director, and Luke Cardiff on camera one – you guys have been with me since the *Naked Chef* days and I love it – thanks for sticking with me. And to the rest of the fantastic on-set team, to camera guys Simon Weekes, Dave Miller and Mike Phaure, to sparks Darren Jackson and Paul Molloy, Gavin MacArthur, Pete Bateson, Matt Cardiff, Ashley Hicks, Calum Thomson, Freddie Claire and Anthony Burke. To Charlotte Chalker, Aman Mistry, Davinia Dillon, Cynthia Osei-Mensah and Max Kinder. Thanks to the hard-working edit gang, Jen Cockburn, Phil Ashton, Hilary O'Hare, Claire Travers Smith, Jude Robson, Dan James, Mike Davey, Danny Cooke, Dan Goldthrop, Tony Greynoth and Joanna Smith. Thanks as well to Barnaby Purdy, Brad Evans, Joe Sarah, Lee Baker, Mauny Wright, Helen Pratt and Kirsten Hemingway. And of course to lovely Julia Bell, Lima O'Donnell and Julie Akeroyd for keeping me presentable on the make-up and fashion front. Big thanks as well to the unstoppable Katie Millard, for all her help getting this project kicked off.

INDEX